# PLAYBILL

A history of the theatre
in the West Country

HARVEY CRANE

MACDONALD AND EVANS

Macdonald & Evans Ltd.
Estover, Plymouth PL6 7PZ

First published 1980

© Macdonald & Evans Ltd. 1980

ISBN: 0 7121 2027 0

Printed in Great Britain by
Clarke, Doble & Brendon Ltd,
Plymouth and London

# Foreword

It is an honour to introduce Harvey Crane's story of the West Country stage. To his qualities as an expert drama critic of long experience he has added the passion of an enthusiast and the patience of a researcher; and the result is the first complete record I know of the stages, that once, theatrically speaking, were practically at the end of the earth. Today, indeed—thanks to Rowena Cade and the Minack at Porthcurno —the theatre has almost reached Land's End.

Naturally Mr Crane concentrates on the great cities of Plymouth and Exeter. What he says of the present conditions of the theatre in the curious pitch-and-toss of our own period is highly important—historians, I am sure, will value it in the years ahead—but obviously any reader will turn first to what he or she has known personally. So in this narrative I have been absorbed in the story of Plymouth during the 1920s and early 1930s.

I had come up then from a county where theatre records were a fragmentary scatter of memories, and actors from Irving to the poorest of strollers were classed indiscriminately as pomping folk; certainly they were in my mother's villages and my own down South:

> They had come down to the river
> By teased and thorny ways
> In the height of the budding summer,
> The sky in a summer haze;
> But who would hear their plays? . . .
>
> Pomping folk from the market square,
> The night, the booth, the torches' flare,

Hamlet, Ophelia, Romeo, turning in silence back;
Only the reeds limp in their hands,
And the royalty of all the lands
Secure within their pack.

Strangely, it was Cornwall that bred Henry Irving during his formative years. He may have been Somerset-born, but he was brought up by an uncle and aunt behind St. Ives, and I have always liked to think that his haunted, imaginative quality derived from those early days in the remote, haunted world of Halsetown.

The metropolis of the regional theatre—and even Exeter, cherishing the name of Kean, will not object—had to be Plymouth where the great Ionic-pillared Theatre Royal was one of the splendours of the West Country. Too often, alas, the productions on its stage could hardly match the external majesty. Even so, there were excitements. No one recalling the 1920s can have forgotten, say, the flash-and-outbreak of the young Ernest Milton's Hamlet; or a visit from the Doran Shakespeare company with what, in later years, would have been a star cast; or Dorothy Holmes-Gore in the first touring company of *Saint Joan*; or the coming to Plymouth of a play, undervalued now, *Outward Bound*, that still tingles in the memory.

It is dangerous, of course, to choose from hundreds of programmes. But let me say, simply, that Plymouth's stage reputation during twenty years depended more and more not upon the splendid Royal, the Palace's relished Music Hall, or the melodramas and revues elsewhere in the city, but upon the achievements of the Plymouth Repertory players on their tea-tray stage at the corner of Princess Square.

Historically, their work has suffered for two reasons. Plymouth, off the main theatrical beat, seldom shared in the publicity given to theatres nearer London. Moreover, local playgoers were apt, I fear, to put size before merit, would praise a second-rate company at the Theatre Royal and ignore the achievements—often startling—on that calm, severe doll's house stage, "the little Rep" on the fringe of the lawyer's preserve.

Today, when Exeter has its Northcott—and I can remember

with excitement Tony Church's opening Shylock—Plymouth should again have its Repertory: no fly-by-night, no seasonal visitor, but a permanent company solidly-established. Harvey Crane would be there to watch it. Believe me, the presence of the right drama critic (as even actors agree) can be most valuable to the regional stage.

Let me say at once that it would be wrong if my own predilections distracted you from the bulk of Mr Crane's affectionately and profusely-detailed book. This is the work of a critic who loves the theatre in all its manifestations; not only those he writes about night by night and week by week, but also the glories of the past, the history of the art he chronicles. Harvey Crane, thank goodness, has never believed that the theatre emerged fully armed from the mists of last Tuesday week. For his probing into the records, his selective command of the most complex of subjects, posterity will be as grateful as the readers and playgoers of his own time (among whom may I put one boy who came up from The Lizard in that primeval world between the wars?).

J. C. Trewin

# Preface

An Arts Council Exhibition of the Georgian Playhouse was held in London in October 1975. Among the exhibits was a copy of James Winston's *The Theatric Tourist* of 1820, which quoted the dismal entry: "Devonshire has never yet been famous for producing theatrical geniuses."

This book was written partly to refute that libellous statement and to chronicle some of those who have spread their influence and talents over the whole spectrum of British theatre. Names ranging from Samuel Phelps, the founder of Sadler's Wells, Thomas D'Urfey, William Farren, Edmund Kean and Henry Irving to Fred Karno, Agatha Christie, Eden Philpotts, Danny La Rue, Wayne Sleep, Peter Cook, Jenny Agutter and Angela Rippon, who represent but a few who have certainly left, or are leaving, their mark on the national theatrical and entertainment scene.

It was also written to redress the balance of theatrical history, for while there have been many volumes published on aspects of the theatre in other parts of Britain, there has never been a comprehensive look at things theatrical in the South West, an area which has often been dismissed in the past as the place of "Theatre Rural" where nothing of any great moment happened or can happen.

The first surprise in a study of the theatre in Devon and Cornwall is to find that one has to go back 800 years to the thirteenth century for its birth. This at once conflicts with the generally accepted view that the dawn of British theatre began with the more widely known Mystery Plays of Chester, York, Wakefield and Coventry, which are decidedly later than the Cornish *Guary* and the *Ordinalia*.

[vii]

Apart from the novelists who conjure up erroneous visions of Glorious Devon in Merrie England being entertained by capering jesters and minstrels and welcomed by the country populace, very few writers have really considered the plight of the Elizabethan strolling player once he had left the outskirts of London.

Yet these itinerant bands of rogues and vagabonds, as they were legally branded, were roughly treated and given scant welcome in the West Country, where they were often prosecuted and banned from playing in many towns, despite their displaying a "licence" from their London Lord and Master.

Again, in the Elizabethan period, it is intriguing to find references to what must be one of the first "documentaries" dealing with a contemporary crime. Although it is one of the "lost" plays of Ben Jonson and Thomas Dekker, there are many instances of money being paid to "bengemyne johnstone and thoms decker in earnest of their boocke wch they be writtinge called pagge of plimoth . . . XXXXs."

In fact *Page of Plymouth* was performed in public, as Henslowe's accounts reveal. It was based on the trial for murder in 1591 of Ulalia Glandfield and George Strangwidge, accused of killing Mr Page, a merchant of Plymouth, and for which they were both hanged at Barnstaple.

Research also revealed the dramatic consequences of the rigid Puritan age and the Bloody Assizes, and their effect on West Country theatre. They were the main cause of the death of the drama in the South West and delayed any advancement for more than one hundred years; while more fortunate parts of the country enjoyed the delights of the Restoration period and came under the influence of Garrick and Sheridan and the Patent Theatres.

Much of the eighteenth- and nineteenth-century theatre scene has been faithfully preserved in the many daybills and broadsheets of that thrifty period, especially in the two principal cities—Exeter with its ancient and continuing line of Theatres Royal and Plymouth with its aptly named "Theatre of Splendid Misery" or Theatre Royal of 1811.

This period redolent with blood and thunder, melodrama, romance, heavy-handed Shakespeare and penny gaffs, is a flamboyant canvas with raffish characters, the drunken

[viii]

"Brandy Company", the notorious Cora Pearl and the early actor-managers, architects of the Stock Companies.

This was the curtain raiser to the present century, whose radio, talking films and television came into common use and spread disaster and disarray in their wake among the hundreds of provincial theatres, of which only a very few managed to survive.

Two world wars, while provid:ng swollen populations during their duration and in consequence bigger audiences at places of entertainment, also decimated the number of theatres, particularly in Plymouth. Thus the Exeter and Plymouth story contains all the familiar ingredients of triumph and disaster endured by the player and manager in conditions which have bedevilled the struggling West Country circuit over the past seventy tumultuous years.

I spent much of my early theatregoing in London, and have since been fortunate in living in and around Plymouth, a city which has so graciously adopted me and which has tolerated my views on the theatre through the columns of the *Western Evening Herald* and *The Stage* for nearly twenty-five years.

I have found over the years that although people from "the smoke" may only regard Devon and Cornwall as that rural and delectable part of Britain which one only visits on holiday, the South West of England has a distinct, and sometimes insular, culture of its own; and it also possesses a way of looking at the world and especially the theatre with a far more perceptive and calculating eye than perhaps the more cosmopolitan Londoner.

Of course I should never have written this book at all. It should have been the work of that famous Cornishman, author and critic, J. C. Trewin, into whose shoes I so unworthily stepped when he left the West Country for the London and world scene.

My debt to John Trewin is immeasurable, not only from his most helpful and detailed correspondence about the pre-war Plymouth Theatre, about which he was a mine of information, but from his many authoritative books (including his works on Macready, Frank Benson, Plymouth, and the Pomping Folk), from which I have extracted much useful information. This I gratefully acknowledge.

[ix]

The research amongst a vast mass of unsifted material, principally in Plymouth and Exeter, has led to many a helpful acquaintanceship and my thanks to those are recorded in a separate list, but a special debt of gratitude is due to my wife Joan who has endured two years of writing and upheaval with tremendous patience and encouragement as well as correcting the final manuscript with some doughty critical comments.

Finally, I doubt if any author could have had such encouragement and kindly assistance as I have received from the Directors and staff of the publishers, Macdonald & Evans Ltd., for which I am indeed most grateful.

1979                                             Harvey Crane

# Acknowledgments

For their generous assistance and advice in the preparation
and providing information during the research of this book, I
am most grateful to those who have volunteered material,
and in particular to the following:

Harry Barnard, Music and Drama Library, Plymouth City
Library.
W. Best Harris, formerly Librarian, Plymouth City Library.
Harold Bettison, Chairman, City of Plymouth Amateur Oper-
atic Society.
John Brettargh, formerly Manager, Palace Theatre, Plymouth.
Jennie Broughton, Music and Drama Library, Exeter Library.
Lilla Cain, theatregoer.
H. Chichester Clark, former Manager, Stratford-upon-Avon
Memorial Theatre.
Paul Clifford, Entertainments Manager for Torbay.
Alan Coleman, theatregoer and member of Plymouth Theatre
Trust.
Angela Collins, actress.
Hilda Collins, musician.
Joan Crane, theatregoer.
Alec Cumming, former curator, City of Plymouth Museum
and Art Gallery.
E. R. Delderfield, author.
Richard Digby Day, Artistic Director, Northcott Theatre,
Exeter.
Ian Fell, Director, BBC, Plymouth.
Paul Filbert, Director, "Medium Fair".

ACKNOWLEDGMENTS

Richard Graham, impresario, London.
Harry Greene, former member of Plymouth Gilbert & Sullivan
    Fellowship.
Jill Griffin, artist.
Clive Gunnell, Director, Westward Television.
W. Harper Cornish, historian.
Peggy Hitchins, actress and theatregoer.
Winifred Hooper, actress and theatregoer.
Geoffrey Irish, Editor, *Western Evening Herald*.
Frank Kempe, journalist, *North Devon Journal*.
Derek Leask, musician.
Malcolm Livingston, Journalist.
Doel Luscombe, actor.
Clive Mumford, journalist and author.
E. O. Parker, former Manager, Regal Theatre, Redruth.
Southcombe Parker, theatregoer.
Donald Pengelly, theatregoer.
Geoffrey Reeves, former Artistic Director, Northcott Theatre,
    Exeter.
Thomas G. Read, member of Plymouth Shakespeare Society.
Terry Roper, former Manager, Palace Theatre, Plymouth.
George Roseman, former Manager, Palace Theatre, Plymouth.
Professor Peter Thomson, Exeter University Drama Dept.
J. C. Trewin, author and critic.
Frank Urell, secretary, Plymouth Gilbert & Sullivan Fellowship.
Sidney Vauncez, *The Stage*.
Ian Watson, Director, South West Arts.
Betty Wright, typist extraordinary.
Ivor Wynne Jones, author.
The staff of the City Library, Plymouth.
The staff of the Devon and Exeter Library.
The staff of the Tavistock Library.
The Librarian, Dulwich College.
The Plymouth Athenaeum.
Plymouth Arts Guild.
The British Broadcasting Corporation, Plymouth.
Westward Television, Plymouth.

[xii]

# Contents

CHAPTER I

# The Awakening in the West

The lights of Shaftesbury Avenue may glitter in the knowledge that it is the centre of the theatre world. Great actors may fret and strut their hour on the Stratford and London stages, and Shakespeare in his tomb provide the bedrock of English plays and players. But did it all begin in far-off Cornwall?

True the troubadours, the English minstrels and the jongleurs from the Continent travelled the country at large before Chaucer, thus setting the pattern for variety artists, Music Hall and, perhaps, the popsters; but, in the light of modern research, it seems more than possible that the dramatic impact of a written play, spoken by a cast of actors, had its British traditions deep down in the West Country with a Cornish audience.

It is no idle reflection that Cornish folk of today still consider that they are different from the "foreigners" of England, and their innate sense of the dramatic, coupled with their refusal to accept the restricted seventeenth-century Puritan view of the stage, reveals an inherited approach that is still very apparent and points to a long-hidden history of things theatrical.

As Robert Louis Stevenson was to find when he first encountered the Cornish in his travels . . . "I can make nothing of them at all," he wrote. "They are a close esoteric family—totally apart from the rest of Britain. Not even a Red Indian is more foreign to my eyes."

For indeed, long before Stevenson's time, Cornwall was another country, cut off from the rest of England by land except for a few hardly used single-track footpaths, remote from London by virtue of the vast and then sparsely populated

[1]

Devon countryside, and peopled with dark-haired Celts, who spoke a language of their own and lived in a country of legend —romantic and magnificent in its scenic beauty.

Seven hundred years ago, before Agincourt and when Richard II ruled England, the Cornish had their own Lydford Law of "hang today and try tomorrow", the cruel primitive code which governed this robust, wild and insular people with their foreign, mystic and gipsy-sounding names, which, like Marazion, Redruth, Truro, Perranzabuloe, Zennor and Lostwithiel, still ring strangely in our ears.

Coming from such a country it is perhaps not so surprising that, on a subject so little known as ancient Cornish literature, which comprises only two or three compositions written in an obsolete language (now almost forgotten except by a few Celtic enthusiasts and scholars), these early beginnings of the British theatre have suffered from neglect.

Theatre historians point to the venerable fourteenth-century York, Chester, Wakefield and Coventry cycles of Mystery Plays as the real birth of the English theatre as we know it in this country; but a much neglected source is the Cornish *Ordinalia* (the plural of *ordinale* meaning a script or wordbook). This is now generally considered to be earlier, being written down around the late thirteenth century, thus putting to paper and to rights the utterances of the peasant players and clerics who acted them in public by rote.

Alfred Herbage's *Annals of the British Drama* dates York as 1352, Chester as 1377, with Wakefield and Coventry coming a little later, but gives the Cornish plays as being extant in 1300–25, preceded only by the liturgical dramas at Winchester; while that carefully-researched volume *The History of the Theatre* by Freedley and Reeves confirms that the Cornish cycle came before Chester. For as J. B. Priestley observes in his book *England*: "Cornwall was Christian long before the Saxons."

The *Ordinalia* was written in the Middle Cornish language, a tongue known to have been in daily use from before 1200 up to the end of the seventeenth century, and was set down by the Canons of the Collegiate Church of Glasney (founded by Walter Brownscombe 1256–1327) which is today part of the Cornish town of Penryn.

[2]

The oldest existing copies, which are handwritten, are estimated to be early fourteenth century, and are held by the British Museum (Harleian Collection) and by the Bodleian Library, and differ in a number of respects from the later Northern plays. Written in a small hand and by no means easy to read, they were translated in 1859 by Edwin Norris, and in recent years by Dr. Neville Denny and Professor Markham Harris.

The Cornwall of 700 years ago, with its well-established stannary towns, primitive laws and own language, was a well-organised community compared with other parts of the country; it was peopled with a race of sea-faring folk, farmers and tin-miners—hardy and industrious men who took their pleasures seriously, leading Carew in his *Survey of Cornwall* in 1602 to remark:

> In past times the Cornish people gave themselves principally (and in a manner wholly) to the seeking of tynne and neglected husbandry.
> They have pastimes to delight the mind, the Cornish men have guarry and three man's songs and for the exercise of the body hunting, hawking, shooting, wrastling and hurling.

With reading and education almost non-existent, the church was the only means of enlightenment; and it was the general practice in the thirteenth century to portray events to an illiterate audience by illustration and example of the Biblical truths of the Fall and Redemption of mankind in churches and chapels, the clerks and monks being the actors and the minor roles and non-speaking crowds etc., being taken by the townsfolk.

The ecclesiastical drama began with the elaboration and symbolic explanation of the Mass itself. This seems to have come about first in France, where liturgical dramas were called *mystères*, and upon their arrival in England at large were variously described as either Miracle or Mystery Plays.

One of the earliest instances was the ceremonial held on Good Friday at Winchester between 956 and 975, when the *Concordia Regularis* of St. Ethelwold records this "trope" or extension of the Mass.

A crucifix was carried in procession and was hidden in a

[3]

sepulchre, specially built for the occasion, near the altar. Four priests approached the sepulchre, one seated himself and, holding a palm, took the part of the angel. The others represented the three Marys who had come to anoint the body of Jesus.

The holy drama was acted out by chant, and so were the simple and beautiful beginnings of the liturgical drama performed inside the church building by the ecclesiastics.

It is here that the Cornish drama becomes unique, for it possesses the sole distinction of being the first to be enacted away from the church, and the first to be performed in the open air, in an arena composed of "rounds" of earth and stone varying between 50ft. and 100ft. in diameter, far smaller and less complicated than the vast third-century amphitheatre built by the Romans at St. Albans for their circus shows of performing animals and trials of strength.

These rounds, known by their ancient Cornish name as *Plain-an-Gwarry*—the "Field of Play"—were found nowhere but in Cornwall, and traces can still be seen in the West Country in such places as Perranporth, with its Piran Round; at St. Hilary, with its windswept Round overlooking St. Michael's Mount; Perranzabuloe, near Redruth, and St. Just near Land's End, where in 1858 Norris, the translator of the *Ordinalia*, surveyed it and found it possessing "some stone benches, but disfigured by recent injudicious repair".

The Rounds should not be confused with the stone circles to be found in other parts of Britain, like those in Wiltshire, Dorset and on Dartmoor, which are, we are told, Bronze Age monuments dating between 2100 B.C. and 1600 B.C. and used as places for prehistoric worship or as astronomical observatories.

There are similar circles in Cornwall, too, but these differ considerably from the earthen ring or round dated by some authorities as tenth-century. These are obviously man-made, forming a continuous raised bank of rock, rubble and earth (that at Piran Round having an apex of some 10ft., the diameter of the circle being about 50ft.) and were patently used for more secular purposes as they form the natural shape taken by onlookers for a happening. It is a pretty conceit of some West Country authorities that the modern British description of plays performed "in the round" emanates from this ancient usage.

The existence of stone benches as Norris noticed at St. Just and the formation of near comfortable tiers set in the grass banks of Piran Round provide further evidence that they were purposely constructed for considerable use and as a place where crowds could be easily accommodated to witness pageants or some other form of organised entertainment.

That such pre-Christian festivities existed in Cornwall before A.D. 1000 is evidenced by those unexplained Celtic relics of the Dark Ages that still exist today: the strange, primitive and almost frightening Padstow Hobby Horse which prances and swirls its unholy way every spring; the fey May Festival of the Helston Flora Day; the throwing of the Silver Ball at St. Ives (similarly the "hurling" at St. Columb) and the old Fair of Bodmin Riding, all of which predate even the ancient Mummers' plays of good and evil that are to be found in various versions up and down Great Britain.

While today the Padstow 'Oss may seem just a quaint old custom fit for tourists, with black swirling skirt and diabolical face mask, its haunting music and its Teaser (the Mayer or May Man), it is without doubt one of the earliest examples in Britain of players making "an effect" upon the onlookers, and on its rare visits to other places in the country it has made many a modern audience tingle and gasp with a strange sense of the primeval to see its antics and listen to the eager cries of "Oss! Oss! Oss!"

Open-air performances of religious plays and pageants were given in France long before such ideas came to this country, notably at Mons and Arras, this last having the honour of presenting the earliest known secular work, the short *Play of the Leafed One* by Adam de la Hale in 1276.

But over 100 years before this the peoples of Southern France with their wealth in land and trade, governed by that "naughty wife" (as the French historians called Eleanor of Aquitaine), were exporting their culture and frivolities, as well as fish and wine, across the Channel to Cornwall. With the boats from Bayonne came the troubadours and jongleurs, the rhymsters and the sound of lute, flute and rebec giving the Cornish a taste of foreign entertainment as well as a digressive,

FIG. 1.—Feats of balancing and dexterity by fourteenth-century strolling entertainers, or *joglars* as they were called in Provence from which comes the present day juggler.

and at times profane, glance towards the strict disciplines of Christian worship.

The proximity of Cornwall to Brittany and Aquitaine, together with their interwoven cultures and language, therefore, makes an obvious stepping stone for the adoption of religious subjects as a living drama for the enlightenment of the people such as had been seen in France. Thus the extension of presenting the Cornish *Ordinalia* in the open air, which in the absence of any other assumption about the construction of the Rounds, entitles us to the fair belief that the earliest of the Mystery Plays were first performed in the twelfth century in Cornwall, from the remembrances of French productions, and these were later given more substance and set down in writing by the Glasney monks.

In common with other Mystery Plays, the *Ordinalia* of

Cornwall consists of three main sections: the *Creation of the World (Origo Mundi)*, the *Passion of our Lord (Passio Domini)* and the *Resurrection (Resurrexio)*—the three groups being divided into some fifty episodes intended to be performed on three separate days, and each possessing an individuality of its own.

It would be wrong to class the plays as merely another collection in the list of Mystery plays such as those from Wakefield, Chester, York and Coventry, for while it is true that they all contain quaint spoken Christian messages from the Old and New Testaments, the Cornish are unique in including scenes and material from local and apocryphal sources which seem to have been inspired by the players themselves. This original stamp is more in common with their Celtic relations just across the Channel who performed in the French Mystery Plays of earlier years, and who also played out of doors (as opposed to the Northern companies who performed either in churches or later upon erected booths or scaffolding in front of the church).

The considerable number of Anglo-French words scattered throught the whole text also gives us good reason to suspect that the plays were first seen by Cornish monks in Brittany and the Cornish cycle was party copied from the French and Latin originals. The *Ordinalia* also possesses a whiff of the rude secularism which developed in the twelfth century and which caused the church in France to thunder against their presentation in that country.

This certain coarseness within a religious theme was noted by Carew in his *Survey*, who reported:

> The Guary, a miracle play, a kind of enterlude compiled in Cornish out of some scripture history with that grossness which accompanied the Romans' vetus commedia. For representing it they raise an earthen amphitheatre in some field having the diameter of this enclose plain some 40 or 50 feet.
> The country people flock from all sides, many miles off to hear and see it for they have therein devills and devices to delight as well the eye as the ear.

On the other hand there is less of life and vigour in the Cornish drama than in the English works of the same sort.

They are permeated with Celtic religious zeal which reflects their dour and earnest approach and there is not so much gross comedy and ribaldry as is found in the more earthy Northern plays.

The Cornish dramas are also distinguished from the contemporary English collections by the simplicity and regularity of the metre in the general dialogue and by the artificial arrangement adopted whenever the writer wished to be more lyrical and to distinguish the diction from that of ordinary recitation.

The episodes which give the *Ordinalia* its style and strength include the black comedy of the Death of Pilate, the farcical blasphemy of the Smith's Wife and, above all, the legend of the Holy Roods, which has high dramatic value as compelling in its strangeness and superstition as that other legend of the Wandering Jew who travels into centuries far beyond the birth of the story.

The play tells of the three roods or twigs. It begins at the death of Adam when Seth places three pips, taken from the apple that Adam and Eve had eaten, into his father's mouth before his burial. (The story of the three kernels is also to be found in the Old English poem *Cursor Mundi*.)

The instructions in the play run: "Let Adam be buried in a fayre tombe with some churche songis at hys buryall," and Seth says "As was formerly ordained unto me, the three kernels are put into his mouth and nostrils."

From these pips sprout three shoots. Later Moses finds these shoots and proves their holiness by curing the sick Israelites with them. As Moses is dying he places the roods on Mount Tabor, and it is to Mount Tabor that King David journeys to collect these "three wands of grace" which by now have grown into saplings.

As David and his court are sleeping, the three saplings become one, and on waking David realises that this must be a miracle, so the tree is left in position. The holy tree is next seen in the reign of King Solomon when the carpenters, needing a piece of wood for the temple, attempt to cut it down. After many attempts, however, this proves useless, and it is rejected.

Again a miracle occurs when the holy prophetess Maximillia sits on a beam of the wood and her clothes catch fire.

[8]

After a few more attempts to get rid of the piece of wood, it is eventually thrown into the River Kedron. This is the same piece of wood which the torturers later use to make a cross on which to crucify Christ.

This great dramatic irony (Christ is crucified on the wood grown from the tree in the Garden of Eden, thereby linking Adam with Christ, the new Adam) makes the legend of the Holy Roods a very simple and effective method of demonstrating to an unlettered person the complicated mysteries of the Trinity as well as providing an absorbing theatrical theme.

Indeed part of the fascination of the *Ordinalia* lies not so much as might be expected in the usual dramatisations of the Old Testament, the Garden of Eden, Noah and his Ark up to the Passion and death of Christ, but in the mixture of styles and the introduction of many local contemporary characters, such as the Smith's wife and the Jailer's boy, or the two Torturers who introduce themselves in rough and rustic fashion. Here, oaths and obscene words are used side by side with religious terms.

In other versions of Miracle plays Jesus may come from Nazareth, but, in the Cornish edition, Pontius Pilate is a "local" and also owns Lostwithiel; and the vulgar scene of the Smith's wife is played out at the same time as Christ is being crucified, which might be a crude medieval technique, but is a classic example of the ironic dramatic idiom still effective in present-day theatre.

The North Country Mystery cycles abound with instances of quaint stage directions and effects to be obtained by the players and presenters, and these are by no means lacking in the Cornish scripts, and with their added French connection on stage mechanics call for slightly different props and scenic structures.

The setting for *The Fall of Adam and Eve* has this poetic instruction:

Let Paradyce be fynely made with two fayre trees in yt and an apell upon the tree and some other frute one the other. Also to have there a fowntaine and fyne flowers in yt painted.

Scenes dealing with Hell and damnation, Satan and devils were of more importance to medieval audiences than those of the gates of Heaven, foreshadowing almost every drama written since, wherein villainy of some sort forms the basic argument and proves the more dramatic.

At Coventry 4*d*. (2p) was paid to a man for "keeping fyer at Hell's Mouth", but in Cornwall Hell's mouth was made to open and shut; such Hell's mouths were the least of the marvels that French audiences demanded. They also required that "devills" should vanish on the instant.

The Cornish *Fall of Lucifer* entreats:

> Let them fight with swordis and Lucyfer voydeth [departs] and goeth downe to Hell appareled fowle with fyre about hem turning to Hell and every degree of devylls of lether and spirytes on cordis running into ye playne and so remayne there nine angells after Lucyfer goeth to Hell.

Similarly some sort of mechanical contrivance must have been in evidence when God the Father appears from Heaven, for the instruction reads: "The Father must be in a clowde and when he speaketh of Heaven let the levys open," which betokens some sort of lever to part the entrance; this would be opposite to Hell's Gate as the following passage in the *Creation* shows.

> The Father cometh before heven and speaketh to Lucyfer. "Ah Lucyfer. Lucyfer. Thou wast all lanthorn [lantern] of Heven and by me certainly always.
> Thou wast exalted soon and thou was sett very high. . . .
> Hell for thee shall be mayde.
> Straightway I command that there though shalt dwell."
> (Let Hell gape when ye Father nameth yt.)

That the fourteenth-century Cornishman was not far behind in his imagination is also shown in the portrayal of the serpent in the Garden of Eden, which is not only made female, but is blonde into the bargain, for the direction reads: "Let a fyne serpent be made with a virgyn face and yolowe heare upon her head," while full dramatic effect is evoked by the players in the *Death of Abel*, where Eve is given this instruction: "Eva is sorrowfulle and tereth her haire and falleth downe upon Adam and he comforteth her."

But the fourteenth-century stage manager's mind must have

boggled at the naïve injunction given in the Cornish version of *The Three Marys* when Christ is crucified. At the moment of death the exquisite stage direction reads: "Then Jesus shall die. Here the sun is darkened."

The performance of all the plays in the *Ordinalia* would call for a very large cast, and whether the actors themselves learnt their roles by heart, read them from a script (if they could read) or were prompted in their lines, is open to conjecture.

It is certain that the principal characters were played by clerics or clerks in the service of the monastery or nearby church, but many of the small parts (and in particular those of "the rude mechanicals") were taken by local inhabitants. It seems they were given their lines by the "ordinary" (the producer, in modern parlance), as Carew points out in his *Survey of Cornwall* some two centuries later; but one is hard put to it to be convinced by the idea of a prompter following about the rough and tumble of the actors in some of the more dramatic parts of the action.

> The players con not their parts without book, but are prompted by one called the ordinary, who followeth at their back with the book in his hand, and telleth them softly what they must pronounce aloud.
>
> Which manner once gave occasion to a pleasant conceited gentleman of practising a merry prank; for he undertaking (perhaps of set purpose) an actor's room was accordingly lessoned (beforehand) by the ordinary "Go forth man, and show thyself".
>
> The gentleman steps out upon the stage, and like a bad clerk in scripture matters, cleaving more to the letter than the sense, pronounced these words aloud.
>
> "Oh (says the ordinary in his ear) you mar all the play." And with this passion the actor makes the audience in like sort acquainted.
>
> Hereupon the prompter falls to flat railing and cursing in the bitterest terms he could devise; which the gentleman with a set gesture and countenance still soberly related, until the ordinary driven at last to mad rage, was fain to give over all; which trousse [jest] though it break off the interlude, yet defrauded not the beholders, but dismissed them with a great deal more sport and laughter than twenty such guaries could have afforded.

[11]

This proves that Peter Quince and Bully Bottom's production of *Pyramus and Thisbe* was not so far removed from fact, and that the presentation of the Cornish Mystery cycle, although intended as a religious festival, was not always staged with the devout decorum that one imagines.

Annual presentations of plays from the *Ordinalia* continued well up to the end of the sixteenth century, after which they began to lapse. This was due mainly to the falling off of the Cornish language, which died out as common speech owing to the fast-growing dominance of English.

Here are the first four lines of *The Creation* in the ancient Cornish tongue, with their equivalent English translation.

> En tas nof y'm gylwyr
> Former pup tra a vyt gyvys
> Onan ha try on yn gyvyr
> En tas ha'n map ha'n spyrys.

> The Father in Heaven I am called
> Creator of all things that are
> One in Three I am in Truth
> The Father and Son and the Spirit.

There is no confirmation that the Cornish players ever ventured beyond the boundaries of the River Tamar, and apart from isolated performances by "boys" from some of the monasteries and schools, neither is there any record of other scripted plays being performed in adjoining Devon around that time.

Accepting that the birth of the British drama began in Cornwall, it seems strange indeed that the movement did not grow into greater things in that county during the following years.

But, apart from that first budding in the fourteenth century, Cornwall subsided into literary obscurity, and right up to the present day as far as theatres are concerned has been renowned for supplying attentive and eager audiences, but never for a great theatrical tradition.

It seems that during that period of Cornish self-expression in drama which culminated in the Renaissance (a period in which English soldiers had won Agincourt, Joan of Arc was burned, the Wars of the Roses were fought at home and Caxton set up his first printing press) the great county of Devon, with its sprawling acres just across the Tamar, was less open to such indulgences as public entertainment of any kind.

Devonshire, with its population of fisher folk and farmers and its almost impenetrable lanes and byways leading westward from Exeter, was visited only very occasionally by the travelling minstrels and interlude players.

That some of them did manage to come so far west is pointed out by Cicely Radford in her piece on "Medieval Actresses" in *Theatre Notebook* of 1953 in which she quotes what must surely be the original instance of the story of the Bishop and the Actress.

She tells of how Robert Busse, the abbot-elect of Tavistock, suffered in the year 1324 a series of accusations, one of which was that:

> In the space of two months at Exeter he gave away trinkets to the value of £60 [around £1,000 today] the property of the house [abbey] and gave them to "ystrienibus maribus ac feminis ac meretricibus et personis aliis levibus ac inhonestis".

Which Latin seems to mean "to stage players, male and female and to whores and other loose and disreputable persons".

Exeter, being the then practical end of the main highway from London and the North, had much better opportunities of seeing some of the more venturesome players of that time. They were becoming something of a nuisance to the peaceful burgesses of that city, for an edict was issued on 11th July 1384 by Bishop Grandisson, directed to the Dean of Exeter, the Archdeacon and the Rector of St. Pauls in the city: "To forbid the performances of a certain harmful and blameworthy play or rather buffoonery in scorn and insult to the leather dressers and their craft, on this Sunday next to come, in the theatre of our city."

This reference to "a theatre" in "our city" is surprising at this very early date, and it possibly refers to a travelling pageant car for which local guilds were responsible, or, perhaps, to a booth set up by itinerant players.

[13]

Such pageant cars were described by Archdeacon Robert Rogers in 1595 during the presentation of the Chester Whitsun Plays:

Every company had his pagiant, or parte, which pagiants weare a high scaffolde with two rowmes, a higher and a lower, upon foure wheeles.

In the lower they apparelled themselves, and in the higher rowme they played, being all open on the tope, that all the behoulders mighte heare and see them. The places where they played was in every streete.

Apart from these sparse events there is little evidence of any further visitations of plays or performers to either Devon or Cornwall during a whole century up to the accession of Queen Elizabeth I in 1558.

This was a century during which the sea route to India was to be found by Vasco da Gama, Martin Luther was to precipitate the Reformation, Coverdale's Bible was to be printed, Calvinism was to come into being, and those early English playwrights John Heywood and Nicholas Udall went into real print to give us—if primitively—a differing kind of play from the old religious mysteries and to pave the way for the glorious and golden age.

CHAPTER II

# Enter the Elizabethans

In these modern times when we read of actors, singers, enter-tainers and musicians receiving fabulous sums and living like millionaires for a few fleeting appearances, it is natural that one should recall through rose-coloured memories their early forbears, the strolling players and minstrels of "merrie England".

So much has been written in romantic vein of the pastoral elegance of Elizabethan England with its innocent and carefree enjoyments, its jovial bands of travelling actors on their carts bringing music and gaiety to backwaters of a contented countryside, that it has come to be accepted that this was in-deed a golden age.

The West Country has suffered most from this romantic misconception, firstly because of its peaceful Devonshire pros-pect which calls forth comfortable illusions of cream, cider and dreamy content, at a time when fast-growing London was the centre of fashion, court intrigue, gay life, executions, commerce and sophistication; secondly because of the over-romantic legends of Hawkins, Raleigh and "that notable pirate, that salt-water thief", Sir Francis Drake; and lastly because theatre folk themselves have epitomised the West Country as a haven of rest and good living, far from the bustle of com-mercial enterprise, and therefore much to be desired—and exploited.

Four centuries ago, Bristol was the third largest town in the country. Exeter easily commanded its position as the captial of Devon and was up amongst the richest in England, standing fifth in the provinces after Norwich, with its popula-tion, at Henry VIII's time, of 5,000 people.

Industriously concerned with the woollen and serge trade it paid its craftsmen 10d. a day and farm labourers 6d a day. A woman servant, living in, received 16s. a year and after some long period of service she might have got 20s.

Smaller Plymouth, with its same-sized population, compressed into less than one square mile, was dependent on wool and fishing. Stonehouse, "a little fishe towne" of a few hundred inhabitants, clung to the beach of the Hamoaze, and Devonport was non-existent. This was at a time when Totnes, Barnstaple and St. Ives were far more important than Liverpool; when Launceston was larger than Sheffield, and Bodmin bigger than Birmingham.

Plymouth's only contact with the outside world in the sixteenth century was either by sea, or by a long and tortuous lane (not mapped via the present line of the motorway) through Tavistock and Okehampton, thence to Exeter, over lonely moorland tracks and exceedingly narrow lanes, where it was almost impossible for two pack horses to pass in comfort, extending over steep windswept hills which time and progress had not yet levelled to aid the motor car to travel at speed.

Within the city gates, the streets, as Richard Carew was to note in 1602, were made of trodden pebbles. "The sea strand also in many places affordeth pebbles, which serve very handsomely for paving of streets and courts."

These pebble pavements, the forerunners of the cobble stones, were also remarked upon by William Strode, the poet from Plympton, who spoke of the wonderment of a country bumpkin having his first sight of Plymouth town.

> The streets be pight of shingle stone
> Doe glissen like the sky-a,
> The zhops ston ope, and all yeere long
> Ise think a faire be there-a.

A few mansions stood around the old church of St. Andrews, the tower of which still remains, and alongside the more salubrious edges of Sutton Pool the few noblemen, the gentry and ecclesiastics lived in robust feudal style in houses with thatched roof, built of timber and wattle daub or, perhaps, of

[16]

local stone with shillet roof which gave rise to their being described on wet days as "made of marble".

In contrast life for the average Plymothian was rough and grim. He eked out his lifespan on pennies in little more than a hovel; his life was bounded by a continual struggle against the sea, and against oppressive and primitively cruel measures from lord and priest; he bartered and bought among his fellows and worked all the hours of daylight in the servitude of his masters.

So it was, perhaps, natural that this closely-confined community whose only communication with the outside world was a visiting ship or occasional visit to the tiny villages just outside the city, should live lives without venturing more than a few miles, and that they should become mercenary and suspicious of strangers.

On the lighter side of life they had their Morris Men, their Maypole romps and the rough and ready roaring ale houses. Occasionally a benign and richer citizen might celebrate with his cronies in public, thus allowing the base, common and popular to watch.

The earliest known of such an occasion was in 1451 when Mayor Thomas Greyle, "a rough gallant man in his home with a goodly train and abundant means for the support thereof did give a most notable feaste on ye Hoe complete with the attendance of nobility and a tournament".

Apart from such events, while the lord enjoyed his punning jester or fool to amuse his "off" moments, the peasants of Plymouth had little to entertain them until the advent of the strolling players, whose first recorded visit to the city was in 1515 (in Henry VIII's time) when The King's Joculars made their appearance at the city gates.

Most of them had already played at Exeter and soon found Plymouth just as rewarding. From then on companies arrived two or three times a year, much to the annoyance of those pious Plymouth fathers who, in common with other elder-men of other towns at that time, would have the city gates slammed in the faces of itinerant actors, even going to the extreme of paying them a pittance "not to appeare".

Thus it is recorded in the Plymouth records of 1599: "Paid 10s to a Nobleman's Players because they would not plaie."

[17]

Barnstaple had the same trouble in the same year: "Given to players on Mr Mayor's order to ridd the Towne of them . . .Xs;" while at Exeter a very righteous town clerk fumed at the brazen effrontery of strolling players who tried to perform inside the city without a licence or official permission from the mayor. Their lord's licence or not, the final decision always came from the mayor, for strolling players were treated much the same way as are the gipsies of today, unwanted in any town or village.

But there were some who contrived to get through the barricades of the bigots, and during the Tudor period some forty companies came to the West Country, playing in the towns of Bath, Exeter, Barnstaple and Plymouth as well as at any village that welcomed them and warranted a few pence.

They came not as the tastefully-dressed Elsie Maynard and Jack Point of *The Yeomen of the Guard*, neither did they travel in comfort on horse-drawn carts carrying their meagre properties, but arrived as weary travellers having pinched, begged and borrowed along the dusty Devon lanes on foot, perhaps if they were lucky, with a small handcart, trudging hopefully between places which fought shy of them.

They might, if lucky, have stolen a horse from the village they had just passed; they might have picked up a starry-eyed yokel to follow them and carry their scant luggage; and they might have been fortunate enough to beg a loaf to sustain them on the road, for strolling players were indeed vagabonds and, according to the law, "rogues and sturdy beggars".

They were harsh days for ordinary folk in Tudor times, with executions by fire and the block for offences ranging from witchcraft to treason, and by hanging for minor offences. There was a sickening persecution of Jews, freethinkers and noncomformists, and compassion was frequently smothered in murderous quarrels about Biblical texts and interpretations. The common man had little redress, and those classed as rogues and vagabonds were liable on summary conviction to be whipped at the end of a cart tail, or to have their ears bored by a red-hot iron.

Apart from the travelling minstrels, jugglers and entertainers, actors were mainly rustics or minor church servants, enrolled or cajoled to appear in the provinces in the Mystery plays and interludes, portraying religious subjects, giving performances prior to this time in churches or schools.

With the arrival of the Morality Plays, which were mainly devoid of humour and dealt with vice and virtue (*Everyman* is the sole survivor), the public began to look for a more secular type of entertainment, and the players, swiftly appreciating whence the applause came, began to look upon themselves as actors and entertainers rather than moral instructors forced to enact according to the dictates of the church.

Thus it came about that during the reigns of Henry VIII and Elizabeth I there began to arise a number of skilled performers and writers whose imaginations rose to the needs of the public, giving us such names as Burbage, Alleyn, Jonson, Dekker, Marlowe and Shakespeare, members of that great band of Elizabethan players and playwrights who were to change the face of English literature and make the British stage unique and the envy of the whole world.

These were in demand with the lords and ladies at the London court, at their private houses and at the newly-erected purpose-built theatres. However, by virtue of their outlawed calling, they commanded little respect and it was only by becoming a servant of a baron of the realm that a common player could escape the rigours of the law.

It then became the custom for the more highly skilled to find a protector, one who would sponsor him as an actor. When he had been accepted he became subservient to his lord and was allowed to wear his livery and badge.

He and his small company of fellow players would perform in the Great Hall on occasions at his master's command, and, in addition, would receive a written licence to perform in surrounding towns and villages when his services were not required in London. This licence took the form of a signed letter which, in fact, only betokened the holder as being the servant of his master.

Such licensed players, when their lord was away or had no present need for their services, sometimes toured further afield to the distant provinces as independent groups, relying on their craft and skill to earn a tentative living; flashing their crumpled and well-used certificate of respectability, with the hope that it might be accepted by a dubious mayor as an official command to let them play in his town and receive payment.

Some from the higher hierarchy travelled with letters patent from the sovereign or Lord Chamberlain, or Master of the Revels, which they presented to the chief citizen with great flourishes, so making it a little more difficult for the mayor's court to refuse them entrance. With this certificate of tolerable respectability in their pockets they began their age-old profession of delightful deception.

It is unfortunate that the West Country had no Pepys or Stowe to record the appearances of these travelling actors, their manner, their style, costume and the kind of fare they provided in the towns and villages far away from the London scene. Details of this kind are sparse and it is only in the cold account books and town records of the period that we can catch a glimpse of their activities; although Phillip Henslowe, the Elizabethan impresario and owner of the three London playhouses, gives in his accounts diary (now preserved at Dulwich College) a capital record of their organisation in London, with occasional references to other places.

It is known that the touring bands of actors generally consisted of some five or six players, together with a boy or two in attendance who would be used to play the female roles, and that apart from the home counties they journeyed west on a number of occasions, particularly to Bristol, Exeter, Barnstaple and Plymouth which were at that time becoming more prosperous than the North.

The earliest instance from Henslowe's record is of the Duke of Norfolk's company which travelled to Norwich and thence to Exeter in 1556.

There were three standards among the professional companies of good standing. The leading members of the company were known as "master actors", and as such were always referred to as "Master Smith", a device which 150 years later was to be converted to "Mister" and which covered all male actors.

Supporting roles were played by adult actors who were given their Christian names, thus "John Smith"—again to be used in the twentieth century, as the accepted mode of billing.

There were three types of "boy" actors. Firstly there were those who were apprenticed at an early age to a professional player by whom they were trained in their craft. Secondly there were the boys from the great choir schools such as the Chapel Royal, St. Paul's and Westminster. Their ages ranged from nine to thirteen and apart from having to learn the art of open-air speaking, they were often taught to sing, dance and play the hautboys, the viol or to beat the drum.

The third type was an adult possessing a falsetto voice and feminine inclinations. The most celebrated being John Pig (Pigge, or Pyk) who was married, and performed for a number of years with Edward Alleyn under Henslowe's management.

The introduction of boy actors in the Elizabethan period has not always been given its full significance, for they brought to plays a gentler and more romantic approach, together with a lightness and impudence that had been severely lacking in the old companies of adult men which were often coarse, rough-and-tumble affairs.

The wages for actors when appearing in a well-established company in London were small. Thomas Hearne in 1597 was under contract to Henslowe at 5s. per week for the first year and 5s. 7d. for the second, out of which he had to provide clothes, wigs, swords etc. as well as keep himself and his family.

When "on tour" they received nothing and were reliant on the good will of their public when they passed the hat around, and perhaps on a few shillings from a beneficent mayor.

But for all their organisation and high-sounding titles, these itinerant strollers were no circumspect body of the "arty-crafty" brigade, as Phillip Stubbes records:

Suche drunken sockets and bawdye Parasites as range the countreys ryming and singing of incleane, corrupt and filthie songs in taverns, ale houses, innes and other public assemblies. For every towne, citie and countrie is full of these Minstrells to pype up and dance to the devill. But some of them will reply "What Sir! We have a lycense from the Justices of the Peace to Pipe and use our Minstrellsie to our best commoditie."

[21]

Cursed be those lycenses which lycense any man to get his living with the destruction of many thousands.

The latter half of the sixteenth century saw an increasing number of such companies making their way westwards. In the Plymouth accounts for August 1560 this item ocurs: "Pd to My Lord Dodlei's Players wch pled in the churche at the Mayor's commandment . . . XXs."

The sum of £1 sterling then would equal at least £20 today, and this munificence on the part of the Plymouth Mayor was soon to be strictly limited when other bands of strolling players came to the city gate in the following years.

Within a few weeks of this performance by Lord Dudley's company, his wife, the unfortunate Amy Robsart (it was believed she was murdered at her husband's behest), was to meet her tragic end at Cumnor Place and a former chaplain of the earl, Francis Babbington, was to preach her funeral sermon and afterwards become Rector of Holsworthy.

Lord Dudley's company toured the provinces for nearly thirty years when not required at court, and included men like Burbage, Wilson, Laneham and Kempe, the comic actor who served under the banner and badge of "The Bear and Ragged Staff". They again appeared in Plymouth and Exeter in 1588, a month before the Spanish Armada sailed up the Channel. The following year they lost their patron and shortly afterwards disbanded.

The Queen's Players came to Tavistock in 1561 and received from the churchwardens Richard Webbe and John Bowdem the reward of 13s. 4d. and then journeyed on to play at Plymouth a few days later.

Other visits at that time include one at Plymouth in 1563: "Item. Paid to the Erell of Warwickeys Plears the IX June for pleying . . . 13/4d."

This was followed by an item for 6th January 1565: "Item. Paid to the boyes of Tottons [Totnes] that played at Mr Mayors . . . Xs."

These children under the charge of their headmaster Roger Cryspyn came to Plymouth on a number of occasions afterwards; so they must have been a great attraction to have

[22]

travelled the thirty-odd miles each way through a none-too-pleasant countryside, to perform.

> 1566. Paied to the scolemr and children of Totnes which played in Christmas . . . Xs.
> 1573. Pd to the boyes of Totnes which played in the churche before the masters of the Towne (the magistrates) . . . Xs.

Not to be outdone, the boys of the old Plymouth Grammar School, which was founded in 1561, also had their day and in 1565 there is an entry of payment to: "Foure boys of the towne that played at the Mayor's . . . Vs."

Totnes in the sixteenth century was a town of some repute, and a play entitled *The Tinker of Totnes* was given its first showing in London in 1596. Henslowe records that it took £3 at the performance in an entry which reads: "18 July 1596. Fr a performance of the tynker of totnes . . . III Li."

These regular visits of professional strolling players spread the desire to witness live and popular performances far and wide. Local companies were formed and we learn that in Plymouth there was a "Company of St. Budoke" in 1576 and that "The Players of Tavistock" performed in 1568; while the Earl of Bath's Company, which had been resident in Liskeard for some months playing the surrounding countryside of Cornwall, toured North Devon as far as Barnstaple.

Performances were often given in the open air, as this Plymouth record of 1575 shows: "Pd to the Pleyers at the brigge [bridge] by commande . . . 6/8d.

The bridge in question was evidently the old Plymouth Bilbury Bridge which spanned the valley at the junction of Bilbury Street and Buckwell Street where into the harbour ran two small streams, now piped away from sight under the present Plymouth bus station at Bretonside.

This sudden leap forward in interest in theatrical fare was no idle flicker, for during the last two decades of the sixteenth century there came a great phenomenon.

The quaint, rigid, homespun comedies were beginning to pall. John Heywood's (1497–1580) farcical play generally known as *The Four P's* from its original title *The Playe called the foure P.P.; a newe and a very mery interlude of a palmer, a pardoner, a potycary and a pedler*, Nicholas Udall's (1505–

[23]

56) *Ralph Roister Doister* (written for the boys of Eton College) and *Gammer Gurton's Needle* (believed to be by William Stevenson 1552) were pale and ineffectual entertainments for the robust Elizabethan citizen who demanded more of real life.

Christopher Marlowe began the revolution with his *Tamburlaine*, followed by Thomas Kyd with *The Spanish Tragedy* —a full-blooded drama—with murders, madness, ghosts and the ever-popular theme of revenge.

Edward Alleyn brought *The Spanish Tragedy* in his repertoire on his travels through the West Country, a woodcut of which is printed on the title page of the 1633 edition.

This early forerunner of the lurid theatrical playbill shows the murderers attacking the doomed Horatio. The stage direction runs: "They hand him in the arbour." The heroine

FIG. 2.—Edward Alleyn as Hieronimo in Kyd's *Spanish Tragedy*, one of the earliest melodramas, from a woodcut. Horatio is found hanging in the arbour and is discovered by his father and the heroine. Alleyn was a member of the Earl of Worcester's Players in 1583 and chief actor of the Admiral's Men in 1587. Of a high reputation and a man of substance, he retired from the stage and founded Dulwich College.

Bellimperia shouts: "Murder! Help! Hieronimo!" while one of the murderers, using what sounds like a modern colloquialism, retorts: "Stop her mouth!" Hieronimo, having heard her cry for help, enters left and exclaims at seeing the body: "Alas it is my son, Horatio!" and so the taste for melodrama was born.

Around 1590 William Shakespeare burst forth on the waiting Elizabethan audiences as a shining sun to end the medieval gloom for all time.

A legend has persisted over the years that Shakespeare once trod the streets of Barnstaple and acted there. He was certainly closely associated with the Lord Chamberlain's Men, or the King's Men as they were sometimes called, a company which toured the West Country on several occasions from 1581, but William did not join them until 1594.

What is certain is that the records show that the King's Men came to Barnstaple in 1605 and again in 1607 when they were given twenty shillings (£1). This was the highest amount ever paid to a company of itinerant actors by the Barnstaple corporation, a fact which might add a little more force to the supposition that this was payment for "a star show".

A little more certain is his appearance in Bath in 1603, for the King's Men were there during the local celebrations for the accession of James I.

Although Henslowe in his accounts diary records many instances of Shakespeare's plays being presented at various places (King Leare and Titus Andronicous in 1593 and Hamlet and Tamynge of a shrowe in 1594), there is never a mention of him by name among the numerous other actors and writers to whom he paid advances on their work.

Such records include a number with West Country connections, the earliest being a reference to a play called Conan Prince of Cornwall or perhaps the Crown Prince. Now lost, it was written by Thomas Dekker in collaboration with Michael Drayton and seems to have been performed on a number of occasions, as three entries show:

Payd to mr drayton and mr dicker the 16 of Octob 1598 in pt of payment for a booke called the conan prince of Cornwell the some of XXXs.

Pd unto Bradshaw [an adult actor] at the Requeste of mr drayton in pt of payment of ther boocke called the conan prince of cornwall the some of Xs.
Layd out for the company of the 20 of Octob 1598 unto mr drayton and mr dickers for a boocke called conan prince of cornwell . . . iiij.

Thomas Dekker, best known for his play *The Shoemaker's Holiday*, had a hand in some forty plays of which only about fifteen survive.

Lord Strange's company performed at Exeter on a number of occasions from 1576 to 1580 travelling under a licence issued by the Privy Council which permitted them to perform in any town which was seven miles from London and "free from infection", in order that the players might keep themselves in practice in their art so that they could perform acceptably before the Queen (Elizabeth) when required.

Edward Alleyn, the chief actor in the Admiral's Men company, who was later to found Dulwich College, and was also reputed to be Shakespeare's first employer as an actor, was also connected with Lord Strange's company which visited the West Country again in 1593; and in a letter to his wife from Bristol in August of that year he mentions a play called *Henry of Cornwall* or, as it has been construed by some authorities, *Henry VI*.

My good sweett mouse I commend me hartely to you and to my father and my mother and my sistere bess hoping in God. Though the sikness beround about you yett by his mercy it may escape yor house therefore keepe yor house fayre and cleane and every eveninge throwe water before yor dore and in yor backerd and have in yor windowes good store of rue and herbe of grace. . . .
I set this from bristol this wensday being ready to begin the playe of harry of cornwell.

Yor lovinge husband      E. Alleyn.

That this play had previously been presented in London is evident from Henslowe's accounts for he records the receipts at two performances in that city: "Rd at harey of cornwell the 25 of Febreary 1591 . . . xxxis vjd. Rd at harey of cornwell the 23 of March 1591 . . . xiijs vjd."

It was during Edward Alleyn's tour that strange stories began to circulate in London of goings on in the West Country —rumours of apparitions appearing at a performance at Exeter where the audience panicked on finding "devils" among the players.

The occasion was a performance of Christopher Marlowe's *The Tragical History of Dr. Faustus*, a dramatisation of the German legend of a man who sold his soul to Mephistopheles.

A British Museum manuscript records this. "Wherein the play of Dr. Faustus the Evil One himself suddenly appeared by the side of Mephistopholes to the dismay of the audience, who fled from the house and to the terror of the players who left the town."

It appears that the actors cast to play devils found as the play progressed that there was one too many among their numbers, and, after a long pause of frightened discussion between themselves, they abruptly brought the performance to an end. "The people also understanding the thing as it was, every man hasten to be the first out of doors and they fled the house. The players spending the night in reading and in prayer (contrary to their custom) got them out of town next morning."

This account is doubly interesting as it is the second recorded incident of a play being performed under a roof in Exeter ("they fled the house") and which might have been the old Seven Stars Inn which was at that time just outside the city boundary.

Ben Jonson, one-time actor, arrogant, quarrelsome, fearless and warm-hearted, author of many plays including *Volpone*, *The Alchemist* and *Bartholomew Fair* with its vivid picture of typical London life, might also have set Plymouth down for posterity in a play, if only (like so many others of that period) it had not been lost.

Written, again in collaboration with Thomas Dekker and called *Page of Plymouth*, it could be considered as one of the first-ever "documentaries", dealing as it does with a contemporary crime and using some of the characters that were alive at the time.

Again, all we have to go on are entries made in his diary by Phillip Henslowe which read as follows:

[27]

Lent unto wm. birde the 10 of auguste 1599 to lend unto bengemyne johnstone and thomas deckers in earnest of ther boocke wch they be writtinge called pagge of plimoth . . . XXXXs.
Lent unto wm birde thomas dowton, wm jube the V of septemb 1599 to paye in fulle payment for a boocke called the lamentable tragedie of pagge of plimoth the some of vj li
Lent unto jewbey and thomas towne the 12 of septemb 1599 to bye womens gownes for page of plimoth the some of Xs.

William Bird (sometimes Borne) was an actor and an important member of the Admiral's Men, while Dowton, Jube and Towne were also actors contracted to Henslowe.

As the methodical and very shrewd Henslowe lent money to buy dresses for *The Lamentable Tragedy of Page of Plymouth*, it can be taken as certain that it was staged in public, but there is no record of where and when.

The sordid details of the murder of a Mr Page, a merchant of Plymouth, by his wife and her lover on 11th February 1591 are well documented in the Roxburgh Collection, in the form of broadsheets of the time, and are also interesting as they are the earliest examples of essentially local "literature".

The broadsheets consist of three doggerel poems of confession and a voluble prose description of the crime, headed: "A true discourse of a cruel and inhumane murder upon Mr Padge of Plimoth the 11 day of February last 1591 by the consent of his own wife and sundry other."

Then there is: "The Lamentation of Master Page's wife of Plimoth, who being enforced by her parents to wed him against her will, did most wickedly consent to his murder, for which fact she suffered death at Barnstaple in Devonshire."

Another version reads: "The complaint of Mrs Page for causing her husband to be murthered for the love of Mr George Strangwidge who were executed together."

A further effusion is entitled: "The Lamentation of George Strangwidge who for consenting to the murther of Mr Page for the love of Ulalia, suffered death at Barnstaple."

Ulalia Glandfield was the daughter of a Tavistock tradesman, and was wooed by a stalwart youth George Strangwidge until their intention to marry was frustrated by their avaricious parents.

[28]

Ulalia pleaded that she was forced to wed Master Page instead, a wealthy widower of Woolster Street in Plymouth, approaching his dotage, and a miser to boot.

The disappointed young Strangwidge, after departing on one of the expeditions to Spain, returned some years later to renew his advances to Mistress Page. There are conflicting stories in the broadsheets that Page was poisoned by Ulalia, and that the lovers bribed two thugs to strangle him.

They were tried at the Barnstaple assizes owing to an outbreak of the plague in Plymouth, and were hanged together with sixteen other persons.

A second attempt to dramatise the crime was made in the early eighteenth century by Lyne Brett, a Plymouth man of letters who was a prominent member of the social circle which met at the Otter club at the Popes Head in Looe Street.

This play entitled *The Merchant of Plymouth* was set in Master Page's house in Woolster Street with all the central characters plus maids and servants.

Written in the moral-stilted style of the period it finishes at the final curtain with old Glandfield railing against his "cursed avarice" and ends with this advice to the audience:

> Ye rigid parents learn from her sad fate
> Never to wed your children where they hate;
> But if chaste passion their young hearts inspire
> With kind indulgence feed the kindled fire!
> For, if by force the bride and bridegroom led,
> Eternal discord waits the nuptial bed.
> Love should be free; it cannot be contained,
> Nor ever bought or sold; it must be gained.

One wonders what the rare Ben Jonson made of the same story and if his lost manuscript will ever be found.

CHAPTER III

# The Blizzard

With the arrival of the seventeenth century, Exeter was growing fast as the first city of Devonshire, and Plymouth had ceased to be a sleepy fishing village and was beginning, in many ways, to stir itself.

The Armada had come and gone, bringing glory to the town and to Francis Drake and those seafaring gallants whose names became everyday words in conversation at the London court.

Shipbuilding became an important industry, bringing in its wake "foreigners" to the city—traders, merchants, hucksters and sailors from other parts of the country. Whereas their sojourn in Plymouth was brief, they left a decided impression on the people giving them new ideas and reflecting a way of life far different from that to which they were accustomed.

Plymouth Castle was crowded with Catholic prisoners captured from the Spanish. Spy fever was rampant and every ship was searched for Papist spies, until James I relaxed the restriction with an order to release a ship from St. Malo which had been driven into port and was found to contain nothing more subversive than "sacred pictures intended for Romish ladies".

This action was not to the liking of the severe Plymouth divines and ecclesiastics now that thoughts at this time were turning to the new Bible, and the atmosphere among mayor and corporation was one of grudging acceptance of the new order. So they vented their spleen by sending all the actors in the city about their business, closing disorderly and superfluous ale houses, controlling the strength of the liquor and

[30]

setting watches on suspected wives, freely using the ducking stool and dipping them into the waters of Sutton Pool.

This action virtually closed the door on the influx of players who during the past thirty years or so had breathed a new life into the dull serf-like existence of the Plymouth peasants, giving them a whiff of the world outside the city walls and beyond the tors of Dartmoor.

But travelling players are hard-faced creatures when their living is combined with finding a place in which to play and which will pay them a modicum of a fee, and some such venturesome companies still continued to come West.

The Prince's Players came in 1617, followed the next year by Lady Elizabeth's Players, with newer and livelier kinds of productions, but they had little success knocking at the gates of the West Country towns.

England was turning sour. The cold chill of Puritanism was spreading through the land, and nowhere more so than Plymouth which, with its narrow-minded pastors and in-bred councillors, was to become a great bastion of the Commonwealth cause and later to be the last to surrender to royal rule.

There were fewer items in the town records of payments to play. Indeed, the actors were often paid small sums to "departe the towne without playing".

Amusements were cut to a minimum and bear-baiting was forbidden (certainly in the case of Puritan Plymouth, as Macaulay remarked, "not because it gave pain to the bear, but that it gave pleasure to the spectators!").

Puritan hands were held up in deprecation of boy-players because they dressed up in women's clothing, quoting Deuteronomy 21:5—"That the woman shall not wear that which pertaineth to a man; neither shall a man put on woman's garment, for all that do so are an abomination to the Lord."

"Plaies will never be supprest," says one Puritan writer whom Sigmund Freud would have diagnosed as having sexual rather than Biblical connotations in mind, "while his majesties unfledged minions flaunt it in silkes and sattens; even in his majesties chappell do those pretty upstart youthes profane the Lorde's Day by the lascivious writhings of their tender limbs and the gorgeous decking of their apparell in the feigning bawdy fables gathered from idolatrous heathen poets."

It was in such outbursts that the killjoys, the Mrs Grundys of olden times, slowly strangled both plays and players in the provincial towns, giving in their place a different kind of entry such as can be found in the Plymouth account books: "Paid to the preacher that preached in the church on the 7 and 8 daies of November . . . Xs."

Apart from earning for itself the name of "Puritan Plymouth", the city was beginning to get a reputation as a money-grubbing, mean and unfriendly place especially for "foreigners"—a description given to anyone who lived more than a day's walk from the city gates.

John Chamberlain wrote in 1620 to Sir Dudley Carleton at the Embassy in Paris, talking of the disposition of a caraque in the British fleet: "Fulke Grivell is gon downe post to Plimoth, and so to the sea to meet her and kepe her from coming into that pilfering towne (as they term it) but bringe her alonge to Portsmouthe."

Such unkind descriptions of the city were to be repeated again and again in the years to come.

But there was a worse fate in store—Civil War and the plague, the side-effects of both of which were to consolidate this suspicion of outsiders and, in particular, of theatrical people, and were to lay the foundations of a continuing feud of Plymouth versus the Theatre which would last the next 200 years.

It is necessary to consider for a moment the state of the West Country during the years up to and during the Civil War, the stand which its leaders took and the situation of the public in general, for as historian Henry Whitfeld so rightly said in his *Plymouth and Devonport in Times of Peace and War* published in 1900: "In the Civil War, Drama was the first casualty and among a large section of the community the habit of theatre-going was lost and was not in fact to return during the next two centuries."

This indeed is most important when assessing theatrical Plymouth, for, looking back over what now amounts to 300 years, the damaging effect of that catastrophe which bred an inward-looking and suspicious approach to the arts (far more intense than the slightly superior attitude exposed by the average Englishman) cannot be over-emphasised, for it left its stamp on the population. Faint traces of this still exist today.

The Civil War affected Devon longer than most other counties. A considerable part of the population of the gentry lived in and around Exeter, which supported the King. At the same time a strong Puritan element existed in the capital city, leaving a cleavage of sympathies, a combination which in the course of time was forced into a peaceable compromise, and both with a much broadened outlook.

But more lasting damage was inflicted by the worst types of Puritans who, in large numbers, were ensconced in Plymouth, and there are many records of their misguided efforts to make life uncomfortable for everyone. It is directly to this oppression that Plymouth's peculiar attitude to professional players may be ascribed.

On the other hand, Cornwall, which was equally strong against the Puritan Levellers and largely favoured the Royalist cause, has never ceased to be a rich catchment area for potential theatregoers, and in spite of the Cornish insularity has, up to the present day, been a faithful source for supplying patrons to the arts in places far beyond its borders.

Perhaps it is understandable that due to its geographical situation and lack of large urban areas, Cornish towns have never been sufficiently affluent to afford the building of large permanent theatres, but this has never prevented their appreciation of things theatrical outside the Tamar.

It may well be that, if left to themselves, the ordinary Plymouth citizens might have weathered the storm years after the leavening influx of Elizabethan foreigners into their close community, but their natural distrust was only fostered and their normal lives restricted by the harsh Puritanical laws such as on profanity, which forbade even the hard-grained seafaring man to utter oaths on pain of a fine of 3s. 4d.—gentlemen had to pay 6s. 8d. for the same offence, and a lord 30s.

With Charles I on a shaky throne, Plymothians sullenly watched the conflict between King and Parliament at a time when the Star Chamber was the supreme court and Popery was in the air. The Devon fisher folk who remembered the Armada had reason enough to be suspicious of Catholics

[33]

anywhere, and inflamed by zealous nonconformists they incurred a rising hatred against the Stuarts, and Catholic witch hunts became rife with prosecutions in the town for those found in possession of "crucifixes, pictures and other superstitious things".

Tempers were roused when a row developed between the Crown and the local authorities. The Star Chamber insisted that the gift of the mother church of St. Andrews was only conditional, and on the appointment of Dr Aaron Wilson as vicar, "a good hater of Presbyterianism", the sparks flew when he charged the mayor and city fathers with trespassing upon the churchyard by their erection of a hospital for the poor.

At this time James Bagg, the West Country sycophant who acted as agent for the dreaded Star Chamber, reported to his masters on the Plymouth situation: "Here they hate all gentlemen, especially such as serve the king at sea."

The Civil War which broke in 1642 found Plymouth ripe for revolution, siding soundly with the Roundheads against Charles' Cavaliers, and so began the long seige of the city which would last for two painful years.

With the Royalist army strategically stretched around the town from Lipson, Mutley, Pennycomequick to Stonehouse and at the vantage points of Mount Edgcumbe and Staddon Heights, the inhabitants within the city gates suffered long hardships and deprivation.

Often reduced to starvation, horrible conditions and with outside assistance only contrived by a very occasional boat slipping through the Sound against the enemy ranged on both sides of the entrance, the citizens in the beleaguered city became more and more resentful. Over 8,000 people died inside the walls during the two long years of siege and it says much for the Plymothians' strength of character that at the end of it they were able to muster enough courage and strength to burst out of the city. In the Sabbath Day Fight on 3rd December 1643, the Roundhead garrison made their great rally and routed the Cavalier army on Freedom Fields.

Under the new-found Commonwealth, conditions in the city were bad; distress and suffering abounded, the town swarmed with destitute soldiers and sailors, shortages affected everyone, profiteering was rife, the castle was full of prisoners

and refugees by the hundred entered the city from the surrounding countryside.

Parliament passed an Act for the total suppression of all
stage plays and the closing of all playhouses, a gesture which
warmed the hearts of the narrow-minded city fathers who
had long striven to forbid such worldly pleasures from con-
taminating the citizens. But this drove the people to find other
ways of escape. Riots occurred in the town almost every day,
drunkenness was widespread and the staple drink, ale, was
badly brewed. A Captain Hatsell reported to the Commonwealth: "The abominable strong drink brewed in this town
is of more prejudice to the state and borough than the heads
of all the brewers and ale house keepers are worth."

It is significant that when Charles II built the Royal Citadel
(however much he denied it) it was erected with guns pointing
inwards, according to local views, "to hold in check the
rebellious spirits in the neighbourhood".

It is also a matter for reflection that if instead of attempt-
ing to cow the city into submission with guns, he had in-
filtrated the town with people of a broader outlook—a few
academics, artists and professional men from the outside
world—he and the city might have gained considerably.

Instead the hard-line Plymothians, while fully justified in
their feelings of making a moral and military stand against
the monarchy and what they considered to be the powers of
evil, showed little magnanimity towards their erstwhile
enemies and continued to harbour their suspicions against outsiders.

So far as the lives of the indigenous population of Plymouth
were concerned, the people were subjected to harsh disciplines
and exhortations; religious observances were flung at them
from every side, and what narrow views they may have
already held, by virtue of their forbears living in a restricted
small town far from the rest of the country, were being
steadily hardened.

Inter-religious strife was rampant and the nonconformists
picked quarrels with all and sundry. Not being content with
being anti-papist, the Presbyterians and Episcopalians united
against the Quakers for their "quaint practices".

Apart from the regular places of worship Plymouth had

[35]

four large meeting houses in the town in 1650 including those of the Quakers and the Anabaptists, and that gloomy old Puritan John Quicke railed and prayed "that this town of my birth should never be a Sodom, but a Jerusalem for Gospel privileges". Up country, William Prynne was inveighing in print against popular stage plays, calling them "the very pompes of the devill which we renounce in baptism".

Alas no "pompes of the devill" came Plymouth's way in those days and the gay extravagances of Restoration London never penetrated so far west.

In their Calvinistic fervour the Puritans described Plymouth as "amongst the best cities of England", but Bernard Gomme, the engineer who prepared the plans for the Citadel, disagreed. He said of Plymouth: "This wilderness town, almost out of the world, where the Presbyterian is in his most Puritanical seat—there is neither company nor woman fit for a gentleman to pass the time with."

Although the seventeenth century was a hard one to bear for West Country folk, there was worse to come; for after the restrictions and deprivations of the Commonwealth came the ill-fated Monmouth Rebellion which tore the great counties apart.

The landing of Monmouth at Lyme Regis in June 1685, his progress through Axminster, Chard and Ilminster and his eventual execution a month later in the Tower provided the forerunner of *The Bluddie West Country Assizes*.

This fearful slaughter, during which no less than 300 folk were sentenced to death and 800 transported as slaves to the West Indies by the dreaded Judge Jeffreys, spread terror to even the smallest towns and villages of Devon and Cornwall.

Maniacal in his cruelty on the innocent and guilty, male or female, old or young, Jeffreys, during his residence in Dorchester and his forays into the country in pursuit of victims, so cowed rich and poor alike that any thoughts of pleasurable entertainment in these dreadful times were banished.

It was amid these calamitous times that the thorny path of the theatre in the West Country was firmly fixed—in the case of Exeter for some fifty years, Plymouth for over a century—for after the Puritans came Quicke, Fox, Wesley and Whitefield, all preaching acceptance of the stern higher life, while London was to enjoy the delights of Congreve and Vanbrugh.

So Plymothians retained their rustic reputation, thus missing the theatrical innovation of the replacement of the old-style boy-actors by the Nell Gwyn set which took the capital by storm.

They missed the time when Davenant and Killigrew were to secure the King's Patent and open the two great London theatres of Covent Garden and Drury Lane. They missed the time of Betterton, Mrs Barry and Mrs Bracegirdle when playwrights like Dryden, Etherege and Wycherley were to struggle out of the stilted straitjacket of pre-Commonwealth drama; and they were to hear little of David Garrick who had yet to stalk the national theatre scene.

Opposition to theatres raged throughout the West Country, reaching as far as Bristol which, despite its size and prosperity, possessed a strong Puritan force ranged against pleasure of any sort.

Bath was the first city to shake off the restricting yoke, and its first theatre was built in 1705 at a cost of £1,300 by John Power, who then cautiously probed the surrounding countryside with a band of touring actors.

The Bath Company eventually succeeded in establishing themselves in Bristol, but it was not until 1729 that the first regular theatre was built in that city.

But the rest of the great South West peninsula remained under the Puritanical thumb, and when it is considered that in the latter part of the seventeenth century the journey from Exeter to London took four days, it is little wonder that Devon folk thought of the fashionable metropolis as another world, and knew but little of the magic that the theatre could really offer.

# CHAPTER IV

# A Turn towards Respectability

Devon and Cornwall have for many generations been considered by members of the theatrical profession and entertainment moguls as backwaters with an apathetic population when it comes to supporting theatrical enterprises. They accuse the people at large of possessing a fear of anything new and of having a firmly conservative and old-fashioned outlook on culture.

While part of this charge can reasonably be levelled against the indigenous population, the reasons for it must be ascribed to the geographical remoteness of the two counties over the past 250 years right up to present memory, coupled with the over-all effect of the constant repression, both physical and spiritual, which cannot be over-emphasised.

This repression left a lasting impression of suspicion of people from "outside" that was not easily changed until the influx of a more sophisticated population caused by the Industrial Revolution and a succession of wars which created garrisons near the major towns.

Exeter at the time of Queen Anne became the fourth largest city in the whole country, and was the first in Devonshire to shake itself free of the dreaded Puritan grip and of the horrors of the Bloody Assize, which, twenty years earlier, had debilitated the surrounding countryside.

Thomas D'Urfey, the bawdy Exeter playwright who is still remembered as the originator of the saying, "our neighbours over the herring pond", had stirred bigoted minds with his *Adventures of Don Quixote* which upset the Puritans and called forth Jeremy Collier's voice to condemn in 1698 "the immorality and profaneness of the English Stage".

But a revival of public interest and reaction after so long a

[38]

period of sullen acceptance could not be denied, and in 1720 the upper rooms of the Seven Stars Inn at Exeter were adapted as a theatre for touring players.

The next year it advertised the talents of a ten-year-old prodigy who performed "many wonderful Fancies as Dancing with swords, by a girl but ten years old, who turns many 100 times round with so swift a motion that its scarce possible to distinguish her face from the hinder parts of her head."

The same year saw the Bath Company of Comedians arrive from Somerset with "a Diverting comedy called the Bisie Body, beginning at exactly 6 o'clock. Prices 1/6d. and 6d."; and soon afterwards followed the play *Love Makes a Man*. So the first real theatre in Exeter at the Seven Stars began to twinkle, showing the way to a number of other enterprising innkeepers in the city who began to open up their premises for similar entertainments.

The Seven Stars' real scoop was to stage the first performance in the provinces of *The Beggar's Opera* a few months after its opening at Lincoln's Inn Fields theatre in 1728.

---

By the Company of Comedians

The Seven Stars, near the Bridge foot in St Thomas
This evening being Friday November 15th 1728 will be enacted
For the last time this season

THE BEGGAR'S OPERA

Written by the ingenious Mr Gay a native of Devon
with all the songs and musick as performed in the
Theatre Royal London

And before the play, at the earnest request of
divers of the Gentry, Mr Radford will perform
his agility, which is the last time he proposes
to do it in publick.

Beginning at exactly 6 O'clock
Prices 2/- and sixpence.

---

FIG. 3.—The text of the announcement of the first performance of Barnstaple-born John Gay's *Beggar's Opera* in his home county Devon, at Exeter on 15th November 1728.

FIG. 4.—Devon-born John Gay of Barnstaple (1685–1732). Gay's light-hearted mixture of burlesque of the eighteenth-century Italian opera and political satire in *The Beggar's Opera*, together with its sequel *Polly*, established him as the author of the first British musical.

This was the first opportunity of Barnstaple-born (in Joy Street, August 1685) poet and satirist John Gay to show his work in his home county. The production was managed by John Rich, who four years later was to be instrumental in building Covent Garden Theatre where the same opera was to be one of the first to be staged in the new building.

This is a chastening reminder that what was to be justly acclaimed as the first-ever British musical came from dreamy Devon.

Gay's *The Beggar's Opera* gave us the romantic highway-man Macheath and Polly Peachum in a light-hearted burlesque and political satire which ousted the Italian opera—then a fashionable cult—and set the pattern which has been followed in all popular musical shows ever since.

*The Beggar's Opera* has withstood many changes and adaptations over the years (it was used by Brecht in 1929 as *Die Dreigroschenoper* when one of its numbers became "Mack the Knife" and known all over the world) and has had many revivals in many countries.

First staged in London on 29th January 1728, it received the following notice in the *Daily Journal* of 1st February:

On Monday was represented for the First Time at the Theatre Royal in Lincoln's Inn Fields, Mr. Gay's new English opera, written in a manner wholly new, and very entertaining, there being introduced instead of Italian airs, above 60 of the most celebrated Old English and Scotch tunes.

There was present then as well last Night, a prodigious Concourse of Nobility and Gentry, and no Theatrical Performance for these many years has met with so much applause.

The combination of Gay's script and the managership of John Rich was so successful that it gave rise to the saying "it made Gay rich and Rich gay."

As E. R. Delderfield records in his book of Exeter's five theatres, *Cavalcade by Candlelight*, the theatre at the Seven Stars Inn soon became fully established as a popular centre and well patronised. It provided more or less regular changes of programme until 1737 when the Bath Company of Comedians, who had played a vital part in Exeter's theatrical rehabilitation, combined with a Mr Andrew Bice and a Mr

Trewman to erect a purpose-built theatre, thus leaving the Seven Stars to be known as "the old theatre".

They chose a site in Waterbeare Street (originally Water-bearer St.) and now foreshortened to Waterbeer, just behind the Guildhall and the Turks Head Inn. Bice and Trewman must have been brave souls indeed for the Bath Theatre itself had just been closed down by the new licensing laws which came into force in 1737.

This Licensing Act abolished at one blow the right of all provincial companies to act for hire, gain or reward, and branded the players once again as rogues and vagabonds, putting them at the mercy of the common informer of whom there were plenty in the Puritan-infested West.

Bice, a forcible character, a champion of the theatre and fighter against injustice, got around the law, like many others throughout the country, by offering free seats for "a rehearsal" and only charged for the sale of a playbill, or, as on one occasion, the sale of a toothpowder, the wrapper of which served as an admission ticket. Others described their productions as concerts giving musical items and dances in between the acts of tragedy or, as in the case of a performance of *As You Like It*, "in the course of the evening two comic songs and a Scotch Pas seul".

The Town Clerk of Exeter, under the guise of being a strictly law-abiding citizen, tried hard to stamp out this evasion of the new law, but he betrayed his own Puritanical zeal when he wrote in revealing terms showing his contempt of actors to the city's Member of Parliament to seek his aid to:

> Suppress Players of Interludes which debauches all Youth and particularly those of this Town. We have a parcell of Fellowes here that will play in Spite of the Magistrates' Teeth, pretending they dont play for Hire. And the intention of our Magistrates is as much as in them lyes to prevent it.

But more was to come. Exeter was to have another touch of what Plymouth had endured for so long—the great Methodist invasion of the West Country was on the way. John Wesley, who had visited Exeter before, came again in

1745 and with religious fervour fulminated against actors who were again persecuted in the towns as vagabonds.

At length the actors were at last obliged to give up their dearly-loved theatre which was at once purchased by the Methodists who, with missionary zeal, turned it into a chapel.

Bice, who by now had become a wealthy man, a newspaper printer and owner, was not one to take a thing like this lying down for long, and he campaigned against this invasion with vigour. He became a real champion of the theatre and began to publish tirades against the iniquitous law which dealt ruin to the players.

Such was his wrath that he stirred the passions of the populace, and the Methodists were mobbed as they attended and left their newly-acquired chapel. Like other campaigners, he used the device of infiltrating the enemy by infiltrating the worshippers with his own men, who, according to one zealot at the time, "beat upon the seats and wainscot with their hands and sticks and halloaed to the end, and then ran out into the street to be ready for us when we came out".

Even the preacher was attacked, with bills posted outside the chapel advertising as if for a performance: "A Tragick Comedy for the benefit of Mr Cennick to which must be added a Concert of Rough Music."

This attack proved too much for the Methodists who were obliged at last to abandon the place to its former owners to whom it reverted, leaving both sides to settle for an uneasy peace.

The theatre in Waterbeare St. continued afterwards with changes of managership, Jefferson from the Plymouth Theatre having a hand at various times as joint manager with Josiah Foote. Productions of plays were somewhat spasmodic and ranged in a wide variety from performing animals, performances of *Richard III* and *The Impostor* in 1764 to a bowdlerised version of *Oroonoko* or *The Royal Slave* in 1771 about which the playbill notes: "The pernicious immorality of the comic scenes and the inconsistencies of the original have been obviated and replaced by new sentiments of fidelity, generosity and affection."

This was followed by a pantomime *Robinson Crusoe* or

[43]

*Harlequin Friday* in 1782 and a locally-adapted play called *The Siege of Exeter by the Danes.*

Some years after John Gay had first shown that Devon could produce men of the theatre, a stage-struck Exeter-born youth called William Dowton got a chance to play at the old Exeter theatre when he was just nineteen years of age.

The applause he received for his first efforts in private theatricals so fired his imagination that he ran away from home (he was articled to a firm of architects) to join a company of strolling players who were appearing in nearby Ashburton.

Suffering many hardships on the way up he was eventually engaged to play at Drury Lane where he was an outstanding success in the character of Sheva in *The Jew*. From there he went to the Haymarket and became one of the most versatile actors on the London stage. Hazlitt called him "a genuine and excellent comedian", and Leigh Hunt considered him to be one of the comic geniuses of the day.

He made repeated return visits to his home town after he had become famous, playing Sheva, Falstaff and Heartall in *The Soldier's Daughter.*

Dowton has the rare distinction among old actors of never being bigheaded about his undoubted success, and his one great peculiarity has been remembered to this day. He would not allow his name to be printed on the playbills larger than those of his fellow players, even though he was often the leading man. His sort are seldom met with in this competitive and cut-throat profession.

The Exeter theatre had a number of alterations and additions to its structure during its changing years, and in 1764 an Exeter butcher named Josiah Foote managed the place. He made a very prosperous job of it, as well as giving the house a touch of respectability.

Josiah brought a completely new approach to theatre managership.

He was first of all a disciplinarian, an efficient manager in financial matters and sufficient of an actor to fulfil general utility parts and know for himself the vagaries of an actor's calling. In consequence he became well liked by his company.

During his regime he staged twenty-three plays of Shakespeare, Restoration comedies and adaptations of the new plays from London. These played invariably to good audiences.

His announcement made in 1766 that "the proprietors are under the disagreeable necessity of exhibiting every night" points to the then custom of changing the bill nightly, so that in one week (if they played at all for the whole week) the actors would have to learn different lines every night.

A feature of Josiah's productions was the occasional use of "costume" for his plays, a rare occurrence in those times. Historical accuracy could prove very costly in both costume and scenery, and even Garrick's productions at Drury Lane were played in the dress of the day and not of the character.

After Josiah Foote's death in 1784, Richard Hughes, who had been with the Plymouth company, succeeded him at Exeter, and being an ambitious and imaginative man (he was the son of John Hughes, manager of Sadler's Wells in 1784) he set about the building of a new theatre.

Opened in 1787 it was built on the plan of London's Sadler's Wells, which he knew intimately, and was sited in Bedford Circus. With the attraction of it being a new building and also an upsurge in the fashion of theatregoing, the place prospered, so that Hughes was able to engage "stars" who included such names as Stephen Kemble, who appeared as Shylock, to be followed later by his brother John Kemble.

In 1789 their sister, the great tragedienne Sarah Siddons, appeared. On this auspicious occasion the astute manager fell into the age-old custom of raising the admission prices to 5s., 3s. and 2s.—a tremendous increase for a provincial theatre in those days.

The Exeter Press gave Mrs Siddons this notice, which typifies the pandering to the public as opposed to reporting real talent:

The Siddons dramatic abilities exceed all description. A circumstance which attended Mrs S' representation of Belvidera evinces her astonishing powers as an Actress when under the agonies of distress in the concluding scene she gave a loud shriek, it was immediately followed by a real hysteric fit in all of the fair and beautiful females who composed the audience.

[45]

Later still, the very talented Charles Kemble and his wife paid a visit to the Exeter theatre and introduced what was to become an integral part of any melodrama—fireworks.

Considering that it was a display within the precincts of the old candlelit theatre, it must have presented a very vulnerable fire hazard; for it probably consisted of the usual "red fire" set alight on a pan backstage, but being a Kemble production it was advertised in grandiose language as consisting of:

> Vertical Wheels of Various Fires, Cyprian Trees of Golden and Silver Fruit, Flower Pots of Golden and Silver Flowers, the Eruption of a Mine and a Bengal Light, such as those used to Illumine Light Houses in the East Indies; the one to be exhibited on the above night is capable of rendering the Faces of 2,000 people perceptible, without the assistance of any light whatever.

Licences issued in Exeter at the time showed that Richard Hughes was forced to relinquish his term of managership in 1799 and the theatre was taken over by Dandford—one of his company. But the latter lacked the taste and control of the players, and in consequence audiences fell away.

But after a short period in the doldrums, due, in no small measure, to counter-attractions appearing at inns in the city, the end of the eighteenth century saw Exeter in full bloom as the No. 1 theatrical town in the West. It gave a wide variety of plays, concerts, extra sketches and interludes of a high quality to an audience that gave the theatre faithful support.

CHAPTER V

# Piercing the Gloom

While the Exonians were the first in the West Country to
battle against the Calvinistic gloom—and even managed now
and then like their modern counterpart, the Northcott Theatre
Company, to send a group of actors to tour the immediate
outlying villages—the rest of Devonshire had remained
theatrically dormant.

Barnstaple, which had been visited on occasions by Elizabethan strolling players, had yet to think for another century
about a theatre of its own, and the scattered towns of Cornwall, which had enjoyed sporadic visits by the strollers, found
with the oppressive laws and current religious outlook that
there were very few companies who would venture so far
West without encountering prosecution on the way.

Stubborn Plymouth sat still and brooded, continuing to ban
all kinds of such frivolous amusements.

At the opening of the eighteenth century it made its own
laws against plays and players, with this entry in the Judicial
Orders of the Plymouth Quarter Sessions for 28th November
1709:

Whereas a Presentment has been made to this Court by the
Grand Jury of this Burrough on their Oathes that Publick
Enterludes and Stage plays are Common Nusances and Tend to
the Increase of Irreligion Prophaneness and Immorality the said
Court doth thereupon order that noe Publick Enterludes or
Stage plays be henceforth Acted within this Burrough and that
in any case any Houses, Boothes or Stages be Erected for the
Acting of any playes or Enterludes that the same shall be pulled
down by the Constables of this Burrough for which this order
of the Sessions shall be their Warrant.

And it is hereby further ordered and declared by the said Court that Actors of any such playes or Enterludes within this Burrough shall be proceeded against dealt with and used as Vagabonds Vagrants and Strolers soe far as the Law has declared them such.

Per Curiam [By the Court]

Plymouth's sanctimonious attitude and parsimony were becoming well known throughout the country, and were blazoned abroad by the poet laureate Sir William Davenant, who was reputed to be the natural son of William Shakespeare by the hostess of the Crown Inn, Cornmarket. There is, of course, no proof, and, like most Shakespeareana, it is shrouded in guess and conjecture. However, it was certain that Shakespeare was well acquainted with his family and that he was Davenant's godfather.

Davenant, in his five-act play *Newes from Plimmoth*, wrote about the town:

This towne is dearer than Jerusalem after a years war. They would make us pay for the Daylight if they knew how to measure the sun by the yard. Nay sell the very aire too if they could serve it out in fine china bottels. If you walk but three times in the High street they will ask you money for wearing out the pebbles.

Meanwhile Plymouth was growing fast, for in 1692 Parliament had voted a sum of £2m sterling "for finishing forthwith their Majestie's Naval Yard at Hamoaze". The Hamoaze was the name applied to the mouth of the River Tamar which divided Devon from Cornwall, and the new township which grew up alongside the yard was unimaginatively labelled "Dock" (later to be changed to Devonport), a town that swiftly spread longer and longer tentacles into the surrounding areas.

Anne had become Queen in 1702, and the Marlborough wars against the French had begun; Admiral Cloudesley Shovell was mourned as a national hero when his ship went down off Scilly; Winstanley's Eddystone light was to flare up in flames in 1703 and be replaced by Rudyerd's lighthouse in 1708; and the first of the Hanoverians, George I, was to succeed to the throne in 1714.

[48]

Plymouth, which had prospered during this time of war through shipbuilding and the addition of increased trade with the military, found itself in 1728 suffering acutely from peacetime depression. Vacant premises multiplied through the city, there was unemployment everywhere and in jumped the Puritans once more with an edict: "To discourage Vice and Immorality." The Freemen rulers of the Hospital for the Poor's Portion (the Workhouse rulers and the only social service then in existence) adopted an inviolable resolution which meant that a starving actor could not demand even a crust from them, but:

> In case of players or actors of interludes, who by statute law are declared rogues and vagabonds, shall presume to act within the borough of Plymouth they should be kept in prison to hard labour till the further pleasure of the Corporation herein; and the Governor and his brother members will indemnifie and defend such constables as may be mulcted or prosecuted for doing their duty.

But peacetime soon gave way to another war—with France this time—and the Jacobite Rebellion was causing unease in the country; so soldiers, sailors and merchants began once more to swell the population. As was to happen so often in the future, when hostilities elsewhere brought a return of prosperity to Plymouth, repressive measures were relaxed as if they were something to be ashamed of when exposed to "foreigners", and at once the natives began to demand the fruits of freedom enjoyed by the outside world and denied to them for so long.

Apparently someone from Plymouth had been to Exeter, seen the success that Bice had made of his Waterbeare theatre and, in spite of the law, and defying the local divines' prejudice, decided to try a similar project in the city.

One can imagine the outcry from the Puritan purists at this blatant effrontery, but they stood little chance against the added force of hundreds of newcomers to the citizenry. Public opinion prevailed and in 1745 the first Plymouth theatre opened in Hoegate Street (then Broad Hoe Lane).

Compared with the Exeter building it was a very makeshift affair, roughly two rooms of a dilapidated house which only

[49]

FIG. 5.—The Myrriorama, a primitive forerunner of the magic lantern which toured the country towns, formed part of the attractions for a population deprived of public entertainment in the early part of the eighteenth-century.

held about a hundred at one time, but it was sufficient to house some of the travelling companies who were only too glad to find a place in which to perform, however ramshackle the surroundings.

The theatre owners cheated the licensing laws by following Exeter's example in performing whatever they thought might slide around the Act. Seeing there was a small advantage in performing some of the classics they staged "*The Tempest—or The Enchanted Island*—with original musick, songs, dances and machinery proper to the entertainment".

Details of other plays presented at the Hoegate Theatre are sparse, but it is known that the Bath Players came to Plymouth with *The Beaux Stratagem* in 1749. By now this company, who were sacked from Somerset and who had taken up residence in Exeter, had become known far and wide as "The Brandy Company"—so described because the majority of them drank themselves to death.

Their dissolute habits soon became a byword even in Plymouth's ale-drinking circles, and the theatre itself also began to make a name itself for riotous entertainment. Fights and quarrels occurred amongst cast and audience until the structure's makeshift qualities began to be felt and it became uninhabitable.

The building was abandoned in 1758 and one of the more sober members of the Bath Company, named Arthur, took over the lease of three partly-built houses in Frankfort Street (the present site would now be roughly in the middle of the Western Approach Road at the end of King Street) and so eager was he to begin operations that for the first week they played without a roof over the heads of the audience. A little later on, so uneasy was the construction that the show had to be stopped as the gallery was swaying, and it was only after being propped up with balks of timber that the performance could continue! It should be borne in mind that "a gallery" in those days was no broad sweep with tiers of seats, but little more than a shelf which allowed a few seats in the front row. The rest of the occupants stood crowding at their backs.

An indication that any kind of theatre would suffice for the drama-starved Plymothians was given when, at the opening performance, £38 was taken at the door—a huge sum in those days—and during the ensuing ten weeks the total takings reached £1,800.

Arthur did not last long at Frankfort Gate, for Joseph Pittard, an actor, took over the theatre soon after the opening. Later that year he acquired the Exeter Theatre from Hugh Kennedy of the Bath Company (the Brandy Company) and in trying to run them both had troubles with his Plymouth audience. The latter, according to Whitfeld, voiced their loud objections when a play billed as *Jane Shore* (a favourite tear-jerker of the time) was dropped and in its place was substituted a poetic prologue by Pittard, a comic dance, a farce *Miss in her Teens* and an epilogue *Everybody*—to be spoken by "Somebody in the character of a Nobody".

For the BENEFIT of
## The Office, Door, & Stage-Keepers.

## THEATRE FRANKFORT-GATE.

*Friday, October 11, 1776, will be perform'd a Concert of Music.*

Between the PARTS of the above CONCERT will be presented GRATIS,

*By Their Majesties Servants, &c. a TRAGEDY, call'd*

# Romeo and Juliet.

Romeo by Mr. WOLFE,
Mercutio Mr. ELLARD,
Prince of Verona Mr. CHALMERS,
Montague Mr. YOUNG,
Paris Mr. CUBIT,
Tibalt Mr. BROWNE,
Page Master VENABLES,
Capulet Mr. MORRIS,
And Fryar Lawrence Mr. VENABLES.
Nurse by Mrs. VENABLES,
Lady Capulet Mrs. YOUNG,
And Juliet Miss USHER.

In Act II. a MASQUERADE and COTILLION, in *Grotesque Characters*, and a MINUET by Mr. ELLARD and Mrs. MASTERS.
In Act IV. *The Funeral Procession, Solemn Dirge,* and *Dead March,* to the MONUMENT of the CAPULETS;
The Vocal Parts by *Mr. Cubitt, Mr. Morris, Mrs. Williams, Mrs. Manning, Mrs. Young, Mrs. Moore,* and *Mrs. Masters.*

*End of the Play a* HORNPIPE *by Master* VENABLES.

*To which will be added a Pantomine Entertainment,* (perform'd here but once these 14 Years) call'd

# Hecate's Enchantment;
## Or, HARLEQUIN SKELETON.

In which will be INTRODUC'D
The DYING SCENE & RESTORATION,
TO CONCLUDE WITH
A TRANSPARENT SCENE of the View of SPITHEAD.
Harlequin by Mr. CHALMERS,
Shatterbrain Mr. ELLARD,
Blunder Master VENABLES,
Porter Mr. J. FOOTE, Cook Mr. YOUNG,
Dwarf Master MORRIS, Doctor Mr. BROWNE,
And Pierrot Mr. MORRIS.
Witches, Lads and Lasses, by Mr. YOUNG, Mr. J. FOOTE, Mrs. WILLIAMS,
Mrs. MANNING, &c. &c.
And Columbine Mrs. YOUNG.

PLYMOUTH: Printed by R. TREWMAN, and B. HAYDON, in PIKE-STREET, where all manner of Printing Work is neatly and expeditiously perform'd, and on the most reasonable Terms.

Apparently Pittard's players (according to Thomas Holcroft in 1780 the common name in the profession for provincial actors was "a spouter") were "on the bottle" or, as one actor was later to put it out in public, "had not got the words"; so he advertised to his patrons his own shortcomings, and said: "In order to make amends I have been over to Launceston to engage some of the best performers belonging to the company there."

Indeed Launceston, once the capital city of Cornwall, had its own company which at the time played at the inns and travelled the villages around during their off season.

The acting seasons for most theatres in those days generally lasted from October to April in the larger towns, but plays were then presented only once a week—on Fridays, except for special occasions. Such occasions would include the Assize weeks at Exeter, when some important visitor was present in the town, or, in the case of Plymouth, the presence of the military or visiting ships which might warrant extra performances.

With many service people around, the West Country was becoming both popular and fashionable. The patronage of influential people was greatly sought after by actors for it gave them the cachet of respectability, and any suggestion that their audience was to be honoured by someone of public stature was immediately advertised on the playbills as: "By the desire and under the distinguished patronage and presence of Major General and the Hon Mrs Murray"; or: "By desire of the Officers and Gentlemen of the Dock Cavalry".

In 1760 there were sedan chairs in the larger cities (Plymouth had six) and these were needed when most streets were just trodden earth and became pools of mud in wet weather. The old rutted footpath between Plymouth and Exeter, while still mostly impassable except on foot, had in places been

FIG. 6 *(facing page)*.—A typical example of the device used by unscrupulous theatre managers to get around the Patent Theatres Act, which forbade the production of plays except at Covent Garden and Drury Lane. This was achieved by describing the performance as "A Concert of Music" when between interspersed songs and dances the main plays would be presented. (Daybill by courtesy of Devon County Libraries.)

widened by use to some 10ft. to 12ft. and was used mainly by pack horses with, very occasionally, a cart. In fact the sight of a horse-drawn carriage, or even a jolting wagon, was very unusual in the overgrown country lanes covered with natural bowers from the overhanging branches, and the appearance of a private coach or carriage was a very rare happening because most visitors came by water.

This was the time when the bucks and the gentry of the navy and military attended fashionable balls and supper parties, especially in the more salubrious Stonehouse (Plymouth's third town), when nights became gayer and the theatre began at last to prosper.

The acme of respectability came when in the mid-1760s Plymouth was visited by George III and his Queen, who, staying at Saltram, were taken by their hosts to the Frankfort Gate Theatre to witness a performance.

How the royal party fared in this rough and ready structure, or what they saw, is not known, but it certainly gave the owners a great lift. Immediately afterwards they called their ramshackle affair "The Theatre Royal" (quite illegally of course—but it was a title which, once achieved and not questioned, was to be passed on to the new building many years in the future).

In the year 1762 war fever was again rampant, with the town full of people and the Sound full of ships. Devonport (Dock) was quickly catching up with its neighbour, having already established itself as a dockyard, and was now rapidly expanding with enclosure of land by Sir William Morice in order to increase its capacity.

With artisans' dwellings being erected at a fast rate to cope with the expansion, Dock became in population figures a much larger town than Plymouth, and the call for entertainment among the dockyard citizens could only be answered by their crossing the ferry at Stonehouse in order to visit Frankfort Gate. The demand became so great that in 1762 a theatre was opened in Cumberland Gardens, opposite the present Old Chapel public house, then a meeting house. It called itself the Dock Theatre, with admission prices Box 2s. 6d., Pit 1s. and Gallery 6d.

Competition between the two towns' theatres was pretty

disastrous for both. Quarrels developed, culminating in a rash attempt to open yet a third theatre in George Street, which soon failed. The theatres eventually settled down to an acceptance of the other's existence with two watchful managements eyeing each other for business; with the result that the Plymouth House became the more respectable of the two (and that is not saying much, for they both had their riotous times) while Dock was more popular with the boisterous "gods" who preferred the "bluer" jokes.

One of the first managers of the Dock theatre was Richard Hughes who was later to take over the Exeter Theatre. He was succeeded by a Samuel Foote, and under the latter's ownership the theatre fared a trifle better than as just a place where sailors, drunks and bawds played havoc with the actors.

Performances as such were more in the form of a two-way conversation between actor and audience. Remarks, shouts and advice were hurled at the players from every quarter— and the actors answered back.

Free fights were commonplace; insults were hurled from gallery to those below in the pit; the players, if not liked, were pelted with orangepeel, bottles, nuts and anything to hand; magistrates tried occasionally to stop the worst of the licentious behaviour, but failed when Jack was out on shore determined to enjoy himself.

There were many examples of the "simple" kind being carried away by the play—and the not-so-simple, too—just as in years to come protests from the audience over some harrowing scene were to become part and parcel of Victorian theatregoing.

Whitfeld relates a remarkable scene during one performance at the Dock Theatre of *Othello*, when the time had come for the tragic Desdemona to be murdered in her bed.

Entering into the spirit of the play in deadly earnest, one Jack Tar shouted: "Is the black brute allowed to cut her life lines? I'm damned if I can stand it any longer." Then throwing himself over the side of the gallery, he ran to the rescue and tore Desdemona from the Moor's grasp. Othello bolted from the stage, greasepaint and all, and rushed in terror through the back lanes to his house—still clutching the dagger.

Not that the Plymouth theatre was at that time any more decorous, for at one performance a female artist, Mrs Bradshaw, was hissed off the stage following a dance. So badly did she take the audience's disapprobation that she had a fit, and, according to Whitfeld, was carried home to die!

It was under these rough-house circumstances that Sarah Siddons appeared at the Dock Theatre in 1785 playing Lady Macbeth with the local stock company, a collection of actors more familiar with the rum bottle than a book.

This was four years earlier than her appearance at the Exeter house when she was thirty years of age, and after her great triumph at Drury Lane. Her appearance at the Dock Theatre (after playing under David Garrick) may, on the face of it, appear rather a comedown; but she was then touring the provinces which had given her the initial experience to enable her to conquer London, and she was under the managership of John Palmer of the Bath Theatre.

This was the company which had provided the nucleus of the Plymouth and Exeter theatres (the Brandy Company) and it was, therefore, natural that Palmer should book her into theatres that were on his old circuit and which were known to him.

It is not on record just how she fared at Dock, but her reputation of paralysing provincial audiences with her great powers followed her everywhere. If there was anyone on the stage at that time who could quell the unruly spirits of Dock, then that was Sarah Siddons.

The frequent changes of management of West Country theatres at this time prove confusing for the historian, especially when only surnames are given on playbills and dates are often dubious.

The title of "Theatre Royal" was bestowed on the Dock Theatre by a new lessee, Samuel Foote (not to be confused with the far greater Samuel Foote, the actor and playwright from Truro who was to be buried in Westminster Abbey). Formerly an army officer called Freeman, he changed his name with his new profession.

Asked upon what authority he called his theatre "Royal" he replied in the best professional tradition: "Well, it's a good travelling name and avoids enquiries."

[56]

His other claim to fame was through his daughter Maria, who, born in Plymouth in 1798, was to become a great beauty and an actress, and was destined to leave her mark on theatre history through scandal.

The year 1779 saw a period of great activity in the Plymouth and Dock theatres with such plays as the much requested *The Tragedy of George Barnwell*, a sentimental tragedy with "an awful warning".

A production of *The Beggar's Opera* was immediately followed by *A Hornpipe by Master Cope* and a farce *Life Below Stairs*, and there were many instances of the oft-repeated device of cheating the Act with such announcements as: "A Concert of Music, between the several parts of the concert will be presented a Tragedy called *Hamlet*." Foote played the King, Jefferson the Gloomy Dane and Mrs Jefferson appeared as Ophelia.

Towards the end of the eighteenth century Plymouth's name was to be heard in other theatres with the production of a new play called *Plymouth in an Uproar*. It was written by Charles Dibdin, composer of "Tom Bowling" and "the Lass that loved a Sailor", songs which were said to have brought more men to the navy in war than all the press gang could muster.

*Plymouth in an Uproar* was written as a musical farce, but it soon became a favourite patriotic piece (it was performed at Covent Garden in 1779), especially with audiences in naval seaports. It contained all the stilted clichés of the day, with a typical and predictable cast for such a play—Lt. Beauclerk, Lord Heartless, Ben and Pipes both Honest Sailors, Emilia the heroine, the wicked Landlord and a band of ostlers, ruffians etc. to do the dirty work.

It finished with the following song of noble sentiment and doggerel verse:

> Proud France and Spain might vainly boast
> In vain with greedy eye they see
> Our roast beef pouring gravy,
> Our lovely dames, our Liberty.
> Which jointly serve to brace each nerve,
> To prove in spite of all their boast,
> No danger shall annoy our coast
> While we've a Gallant Navy!

* Plymouth was indeed in an uproar, outside the theatre as well as in. It was unruly, stinking, greedy, grasping and fearful of what the next day would bring.

W. G. Maton, a visitor in 1785, wrote:

> The Town of Plymouth is a large, but ill-built disagreeable place, infested with all the filthiness so frequent in seaports and there is a great exportation of pilchards to Italy and other Catholic countries. From the bustle and continued passing of people we could fancy ourselves in the outskirts of London.

while Captain Marryatt, author of *Mr Midshipman Easy* and *Masterman Ready*, gave the following vivid description of the town when wars were rife and the press gang was at its cruel best.

> Disorder reigned supreme at Mutton Cove as stock and spares were hurried aboard. "Jump into the cutter sir, and go to Mount Wise for the officers, and be careful that none of your men leave the boat," shouted the first lieutenant. At Mutton Cove foul oaths escaped the seamen as they dash their hooks into the watermen's craft. A sergeant of marines was sent in search of absentees, whom he picked up roaring drunk in one of the neighbouring inns, and their arrival made it worse as it was impossible to control those that were sober.

On the other hand "paying-off" time in the Dockyard came to be feared by the populace and welcomed by the tradesmen who always knew when the men were to receive their money.

Bumboat men, trading sharks, women wanting long arrears and shopkeepers waiting for settlement of debts surrounded each ship's company as it came ashore amid a babel of bawling, threatening, laughing and crying.

"Spend it quickly before we sail again," was the watchword, and the ale houses, dens, bawdy houses and theatres took the majority back into their clutches for the town was beginning to see where its destiny lay. A way of life that in the years to come would rely for the most part on the prosperity of the navy was evolving, making Plymouth rich in times of war, and parsimonious in peace.

*A Picture of Plymouth*, published in the 1790s, says of the Dock Theatre:

It has nothing to recommend it in its outward appearance, it is neatly fitted up in the interior and sufficiently spacious for the inhabitants who are not very constant in their attendance. It derives its support chiefly from the Army and the Navy and is generally open during the winter months and has a tolerable set of Comedians from the Exeter and Plymouth stages.

Inside, its atmosphere was little more than a circus. Repartee between actor and audience in the middle of a play was commonplace; patrons who stood or sat upon benches drinking and smoking conducted ribald backchat with their neighbours and were far from acquainted with the refined niceties and genteel approach of modern theatregoing. The fare was appropriately designed to measure up to their taste.

James Winston's *Theatric Tourist*, published at the end of the eighteenth century, has a word on West Country aesthetic appreciation.

ON AUDIENCES IN PLYMOUTH. The Plymouth taste like that of most other country towns is very far from refined one, preferring buffoonery to the chastest acting.
ON THE LICENSING AUTHORITIES IN DEVONPORT. This house (The Dock Theatre) is a nightly scene of riot and debauchery notwithstanding the presence of the Magistrates who use their privilege of admission not only for themselves, but for their friends.
ON ATTENDANCES AT EXETER. There, as in most other cities, the theatre is not attended in proportion to the population; the company, generally speaking, is respectable; but Devonshire has never yet been famous for producing theatrical geniuses.

Perhaps not at that early date—but they were on the way.

At the turn of the century Nelson was supreme, the dour Puritans of Plymouth were once again submerged by a flood of "foreign" labour with artisans, soldiers and professional men coming into the town, which by now had spread itself far beyond the old boundaries and extended west to the end of the present Royal Parade, and north as far as Portland Square encompassing a population of 30,000 souls.

Its adjacent towns were growing fast, too. Stonehouse now had a residential population of 6,000 around Durnford Street and parts of Stoke; while Dock, which was soon to outstrip

THEATRE, FRANKFORT-GATE.

## By Their Majesties Servants.

On WEDNESDAY, July 19, 1780,

Will be PERFORM'D

# A CONCERT of MUSIC.

BOXES 3s.— UPPER BOXES 2s. 6d.— PIT 2s.— GALLERY 1s.

TICKETS to be had at Messrs. Wallis and Haydon's, Booksellers; Mr. Weatherley's, Printer; King's-Arms, and London Inns; Mr. Ord's Tavern, Plymouth — The Fountain, and King's-Arms, at Dock; and at the Theatre, where Places for the Boxes may be taken.

*The DOORS to be opened at SIX, and begin precisely at SEVEN o'CLOCK.*

Between the several Parts of the CONCERT, will be presented GRATIS,

*A New COMIC OPERA, call'd*

# The DUENNA:

## Or, The DOUBLE ELOPEMENT.

Don Anthonio by Mr. CUBITT,
Don Ferdinand by Mr. BARRYMORE,
Don Carlos by Miss JARRATT,
Isaac Mendosa by Mr. T. BLANCHARD,
Father Paul by Mr. BROWNE,
Father Augustine by Mr. BLANCHARD,
Lay Brother by Mr. THORNTON,
Lopez by Mr. SMITH,
And Don Jerome *(for the first Time)* by Mr. FOOTE.

Donna Louisa by Mrs. WELLS,
Donna Clara by Mrs. JEFFERSON,
Nun by Mrs. DAVIS,
And the Duenna by Mrs. THORNTON.

*End of Act I. a* DANCE, *by Miss* BRADSHAW.
*End of the Opera a* HORNPIPE *by Mr.* T. BLANCHARD.

To which will be added a FARCE, call'd

# *Three Weeks after Marriage:*

## Or, What we must all come To.

Sir Charles Racket by Mr. JEFFERSON,
Mr. Woodley by Mr. THORNTON,
William by Mr. SMITH,
And Old Drugget by Mr. FOOTE.

Lady Racket by Mrs. JEFFERSON,
Dimity by Mrs. THORNTON,
Nancy by Mrs. WELLS,
And Mrs. Drugget by Mrs. BRADSHAW.

N.B. No Person can possibly be admitted behind the Scenes; at which, it is humbly presumed, no Gentleman can be offended.

PLYMOUTH: Printed by R. TREWMAN, and B. HAYDON, in Pike-Street.

them all, was furiously busy with extensive additions to the dockyard and a large shipbuilding programme, which brought in its wake houses for officers in Morice Town and Keyham with workers' dwellings crammed in between. It had its own rapidly-growing local authority supporting a population of 23,000.

Amid this great expansion the theatre had made another big step forward with the passing in 1788 of an Act which went a long way towards legalising acting in the provinces by giving Justices power to license plays for sixty days at one time. Licences were granted at Quarter Sessions to the manager of the company and this had the effect of giving a greater air of respectability to the "rogues and vagabonds" of previous enactments. It also, to some extent, put a stop to the absurd situation whereby only the two Patent Theatres in London were allowed to present full-length plays.

Needless to say, the city fathers were not over-pleased with this recognition of common players and gave only grudging permission for licences to be issued.

A typical petition to the Council presented by the lessee of Frankfort Gate Theatre, Samuel Foote, is still preserved in the city archives and reads:

To the Worshipful the Mayor and Others Justices of the Peace of the Borough of Plymouth in the County of Devon in Quarter Sessions Assembled.

The humble petition of Samuel Foote Sheweth that your Petitioner did upwards of three weeks before this application wait upon, and give notice to the Worshipful the Mayor of this Borough, of this his intention to make the present application And in pursuance thereof, and of the Act of Parliament passed in that behalf, your Petitioner does now humbly Petition for your Worships to grant him a Licence for the performance of all such Tragedies, Comedies, Operas, Farces, Interludes and every such other Dramatic Entertainments as have or may be presented at either of the Theatres Royal within the City of Westminster, at the theatre in Frankfort Gate within the

FIG. 7 *(facing page)*.—In order to pare the cost of engaging actors the manager invariably appeared himself, and Foote's name on the playbill was a regular feature during his time at Frankfort-Gate theatre.

Borough of Plymouth aforesaid for the number of sixty days within the space of four months conmmencing on the first of June one thousand eight hundred and two, and to continue for four months as aforesaid, agreeable to the said Act of Parliament; And your Petitioner shall ever pray

Signed Sam Foote.

While the last four decades of the eighteenth century had certainly seen an awakening of theatrical interest—albeit a coarse and crude one—in the long depressed area of the West Country, it was hardly spectacular when set alongside the London scene. However, it had sparked off imaginations and bred the seeds of greatness among a few.

William Farren, the head of a distinguished theatrical family, made his debut in Plymouth under his brother's management during those early years, and shortly afterwards appeared at the Exeter Theatre. He rose to fame in after years for his portrayal of Sir Peter Teazle, which he had played at Covent Garden and Drury Lane among other classic roles.

The elder Jefferson, born in Ripon in 1728 and previously mentioned as taking over the old Exeter Theatre, went to London in 1746 to become a member of Garrick's company at Drury Lane where he was quoted as being "Garrick's favourite Horatio in Hamlet". He came back to Plymouth where he managed the theatre for some time. His Hamlet, with his wife's Ophelia, was seen at the Frankfort Gate Theatre in 1774.

His son Joseph Jefferson was born in Plymouth in the same year, was carefully groomed for a career on the stage and appeared at the Plymouth Theatre while still a youth. However, as soon as he became of age, he emigrated to America and founded the famous Jefferson acting family in that country.

His relationship with President Jefferson with whom he was on friendly terms suggested that they were of the same family, but whereas Joseph was born in Plymouth, the President claimed his ancestry was of Welsh extraction and no connection could be traced.

These above-mentioned names and the occasional visits by such "stars" as the Kembles, John Gay and Mrs Siddons all helped to form the first footprints of what was to become the well-trodden West Country circuit—prints first sketched out by those strolling players of Elizabethan times in a circuit which took in such places as Bristol, Bath, Exeter, Plymouth and Weymouth, with occasional deviations into Cornwall and the smaller towns of Devon.

As yet these were but tokens of what London theatres had enjoyed since just after the Restoration, but, at long last, the curtain was to open in the West Country on the wide cyclorama of theatreland, and its citizens were to see what had been denied them over those long intervening years.

CHAPTER VI

# Blood and Thunder

It is a sad reflection on human nature that the arts flourish most in England during times of stress and turbulence. While this is a national phenomenon, it abundantly illustrates Plymouth's later emergence, for a brief period, as a No. 1 theatrical city (one day to house seven theatres all at one time), a situation which in turn opened the way for other West Country towns to the joys of theatrical art and entertainment.

The belated deliverance from the dismal Puritan outlook on pleasure, entertainment and enjoyment was brought about by war, and, as was so often to happen in the city's history, the sour kill-joys were forced back into their narrow-minded cells by the sheer mass of numbers from outside, who in turn influenced the slower-minded but purposeful Plymothian to action.

During the early days of the nineteenth century Plymouth's population had swollen to nearly double that of Exeter (then 17,000) and the Napoleonic wars on sea and land, with rumours of invasion from the French, had brought the city not only to a high pitch of feverish industry through ship-building and trade in general, but into the bargain had come an invasion of British workpeople from up-country, resulting in overcrowding in the still small town. With them came the worst excesses of wartime fever.

Both civilian and military demanded recreation in their off times. Inns and ale houses opened at 6 a.m. and remained open most of the night; the ladies of Devonport (and of Plymouth for that matter) advertised their charms by dropping cards on unsuspecting officers; gambling, drunkenness and muggery in the streets were commonplace.

Vandalism was an everyday occurrence. A Mr Wm May of 4, Chapel St. advertised: "I promise a reward of £100 if those pests of society are prosecuted to conviction," and asked the Gentlemen of Dock whether it would not be desirable to approve a nightly watch "as we have so many strangers and foreigners about".

Coiners and forgers, who were busy conterfeiting money over at Cawsand after Waterloo, did fine business until they were eventually caught and hanged at Bodmin.

Magistrates tried in vain to curb riots. Public whippings were imposed and the stocks and ducking stool used frequently, but with poorly-lit streets and order maintained by Rounders and Watchmen armed with staves, lanterns and rattles, the title of a Naval seaport was quickly being earned.

Amusements, such as they were, could only be found in Plymouth at the ramshackle Frankfort Gate Theatre and the barn-like structure at Dock where the main bill of fare consisted of repetitions of *George Barnwell* with its trite moral "Learn to be wise from Others Harm and you shall do Full Well", and freely-written topical plays *The Sailor's Hobby*, *Naval Revels* (or *All Alive at Plymouth Dock*) and *A British Sailor's advice to the Volunteers*.

Now and again the managements would engage a better attraction. On the West Country circuit in 1806 came the Boy Wonder, Master William Betty. The Young Roscius, as he was called, was then aged fourteen and had already played at Covent Garden and Drury Lane in all the great tragic roles.

By 1806, however, his brief and hectic success was waning, and after appearing at Exeter where he earned lukewarm praise from the critics, he came to Frankfort Gate in November and a local theatregoer recorded his impressions.

> Master Betty appeared in Hamlet, Romeo and as Frederick in *Lover's Vows*—in all which parts his wonderful powers astonished my weak mind—and methinks to myself, many other weak minds.

In June, 1810, the Dock Theatre enjoyed a visit from the "First Comedian of the English Stage", Joseph Munden, of whom Charles Lamb had written: "He and he alone, literally

[65]

# Theatre-Royal, Plymouth.

## This present Wednesday, June 16, 1802,

Will be acted the favorite PLAY of

# The Castle Spectre.

In Act 2, The Armoury and the Gothic Chamber.

In Act 3, The Cedar Room, and a Transparency of a Roman Oratory, with a grand and awful Appearance of the Spectre of the Castle.

In Act 4, View of Conway Castle, at Sun-set.

In Act 5, The Outside of the Castle, and a subterraneous Dungeon.

Osmond, Mr. SMITH,
Percy, Mr. GORE, Hassan, Mr. MILLS,
Kenrick, Mr. WESTERNLY, Father Philip, Mr. MATTHEWS,
Saib, Mr. DENHAM, Muley, Mr. GRANT,
Motley, Mr. FREEMAN, Allan, Mr. BROWNE,
Reginald, Mr. HAGUE.

The Spectre, Mrs. WESTERNLY, Alice, Mrs. GORE,
Angela, Miss HAGUE.

END OF THE PLAY,

A favorite new SONG by Mr. GORE,

To which will be added the MUSICAL FARCE of

# The Agreeable Surprize.

## Lingo by Mr. WINSTON,

Compton, Mr. GORE, Chicane, Mr. BROWNE,
Eugene, Mr. MILLS, John, Mr. MATTHEWS,
Thomas, Mr. GRANT, Cudden, Mr. DENHAM, Stump, Mr. WESTERNLY,
And Sir Felix Friendly, Mr. HAGUE.

Laura, Mrs. MILLS,
Mrs. Cheshire, Mrs. GORE, Fringe, Miss HAGUE,
And Cowslip, Miss GRANT.

Tickets to be had, & Places in the Boxes taken, at *Browne's Circulating-Library*, N°. 13, Frankfort-Place;

BOXES, 3s.——PIT 2s.——GALLERY 1s.

Second Account to Boxes, 2s.—to the Pit, 1s. 6d.—but nothing under Full Price to the Gallery

☞ Doors to be Opened at SIX, and begin precisely at SEVEN o'CLOCK.

HAYDON, Printer. Stationer. &c. Market Place. Plymouth.

[66]

*makes* faces . . . Munden stands out as single and unaccompanied as Hogarth."

Farren and Hughes appeared at Dock the same year in *The Belle's Strategem*, a farce *The Sultan*, a comedy called *The Wonder* and another entitled *The Wedding Day*—all in the same evening.

Going to the theatre in those days was no elegant outing for the family, an evening of culture or three hours of enlightened entertainment. Instead, it was more a case of free-for-all among the audience and "take what you get" from the actors.

"Country versions" of the classics were regular offerings from the semi-literate stock companies. They were easier to play and cheaper (using less actors) to present.

Productions of *Romeo and Juliet* generally began with Mercutio's entrance in I, iv. Many of the lesser characters were left out entirely and other parts were doubled (and if possible, trebled).

Production and properties were of the most primitive kind, and words were interpolated by the actors to cover every contingency. One Plymouth presentation of *Othello* had Desdemona discovered on a bed composed of a plank placed lengthways between two chairs, and in trying to maintain an equilibrium during the long death scene she conducted a *sotto voce* conversation with the Moor and the prompter to prevent her from falling off.

| | |
|---|---|
| DESDEMONA. | O, banish me, my lord, but kill me not! |
| OTHELLO. | (Keep yourself up) Down, strumpet. |
| DES. | Kill me tomorrow; let me live tonight. (I shall be over.) |
| OTH. | Nay, an you strive—(Lie still you bitch.) |
| DES. | But half an hour! (I'm falling.) |

FIG. 8 *(facing page)*.—*The Castle Spectre*, written in 1797 by Matthew Gregory Lewis, was highly popular at the turn of the eighteenth-century. A hotch-potch melodrama, it had everything—villain, hero, maniacal romance, distressed maid and a horrifying spectre who, according to the prologue, "Oft with glimmering lamp, near graves, new open'd, or midst dungeons damp,/Drear Forests, ruin'd aisles, and haunted towers,/Forlorn she roves, and raves away the hours!"

OTH.      Being done, there is no pause.
DES.      But while I say one prayer! (I'm off.)
OTH.      It is too late.

And in his eagerness to keep her steady Othello placed one knee upon the bed, which at once capsized leaving him bestriding her in a most uncultural position.

Bottles, rotten apples and other missiles were often thrown at the actors, who, in turn, would throw them back over the rows of flickering candles into the darkness of the audience with the added force of a blistering curse.

During those first years of the new century all places of amusement suffered a great deal of rowdyism, as the audiences were composed mostly of the rougher elements of the town, raucous sailors and soldiers and the more venturesome of the civilian population. The more genteel and respectable folk were afraid to go into such places, not so much because of the boisterous crowds, but for fear of the ever-present press gang who conscripted any able-bodied man on sight.

The dread of these official kidnappers had been a part of naval seaport life for many years, and their activities were intensified at the time of Trafalgar. This dread was reflected in the revival of an old ballad first heard in 1796 called "Sweet Poll of Plymouth". The grief and despair endured by ordinary folk at the rough handling they received from the press gangs is shown in the first verse:

> Sweet Poll of Plymouth was my dear
> When forced from her to go;
> Adown her cheek ran many a tear,
> Her heart was fraught with woe.
> And they have torn my love away,
> And is he gone? She cry'd,
> My Love, the sweetest flower in May
> Then languished, drooped and died.

Set to music by Thomas Arne, it was sung by Mrs Kennedy in a play called *The Positive Man*, became one of the popular "hits" of the day and lasted so for many years.

Years later, the nautical melodrama *Sweet Poll of Plymouth* was written by Douglas Jerrold in 1829, and later the title

SWEET POLL OF PLYMOUTH.

FIG. 9.—An old print of Sweet Poll of Plymouth and the press gang first published in 1796 and reprinted at the time of Trafalgar.

was changed to *Black Eyed Susan*. It became a great favourite after T. P. Cooke made a hit as the flag-waving hero William at the old Surrey Theatre in London.

As Maurice Willson Disher records in his book *Blood and Thunder*:

[69]

No drama was ever more nautical; no other seamen so redolent of tar, so virtuous compared with landsmen; so full of seafaring oaths, exclamations, similes and metaphors—salt water is rarely out of their mouths and often fills their eyes.

William never utters a phrase that is not seaworthy . . . and when all is ready for the hanging from the foreyard, Crosstree rushes forward with a pre-dated discharge saying "When William struck me he was not the King's sailor—I was not his officer!"

To resounding patriotic cheers and red fire, *Black Eyed Susan* or *Sweet Poll of Plymouth* was to be revived over and over again in the Plymouth and Dock theatres where it was invariably received with rousing shouts of approval.

Jerrold was to write less for the theatre when he became associated with the foundation of *Punch* in 1841, and in later years lost his taste for the theatre altogether and referred to *Black Eyed Susan* as "Surrey Trash".

But, despite the glorified patriotism of the melodrama of the day, the nefarious press gang hunted and thrashed into submission many citizens, able-bodied or not, from all over the West Country. No town or village escaped their bullying entry into inns, theatres or meetings for a period of some forty years; in consequence fear kept people closely to their homes, and they were restless.

But amid these distressing times a new spirit was felt in the air. Victory came at Trafalgar—a glorious prelude to another victory at Waterloo and the subsequent banishment of Napoleon, whom Plymothians were to row out to see in the *Bellerophon* in Plymouth Sound, events which in the space of ten years created a happier and more optimistic atmosphere among the people.

Up to the turn of the century the Plymouth Corporation's power of initiative was mainly confined to the collection of tolls, dues and profits arising from the letting of fish, fruit, meat and vegetable stalls, the sale of dung, dirt and ashes, and a niggardly administration of the town, with little thought to municipal development.

But the wars had brought new blood, skill and professionalism into the town, and a new kind of citizen took up permanent residence in the more salubrious parts. Their gradual infiltration into the minds, ranks and workings of the corporate body was to have revolutionary results.

Who would have dreamed that the closely-knit small town of Puritan Plymouth of over 150 years ago would conceive the building of a social project complete with hotel, assembly rooms and a majestic theatre, describing it as "for the greater convenience, accommodation and amusement of persons resorting to this town" (not for the citizens, mark you) and, what is more, finance it from the proceeds of a lottery and the sale of religious benefices?

The place originally chosen by the corporation for the new complex was on the same site as the old theatre in Frankfort Gate. But they had engaged an architect with a mind and a will of his own, John Foulston, who roundly declared that such a fine building as he had in mind would be lost in such a position, and he opted for an unoccupied space in front of George Place, once used by one Ryder who had a cherry garden there.

When the corporation objected that this site was too isolated from the rest of the town, Foulston retorted: "Isolated! Let me raise the fabric and you will soon see a vast addition of houses in that locality." The citizen of today can see just how right he was, for he chose the very heart of the city.

It is difficult to imagine these days how this highly imaginative plan was ever carried through. In 1810 the town of Plymouth ended just west of St. Andrews Church, and where Derry's Clock and the ABC Theatre now stand was marshland with a creek running the length of Union Street. Contact with Stonehouse was via a narrow winding, muddy footpath through fields and with Devonport by ferry instead of over the present Stonehouse bridge.

Yet this was the site he chose, and his plan, envisaged in association with local architect George Wightwick, embraced a great hotel, assembly rooms that could be used for music, concerts and conferences, dining room, club, coffee rooms, theatre and stables, all built around a square courtyard, and entered through majestic columns. The cost was £60,000, which by present-day standards would be around the £10m mark.

The way in which the city fathers obtained the money is curious and unique in the annals of a corporation devoted to strict, careful and quasi-religious methods of local government.

They held the advowsons of the parishes of St. Andrews and Charles Church, which had the right of the presentation of benefices to these two churches, and, considering that there was no pecuniary reward in appointing two vicars, decided to sell the advowsons and nominate instead a theatre manager.

Such a scheme, of course, raised the ire of the nonconformists who were thinking more of pleasure-banning than the effect on the established church, but their criticism became more vociferous when they heard of the next move.

The money from the sale of the advowsons was not half enough, and a further £20,000 was raised by a tontine, or lottery. This was a most outrageous method in Puritan eyes, but not so in the country at large as funds for the erection of the British Museum and the first Westminster Bridge were also raised by this method.

The sum was collected by annuities on lives nominated by the subscribers, and the annuity was paid up to the death of the last, so that subscribers of £10 each on such last nominees received a net income of £100. The payments were secured by bonds issued under the seal of the corporation, and the mayor "presented a lottery ticket to each class of subscriber, thereby affording a chance of an immediate return of their money".

Applications were enormous, and by this means some £46,000 was accumulated within three months.

Work began in 1811, and the foundation stone was laid by Edmund Lockyer, the mayor. The streets were decked with flags and there was a procession with the Royal Marines Band playing national and patriotic airs. It was stated at the time that beneath the stone was laid a Plymouth porcelain vase (by

FIG. 10. *(facing page)*.—Foulston's imaginative leisure complex in Victorian times, then sited on the outskirts of the growing town of Plymouth. The Theatre Royal can be seen to the immediate right of Derry's clock, the only feature which still exists today.

William Cookworthy) containing silver coins and a com-
memorative medal.

In 1978 the stone was lifted after being buried for some
thirty years by Blitz rubble, but alas there was no Plymouth
porcelain vase. Under the stone was found a cheap earthen-
ware tray containing a few coins of the period, a commemora-
tive medal and a printed slip of paper giving the names of the
mayor and councillors concerned in the building project. They
are now in the Plymouth Museum.

With their new found cultural enlightenment the corporation at once took harsh and oppressive measures to make sure
that their take-over of things theatrical should be absolute, and
with good business acumen adopted repressive attitudes towards low-class competitors.

In 1812 John Kelland, who owned a hostelry near Frankfort
Place called "The Fox and Goose" and ran a sort of penny gaff
for youngsters of the town, was summoned and warned to "be
more circumspect".

The actors were put in the dock and the magistrates, with all
the hypocrisy of the poacher-turned-gamekeeper, solemnly
proclaimed:

> The evil tendency of these meetings as affording incentives to
> vice, is so evident and their immediate suppression a matter of
> such imperative necessity, that the Mayor feels it is his
> bounden duty to declare his fixed determination to punish all
> future offenders, after thus public notice, with every severity
> of the law.

The Theatre Royal, as it was naturally to be called, was an
impressive structure from the outside with its graceful columns
following the lofty and majestic style in keeping with the
ideals of the times. Simon Tidworth, in his *History of Theatres*,
described it as "in the Georgian English style . . . a specially
interesting example of the transition from the neo-classical
era and the plainness of the Georgian provincial playhouse,
developing into Victorian opulence".

Seating 1,200, it boasted a spacious vestibule, first and
second circle, upper boxes, pit and gallery, and the auditorium
was ornamented with a series of paintings from events of the
*Iliad*. The ceiling represented an open dome adorned with the

signs of the Zodiac through which Fame with two attendants were seen flying through the blue sky.

The stage itself was furnished with the latest modern fittings where "the Olympian machinery of moon-light, thunder, lightning and rain is furnished from the spacious scene loft above."

In common with other theatres of the day there were two drop curtains of classical design, one painted from a Foulston sketch representing a magnificent hall interior with statues and columns, and the other a view of the Acropolis of Athens.

The stage was designed to accept the then very modern wingsets, with three grooves each side into which they could be slid, and the stock of scenery consisted of a Palace, Interior Chamber and a Tree set, all of which could be interchanged to suit a particular play. To defeat the attempts of over-enthusiastic members of the audience from clambering onto the stage, a row of iron spikes rose in front of the orchestra pit.

The Theatre Royal, Plymouth, opened in all its glory on 23rd August 1813 under the management of Farren and Foote with a playbill that announced:

AN Occasional Address" after which Shakespeare's celebrated play of "As You Like It" to which will be added the farce of "Catherine and Petruchio".
Boxes 4/- Pit 2/6d Gallery 1/-
Doors open at six and begin precisely at seven o'clock. Ladies and Gentlemen are respectfully requested to send their servants to keep place at half past five o'clock.

The company who performed that evening included such people as Mr Hughes, Sandford, Congdon, Hayden, Mrs Bennett, Andrews and Mrs Windsor, names which were to become familiar as the Plymouth Stock Company in the months to follow.

At the first performance there were 1,149 persons in the house, and total receipts amounted to £152 14s.—good business for a provincial theatre at that time, but it did not last long.

It was a very big house to fill in such a small town in which the general populace were lowly paid. They fought shy of such a palatial edifice, being more accustomed to a rougher and more homely atmosphere.

It was also exceedingly cold in winter, so much so that the management were forced into the primitive device of burning large fires in the pit in an endeavour to keep the place warm. Farren and Foote soon found it financially impossible to carry on and relinquished the management to Hughes who had been running the Dock theatre. He was succeeded by John Brunton, also from Dock, and a man later to become lessee of the Exeter theatre.

But the 1820s and 30s were not kind decades to the theatre in the West. Smallpox and cholera epidemics decimated audiences drastically; the law fell harshly on the poorer classes; transportation was a regular sentence and Plymouth became the base from which the convict ships sailed for Australia.

Stagecoaches were the main means of travel between cities. The Celerity coach left Hannaford's Commercial Inn, Plymouth, at 9 a.m. for London, via Ridgeway, Ivybridge, Ashburton, Chudleigh, Exeter, Honiton, Axminster, Bridport, Blandford and Salisbury arriving at the Saracen's Head in Snow Hill in twenty-eight hours. Durnford Street became fashionable, while Stonehouse was described as "a handsome and increasing town"; houses were built in Morley Street, Plymouth, "a genteel neighbourhood"; Roborough was not yet so named, being called Jump; and tablecloths at the Belfast Linen House in Devonport were advertised at 1s. 8d. for 1 ½ yards long and stout linen at 6½d. per yard.

The nonconformists had their ranks expanded by the Exclusives, the Kellyites, the Newtonites and Bethesda; while the Plymouth Brethren settled in the city in 1830, bringing with them even harsher doctrines which spelt death to the theatre.

The decline in support for the brave new Plymouth Theatre led Brunton to announce:

Whether the want of success may be attributed to the embarrassment of the County or to the hostility of a presumed Moral Principle I am not prepared to say. The opinion among

[76]

certain classes which appear to gain ground is that the stage
is positively injurious to the weal of mankind.

Shall we listen to the Cant of the Day against the Drama
because its language is not always what an innocent old Maid
of three score would wish?

It was at this time that a future theatrical pattern was to
evolve that was to show the difference in style between the
two major Devonshire towns. Exeter, the long-established
capital and cathedral city, while small in comparison with
the growing Plymouth, had a more or less static population
who, though enjoying the simpler entertainments of the crude
melodramas, occasionally appreciated higher things with revivals of the classics and plays by Shakespeare. In this they
were supported by the local gentry of long lineage, and by a
nucleus of learned and professional men and well-established
merchants.

Plymouth, on the other hand, reinforced by the large dockyard force, went in for popular plays, local attractions and
rip-roaring comedy and dramas of which there were plenty
among the repertoires of the stock companies.

Their backing came from the naval and military portion of
the audience, who, while adamant in their high patriotic
beliefs, valiant in war, and useful spenders in peacetime, had
small pretensions to academic scholarship, and who, like some
of their successors, came to the theatre for "the funny jokes"
and as a social duty.

This was exemplified in the many productions at the Plymouth theatres of plays dedicated to the various regiments,
with such servile playbill headings as:

The Management Humbly Solicits the support of the Ladies
and Gentlemen of the Army, Navy and Public, and assures
them that nothing shall be wanting to render the evening's
amusement worthy of their distinguished patronage . . .

and occasionally by the number of amateur presentations
given by the resident services, wherein the cast were all
officers or the gentry, with never a mention of the lower
ranks. This led to those distasteful headings on the bills of
"Fashionable Nights", which the *hoi polloi* were discouraged
from attending.

[77]

Yet during this depressing and doleful period, a spark was to kindle a theatrical fire in sleepy Devonshire, from which there was to emerge a name that was to ring throughout the country and down the coming years as the greatest of them all.

On a cold December day in 1811 there slouched into the city streets of Exeter a tired, bedraggled group—a rough, tough young man in his early twenties, trailing a wife and two children. Black-haired and with a wild eye, he looked like a gipsy or a throwout from some provincial fairground as he made his way to the Exeter theatre to ask for work.

Antecedents unknown, he may have been a gipsy, or, as Macaulay declared, descended from George Savile, Marquis of Halifax.

He was called Edmund Kean—a name that was to resound through the annals of the theatre right up to the present day whenever is heard that electrifying line spoken by Sir William Gower in *Trelawny of the Wells*: "—*I've* seen Edmund Kean . . ." words which can still send a quiver down the spine.

Kean, the man of whom Hazlitt wrote: "His fame shall last as long as the heart of a man shall beat in response to the call of nature"; Kean, the womaniser, the drunk, the moody and the genius, was to startle the theatrical profession out of its stupor and to create an entirely new conception of the traditional characters.

He did not play Shylock as the red-wigged dirty Jew of Restoration times, but gave him a character of dignity and pity. Kean was to take London by storm, tour America, play Macbeth, Richard Crookback and Iago in such a style that it would change the face of contemporary acting from the wooden, artificial posturings to real life, causing the poet Coleridge to proclaim: "To see him act is like reading Shakespeare by flashes of lightning."

Entirely unknown, he had played briefly in Belfast, Gloucester and Bath and he was cautiously admitted to the Exeter theatre company with some misgivings on the part of the management to "play everything"—which included comedy, tragedy and even Harlequin, which he hated, as he considered himself only as a tragedian.

[78]

But whatever he or the management thought, the audience received him with enthusiasm, for he brought new life to the old classic roles. They flocked to see this lithe, curiously-dressed creature from nowhere who probed and thrilled their emotions and then sent them home happy at the end of the performance with his agile Harlequin.

The local Press on that first occasion in Exeter wote of him :

> The principal is Mr Kean, who though his figure is rather below the standard of a hero, appears to possess a considerable degree of merit, and a versatility of talent rarely combined in one actor. He is equally at home in tragedy, comedy and pantomime, and bids fair to be a great favourite with the public.

Most of Kean's life is a tangle of legend and hearsay, making it difficult to ascertain clearly the details of his time in the West Country.

But it is known that the family took lodgings over a china shop at 211 High Street, owned by a Miss Hake, who was an ostrich-feather dresser who lived with her sister and "took in" genteel travellers.

Local legend has it that the two ladies, respectable and precise, were very particular in their lodgers, and were completely unaware of the wild 22-year-old actor's penchant for brandy. It must have been in one of his more sober moments that they let their rooms over the shop to him.

Apparently all went well at first and he remained circumspect in their presence, never returning home from the theatre until long after the Misses Hake were in their beds.

After playing the enforced role of Harlequin one night, he visited the tavern as usual where he fell into an argument with a man who told him he disliked his performance. Words led to blows and the impetuous Kean suggested swords.

He ran across the road to his lodgings for the weapons, still in Harlequin costume, bounded up the stairs and burst clean through the glass door at the top. The two Misses Hake, in their nightdresses, peeped from their bedroom door; Mrs Kean appeared at the other; and the lodger, a solicitor Mr Cawsey, watched in amazement. The tipsy Kean, swords in hand, gave one bound and disappeared down the stairs. During the following three days he was neither seen nor heard of by his wife and family. Then he returned saying he "had been doing a noble action", and informed his wife Mary that he had been drinking for three days, with an actor who was about to leave Exeter, in order "to keep his spirits up".

FIG. 11.—Edmund Kean. This sketch, attributed to T. Wageman (date unknown), is possibly the most faithful likeness of the man among the very few paintings representing Kean in character. (By courtesy of the National Portrait Gallery.)

He did not last long at Exeter this time, and tramped all the way back to Bath seeking a job there at 30s. a week. This was refused and, dragging his wife and children with him, he trudged through the country looking for work from anyone who would pay him the price of food and a bottle of brandy. But apparently nobody wanted anything to do with him and once again he presented himself at the Exeter theatre where he managed to persuade Hughes, the manager, to take him back into the company.

Local gossip magnified his dissolute off-stage habits and told how he would have to be fetched from the inn and roused from his stupor by the pump and cold water before he could take the stage—but, once there, his very nature would seem to change. Such stories should be treated with suspicion, for, as any actor worth his salt knows full well, it is impossible to sustain any role of length without an alert memory, and one that is in the least fuddled by drink spells disaster.

The audience, despite his reputation for drunkenness, loved him and he stayed on to play at Exeter for forty nights. During this time he acted triumphantly, got drunk, refused to appear and once jumped through a burning beer barrel because the management called for it.

A playbill of that time shows that he appeared in a much truncated version of *Macbeth*. Kean played the leading role, with Hughes, the manager, appearing as Malcolm and as one of "The Singing Witches"; a Mr Condon played another and also took the part of "The Bleeding Captain"; while Miss Rivers appeared as Lady Macbeth, Mr Worsdale as Duncan, Mr Mason as Macduff and Mr Perkins as Banquo. But there is no mention in the list of Donalbain, Lennox, Ross etc. nor of Lady Macduff, Fleance and Siward.

But it was this Macbeth (first seen by the Exeter theatre-goers in 1811) that was to be described, when he played it later in London, as "heart rending, and on coming to himself after the murder his voice clung to his throat at the sight of his bloody hands".

Kean's time in Devonshire was running short, and despite the rustic set-up of the Exeter theatre company and its acceptance of brandy as part of life itself, the manager's patience was being exhausted.

Once Kean was so intoxicated that Hughes had to take over his part. During the play Kean staggered into the box and in a mocking voice, jeered and shouted "bravo" every time Hughes made a speech. Hughes had had enough, and Kean got the sack.

The family, consisting of Kean, his wife, Howard (the eldest

# EXETER THEATRE.

Bombastes Furioso having been received with such universal Approbation, will be repeated this Evening.

## ON WEDNESDAY, DECEMBER 16th, 1812,

Will be presented the celebrated TRAGEDY of

# MACBETH,
## *KING OF SCOTLAND.*

Macbeth Mr. KEAN,
Banquo Mr. PERKINS—Duncan Mr. WORSDALE,
Malcolm Mr. H. HUGHES,—Bleeding Captain Mr. CONGDON.
Macduff Mr. MASON,
Gentlewoman, Mrs. WORSDALE,—Lady Macbeth Miss RIVERS,
Hecate Mr. BENNETT.
1st Witch Mr. Tokeley,—2nd ditto Mr. Loveday,—3rd ditto Mrs. Loveday
Singing Witches Messrs H. Hughes, Esword, Congdon &c.
Mesdms. H. Hughes, Bennett, Kean, Worsdale, &c. &c.

## A SONG by Mr. CONGDON.

To which will be added (Second Time) the popular
BURLESQUE TRAGIC OPERA, called

# *Bombastes Furioso,*

As performed upwards of 100 Nights at the Theatre Royal, Haymarket
Artaxominous (King of Utopia) Mr. TOKELEY,
Fusbos (Minister of State) Mr. PERKINS,
First Courtier Mr. H. HUGHES,—Second Courtier, Mr. CONGDON,
General Bombastes Mr. BENNETT,
Distaffina Mrs. H. HUGHES.

Doors to be opened at *Six* and begin precisely at *Seven* o'Clock.
BOXES 4s.—PIT 2s. 6d.—GALLERY 1s.
Season Tickets—to the Boxes, Transferable 4l. 4s.—Not Transferable, 3l. 3s.
to be had of Messrs. Trewman and Son.
TICKETS to be had of Mess. Trewman and Son ; and of Mr. Dryer, of whom
places for the BOXES may be taken.

## A NEW HARLEQUINADE is in Preparation, and will be produced in the Holidays.

On Friday Evening,
## She Stoops to Conquer, and The Irishman in London.

Trewmans, Printers, Exeter.

boy) and the baby Charles, left Exeter in distress, and tramped all the way to Dorchester where Howard, overcome by the privations suffered on the journey, died, leaving Kean distracted by grief.

But good fortune followed afterwards, because an Exeter theatregoer, impressed by Kean's acting, had told Dr Joseph Drury (headmaster of Harrow School who was holidaying in Devon) to look out for him at Dorchester. Drury recommended Kean to Samuel Arnold, the manager of Drury Lane. The latter travelled to the West Country, saw him and suggested he came to the metropolis when his Dorchester date was over.

Upon presenting himself at Drury Lane Kean obtained an engagement at that theatre, where he signed a contract for £20 a week. Shortly afterwards the committee of management of Drury Lane added 50 guineas as a token of their appreciation of his powers.

His later successes in London brought forth shouts of approval from a highly critical audience. He lived a still riotous life, but earned a place at Eton for his son, Charles, and became himself a legend.

Much mystery and conjecture surrounds Kean's life and appearances in the provinces, but a local eyewitness was one Paul Ourry Treby, an officer and gentleman of Goodamore, near Sparkwell, who was born in 1785, went to Plympton Grammar School and thence to Eton. He was a man widely read who enjoyed his theatre. Fortunately, he kept a journal which has been preserved by his kinsman Harry Chichester Clark of Tavistock. Under the date London 1st May 1815 he writes:

---

FIG. 12.*(facing page)*.—This was the Macbeth which, when performed later at Drury Lane, was to be described as "heart-rending" and of which was said: "on coming to himself after the murder, his voice clung to his throat at the sight of his bloody hands." It is possible that this production at Exeter in 1812 was the one in which Dr. Joseph Drury, headmaster of Harrow School, first saw Kean act. Afterwards he recommended him to Samuel Arnold, manager of Drury Lane, who in turn eventually saw him play at the Dorchester Theatre and invited him to London to appear at the Patent Theatre.

[83]

I saw Kean this evening in the character of Richard III at Drury Lane. On 4 May I saw him in Othello with Pope as Iago. Kean played very well. On 6 May I saw Kean as Iago with Sowerby playing Othello very wretchedly. Kean best in Richard III.

Kean was to come back to the West Country on a number of occasions, playing again in Exeter and at Plymouth in 1816 at the New Theatre Royal. A local critic wrote of him:

Kean gave Shakespeare with commendation.
He leant to the romantic, was all passion and intellect was really the medium of expression.
Kean could not render Macready's classic roles, and Macready could make nothing of Kean's, but those who felt deeply with Kean were as affected by Macready, although it is hard to say to whom the locality voted the palm.

But Thomas Barnes, the pungent critic of *The Examiner*, was to be more gracious:

He had not been on the stage two minutes, nor repeated half a dozen lines before there was an universal feeling that no common being had now come forward to challenge our attention, and when he finished the soliloquy he left the audience in admiration of the power of his understanding.

Theatregoer Ourry Treby was in Plymouth, too, on that occasion, and he wrote in his diary:

I saw Kean play Othello at Plymouth to a house half filled. On 30th I again saw him and as before most amazingly admired Kean in the character of Hamlet.
Either from lack of cash, or from want of wit, he played to empty houses, half full pit.
Plymouth for shame!!

This remark, written by a Devonian living not far from Plymouth 160 years ago, was to become a text which applied to almost every production, to every star and to every innovation in the theatre for years that followed. It was to give the basis for that oft-repeated saying in the theatrical profession that "Plymouth is death to the pro".

[84]

This peculiar outlook that anyone (or anything) new is to be viewed with suspicion, and can only be accepted after it has been "tried on the dog" or after someone else has passed it as acceptable, was to occur again and again, and the historical fact that the Plymothians of 1816 spurned Edmund Kean must inevitably do them discredit.

The same attitude (this time to one of their own citizens) was to be revealed but a few years afterwards as if to underline their refusal to accept talent and make a judgment of their own.

At the time Kean was playing Exeter, a young boy of nine, Samuel Phelps, was about to begin his lessons with Dr Samuel Reece at a classical school in Saltash.

Born on 13th February 1804, the son of a shopkeeper at No. 1 St. Aubyn Street, Devonport. Phelps was destined to become apprentice to a Plymouth newspaper as junior reader. But his heart and imagination had been fired by the theatres at Dock and Plymouth.

Feeling frustrated at his limited prospects he left home at the age of seventeen with only 14s. 6d. in his pocket. He walked all the way to London to seek his fortune, and not finding it there joined a band of players who toured many of the Northern cities. He quickly learned their art and craft.

He was engaged by the great actor Macready to appear at Covent Garden, at which theatre he graduated to play such roles as Shylock, Hamlet and Othello to Macready's Iago. Phelps made part of theatrical history by up-staging Macready —so putting another word in the long list of theatre jargon.

Jealous of his growing reputation, Macready then gave him inferior parts, causing one critic of the day to remark:

> Depriving Phelps of an opportunity of proving to the town that the high promise which he gave was capable of standing the test of the widest range and the most arduous characters of the legitimate drama.
>
> If Mr Macready thinks he can keep down talent by virtue of the position he occupies he mistakes his powers and fails to the due discharge of his compact with the public.

Samuel Phelps returned to his native West Country in 1836. When he appeared at the Exeter theatre the editor of the

FIG. 13.—Samuel Phelps (1804–78), who ran away from his home in St. Aubyn Street, Devonport to become the first manager to take advantage of the abolition of the Patent monopoly by opening Sadler's Wells and running it as a free playhouse. He rivalled Macready as an actor, and as the manager of the Wells he staged no less than thirty-four of Shakespeare's plays during his twenty-year reign. (By courtesy of the National Portrait Gallery.)

[86]

*Plymouth Journal* considered him a rival to Edmund Kean—
and this was proved by the actor subsequently filling that
theatre for four and a half months.

He went on to play at the Plymouth theatre, as Richard III,
Othello and Sir Giles Overreach, expecting great things from
his home town.

At least he was due to play Othello, but the local stock
company which was not one of the best (as Macready found)
posed difficulties, and Phelps was obliged instead to play Iago,
because the actor due for that role, a Mr Mude, "could not
get the words".

But alas, little honour awaited him in his own city where
his King Lear was condemned by the Plymouth Press as "a
distorted skeleton" and his Hamlet as "too original". This was
an early view of what Plymouth audiences of the future
were to say about anything new, a spectacular example being
in the late 1940s when Sam Wannamaker first tried out *The
Rainmaker* to empty houses at the Palace Theatre.

In other towns in the provinces Phelps received a more
generous welcome, even though he had to contend with the
jealousies of Charles Kean and other stars. "Kemble," said
Kean, "did all he could to prevent me from supplanting him,
and I owe it to my family to do all I can to prevent Phelps
supplanting me."

However, Samuel Phelps, from Devonport, who could play
Bottom as well as the great tragic roles, grew in theatrical
stature and in 1844 took over Sadler's Wells theatre and held
sway there until 1863. Many a young actor of the time was
later to proudly boast that he had played Shakespeare at the
Wells under Phelps.

Another gifted Plymothian was Sheridan Knowles, a member
of a literary family who became a friend of Hazlitt and
Coleridge. He was a cousin of the great playwright Richard
Brinsley Sheridan. His most successful play, *The Hunchback*
(1832), was given a number of productions at both the Plymouth and Dock theatres.

The local comic at that time was James Doel, whose style
was one of dry humour with a poker face. He had only to
walk across the stage and ask: "What are you laughing at?"
(like the late George Robey) for the audience to fall about.

Doel was also a Devonport man, and he became a tradition in the town, having played first gravedigger to Edmund Kean and first witch to Macready's Macbeth. Later he took over the managership of the Dock theatre in which he appeared regularly for many years.

FIG. 14.—James Doel, the comedian from Devonport Dock Theatre, who later became a legitimate actor to appear with Edmund Kean and William Macready.

But as times grew harder he became disillusioned with the theatre and with actors, and in an interview given after he had retired from the stage and taken over a pub in Edgcumbe Street, he revealed himself to be more of what we would call today a variety artist rather than a legitimate actor. When asked the question if he thought that his generation of actors did not match up to those of bygone days, he replied:

> They have all too much learning. They study their parts too much. They are too precise. They endeavour to reach perfection by art, and in so doing lose not only the touch of nature, but also the touch of the heart. It's all beautiful elocution, hour long discussions about the meaning of this phrase or that, and about the pronunciation of this word and that—and over these pretentious trifles they forget that the author meant these men to be living creatures, swayed by passion, and not at all absolutely correct in their pronunciation of words.

This provides a revealing clue to the great difference between the acting styles of the Georgian "ham" and the Victorian heavy-handed approach (which makes one wonder what James Doel would have thought of method acting).

The Exeter theatre was lit by gaslight in 1817, one of the first in the country to try out this new form of stage lighting. But it was not for long, because after a few nights there was an explosion during a performance and back they went to candles again, or as was announced on one playbill: "The House is illuminated by wax."

Gas came to Plymouth in 1825, a year after Dock ceased to be and was henceforth called Devonport, while Plymouth, like a haughty hen, tried not to notice the change and the growing importance of its close neighbour.

The celebrated comedian Charles Mathews visited Plymouth a number of times at this period, an actor who developed into a one-man show in his later years.

Friend of Sir Walter Scott, a mimic, wit and jovial companion, Mathews made a number of friends in the city; notably George Wightwick the architect who introduced him to the Blue Friars—a select dining club whose members dined in monk's garb, drank deeply and published their lively discussions in pamphlet form.

Mathews was taken ill in Plymouth in the summer of 1835 after he returned from appearing in New York, and died shortly afterwards. He was buried in St. Andrews Church where a plaque to his memory stands to this day on the wall

[89]

*35a*

# THEATRE  ROYAL,

#### PLYMOUTH.

Lessee and Manager .. .. .. Mr. J. R. NEWCOMBE. 1868.

By the kind permission of Mr. Newcombe, the Theatre will open for One Night only,

## MONDAY, MARCH the 30th,

FOR THE

### Thirty-seventh Annual Benefit

OF

# MR. JAMES DOEL,

## UNDER DISTINGUISHED PATRONAGE.

Mr. Doel most respectfully solicits his Patrons and the Friends of the Drama to pay him a Visit on this occasion, he having selected for their gratification and amusement one of the best Comedies of the OLD Masters,—COLMAN *the Younger's*

### "HEIR AT LAW;"

And he assures them that nothing shall be wanting on his part to render the Evening's entertainment a source of enjoyment to all.

## On MONDAY, MARCH the 30th,

Will be presented COLMAN the Younger's's celebrated Comedy, in Five Acts, entitled The

# HEIR AT LAW

## OR £20,000 IN THE LOTTERY.

*WITH THE ORIGINAL EPILOGUE BY THE CHARACTERS.*

Dick Dowlas ........Mr WALTER KEEBLE    Dr. Pangloss........Mr FRANK KILPACK
Zekiel Homespun ........................................................ Mr JAMES DOEL
The other Characters by the Strength of the Company.

To which will be added the Laughable Piece of

# THE LOTTERY TICKET.

Wormwood ..................................................... Mr JAMES DOEL

To conclude with

# RAISING THE WIND

## OR HOW TO GET A BREAKFAST.

Jeremy Diddler.......................................................Mr J. R. NEWCOMBE
Sam ............................................................... Mr JAMES DOEL

☞ Doors open at half-past Six; to commence at Seven.

PRICES :—Orchestra and Dress Balcony Stalls..3s.    Upper Boxes..2s.    Pit Stalls..1s. 6d.
Pit..1s.    Gallery..6d.    Private Boxes, One Guinea and a Half, and One Guinea.
Second Price at Nine o'Clock, or as near as possible to prevent interruption to the Performances.
Orchestra and Dress Balcony Stalls..2s.    Upper Boxes..1s.
Children from Five to Twelve years of age admitted to the Boxes at Second Price from the
commencement.    Children under Five Years not admitted.
Tickets for the Orchestra and Dress Balcony Stalls may be had of Mrs. P. E. ROWE, George Street,
Plymouth, and of Mr. JAMES DOEL, Prince George Hotel, Stonehouse.    [KEYS, TYP., PLYMOUTH.

at the western end of the church, bearing the following inscription:

Near this spot are deposited the honoured remains of
Charles Mathews
Comedian
Born 28th June 1776
Died 28th June 1835.

That same year Charles Kean, son of the great Edmund, came west. appearing at Plymouth and Exeter and at the last theatre played for five nights for one third of the gross receipts which were:

| July | 27 | Giles Overreach | Gross receipts | £17. 5. 6. |
| | 28 | Othello | ,, ,, | £18. 8. 0. |
| | 29 | Merchant of Venice | ,, ,, | £30. 3. 0. |
| | 30 | Hamlet | ,, ,, | 30. 9. 6. |
| | 31 | Richard III | ,, ,, | 38. 3. 6. |

Kean's total for the week thus amounted to about £45.

Business continued to be bad everywhere, apart from one or two flashes of minor successes, and when the brief euphoria of new patriotic plays, occasioned by the young Victoria succeeding to the throne in 1837, finished, the theatres had another bad patch.

A plea that was to echo through the ages was made by the licensee of Plymouth's Theatre Royal, a Mr Hay, who declared after a particularly disastrous period: "It is impossible to make the theatre pay. It is too large for the town, very frequently it is a mere wilderness and represents a most melancholy and comfortless sight, and it is impossible for the actors to dispel the prevailing sadness."

According to Whitfeld this "was largely due to private theatricals. At the local mansions, festivities of this kind were

FIG. 15 (facing page).—James Doel's thirty-seventh annual benefit in 1868. As a local actor of repute he had played at all the West country theatres, and in 1845 had become manager of the Devonport Theatre which he gave up in disgust after ten years, describing it as "a heart breaking experience". However, he continued to play at the Plymouth theatre for many years afterwards.

# THEATRE ROYAL,

### PLYMOUTH.

W. 21.]     Lessee and Manager.................................Mr J. R. NEWCOMBE.     [N. 122.

## LAST WEEK OF THE SEASON.

### FOURTH NIGHT OF THE ENGAGEMENT OF
### MR. & MRS.

# MATHEWS

## On THURSDAY, MAY 26th, 1859,

The Entertainments will commence with Dion Boucicault's fashionable Comedy entitled

# LONDON ASSURANCE

| | |
|---|---|
| Sir Harcourt Courtley | Mr W. S BRANSON |
| Max Harkaway | Mr LOOME |
| **Dazzle** | **Mr CHARLES MATHEWS** |
| Charles Courtley | Mr E. F. EDGAR |
| Dolly Spanker | Mr A. WOOD |
| Mark Meddle | Mr C. LLOYDS |
| Cool | Mr ELLISON |
| Simpson | Mr C. MORELLI |
| Martin | Mr BRIDGEFORD |
| James | Mr McINTYRE |
| Solomon | Mr WATSON |
| **Lady Gay Spanker** | **Mrs CHARLES MATHEWS** |
| Grace Harkaway | Miss KATE CARSON |
| Pert | Miss ELIZA JOHNSTONE |

To conclude with RICHARD BRINSLEY SHERIDAN'S Dramatic Piece, in Two Acts, entitled

# THE CRITIC

## OR A TRAGEDY REHEARSED.

### CHARACTERS.

| | | | |
|---|---|---|---|
| Dangle | Mr W. S. BRANSON | Sneer | Mr ELLISON |
| Sir Fretful Plagiary | | | |
| Puff | | } Mr CHARLES MATHEWS | |
| Mrs Dangle | | Mrs H. VANDENHOFF | |

### CHARACTERS OF THE TRAGEDY.

| | | | | | |
|---|---|---|---|---|---|
| Lord Burleigh | Mr C. MORELLI | Governor of Tilbury Fort | Mr LOOME | Earl of Leicester | Mr C. H. STEPHENSON |
| Sir Walter Raleigh | Mr FRANK ALLEN | Sir Christopher Hatton | Mr C. LLOYDS | Master of the Horse | Mr BRIDGEFORD |
| Beefeater | Mr WATSON | Don Ferolo Whiskerandos | | Mr A. WOOD | Call Boy | Master NEWTON |
| | | First Sentinel | Mr McINTYRE | Second Sentinel | Mr DARNELL |
| Tilburina | | | | **Mrs CHARLES MATHEWS** | |
| First Niece | Miss KATE CARSON | Second Niece | Miss ELLEN BEAUFORT | Confidant | Mrs F. RAYMOND |

On FRIDAY,—"MILLINER TO THE KING." Flormel...Mr CHARLES MATHEWS    Nanette...Mrs CHARLES MATHEWS    And "HE WOULD BE AN ACTOR." Motley...Mr CHARLES MATHEWS. **For the Benefit of Mr. & Mrs. MATHEWS.**

FIRST PRICE:—DRESS BOXES, 3s.    UPPER DITTO, 2s.    PIT, 1s.    GALLERY, 6d.
SECOND PRICE:—DRESS BOXES, 2s.    UPPER DITTO, 1s.
Second Price at Nine o'clock, or as nearly as possible, to prevent interruption to the Performance.
PRIVATE BOXES TO ACCOMMODATE SIX PERSONS, ONE GUINEA AND A HALF;—FOUR PERSONS, ONE GUINEA.
Children from Five to Twelve years of Age admitted to the Boxes at Second Price from the Commencement. Children under FIVE YEARS of Age not admitted.
DOORS OPEN AT SEVEN.    TO COMMENCE AT HALF-PAST SEVEN.
Tickets and Places to be had at Mr. HENRY REED'S Musical Establishment, 20, Union Street.

Printed at I. W. N. KEYS'S Commercial and General Printing Offices, Bedford Street, PLYMOUTH.

given by Lady Morley, Lady Elizabeth Bulteel, Lady Whitmore, the Hon. Mrs Edgcumbe, Sir Henry Blackmore and Sir
George Whitmore."

The versatile architect George Wightwick wrote a prologue
to a piece called *Perfection at Saltram* which reflected the
doleful situation:

> In Plymouth, vis-à-vis, to St George's Place,
> Rising in column'd pride and Attic grace,
> The portals of the Playhouse greeted me
> With hopes of some advancement; for, you see,
> I'm a poor actor, wand'ring on, to seek
> For bread and fame at one-pound-one a week.
> I battered at the door—a hollow sound
> As from some dark and murky cave profound
> Cried "Who comes here, to pierce this fearful gloom!
> "The Drama's Ghost disturbing in its tomb! . . .
> "Tremble ye cobwebs! Fly each fleeting mouse!
> They mean to make the play—a Meeting House!"

FIG. 16 *(facing page)*.—Charles Mathews senior died in Plymouth in 1835.
His son Charles had married Mme. Vestris, the opera singer who took
over the Olympic in London, after a disastrous early life touring America,
Australia and India. On their return, they made many visits to the
provinces notably with *London Assurance* with Mathews in one of his
best parts as Dazzle.

# CHAPTER VII

# Theatre of Splendid Misery

The building of a "respectable theatre" in Plymouth did not mean an overnight change in either the tastes of the audience or to the actor's approach. However, it did bring with it an awareness of what was going on in the more sophisticated parts of the country—an awareness of a glittering life far removed from the drab, crude and often primitive existence which surrounded the first quarter of the nineteenth century.

These were the years which inspired Pollock's popular cardboard cut-out theatres sold as "Penny Plain and Tuppence Coloured", their crude print illustrating some of the old Surrey melodramas of Thomas Dibden, *The Bride of Lammermcor* and *Ivanhoe*. They were horribly adapted from Walter Scott into plays which ideally suited a provincial audience's thirst for plenty of meat and action, with the words cut to a minimum.

Both Exeter and Plymouth audiences became addicts of blood and thunder, but moved swiftly into the Victorian pastime of weeping many tears for "the rewards of virtue" and "tempting providence". They looked with some envy at the plays of *la femme fatale* and those whose moral was "the wages of sin" and gave good support to such works as *The Somnambulist*, *The Italian Wife* and *The Chamber of Death* which became regular features during the years 1820–40.

The players themselves, for so long content to accept their lowly station as subservient creatures, were gradually coming —at least on the surface—to behave in more circumspect fashion when performing before the public. But they continued their own raffish style when not on stage in what was soon to be called Bohemianism.

[94]

It was a time of turbulence, particularly in London then still the Mecca of every aspiring actor, and a time of jealousies, posturings of the star, intrigues, mismanagement, libels, fights and innuendoes that make the twentieth-century "pop" scene appear like a children's party in comparison.

Following in the long tradition set by Nell Gwyn, females were being engaged more for their looks than for their talents, and small-time actresses were beginning to capitalise on their powers of attraction with the more fashionable element in their audience, who, in turn, were infiltrating the more robust, earthy and rough-house portions of "those in front".

It was not always London that produced these blots on the theatrical escutcheon, for Devon in the quiet West Country gave birth to two *causes célèbres* which were to resound nation-wide.

Scandal and gossip were to be had all over the country, especially where the theatre was concerned, and, as if to give substance to the Puritans of Plymouth who considered that even to go inside a theatre was sinful, two seamy scandals concerning two local girls burst upon those late Georgian and early Victorian days to such an effect that they became household names.

Mention has already been made of Maria Foote, the Plymouth-born daughter of Samuel Foote (formerly Freeman) who acted as Juliet in the Dock Theatre at the age of twelve. She became a successful singer—or at least she sang songs sweetly if not very well.

By the age of seventeen, Maria had grown into a beautiful woman and had obtained an engagement at Covent Garden where she appeared as Amanthis in *The Child of Nature* which proved such a success that she was given a permanent engagement during which she appeared as Miranda in *The Tempest* and also played with Master Betty the boy prodigy.

Never a great actress, she earned countrywide fame in a notorious breach of promise case in 1824 in which it was revealed to horrified matrons that she had been living in sin with Colonel Berkeley, the eldest son of the Earl of Berkeley and had two children by him.

The case was brought by Maria against "Pea Green" Joseph Hayne (so called due to the highly-coloured suits he habitually wore) a wealthy young dandy who possessed a fortune of some £187,000 and was a friend of Beau Brummell.

He became infatuated with Maria and engaged to her, but upon hearing of the liaison with Col. Berkeley, he broke it off. Later he relented and even offered to accept custody of the children, but the engagement ended again.

The evidence given at the hearing heaped scandal upon scandal. Hayne was called a public fop who did not know his own mind; Maria was described as a scheming, unprincipled

MISS FOOTE.

AS MARIA DARLINGTON.

FIG. 17.—Plymouth born Maria Foote (1797-1867), one time actress at the Dock Theatre and later at Covent Garden, whose love affairs scandalised society in the notorious breach of promise case in 1824.

woman; and Col. Berkeley emerged as a man who could not be relied upon to keep his promise.

Maria won her case with damages of £3,000 but received little sympathy from the public, and in 1832 she retired from the theatre and married the eccentric 4th Earl of Harrington to become his countess.

A more unsavoury episode occurred in later years concerning Eliza Emma Couch, the eldest daughter of F. Nicholas Couch of Devonshire Place, Plymouth. He was a musician, and earned recogn'tion as being the composer of "Kathleen Mavourneen", a song which he sold outright and afterwards deserted his family to shake off his creditors.

Emma was born in Caroline Place, Stonehouse, in 1836, and achieved her greatest glory outside Britain among the distinguished whores of the day. She enjoys the repute of being included in the Dictionary of National Biography as the top-flight *demi-monde* of the Second Empire.

Eldest of sixteen children, she christened herself Cora Pearl, and went to Paris with a lover. By bestowing her favours judiciously she found that money showered on her bed so much so that she became overwhelmed with jewels, treasures and gifts from her admirers and was recognised as the uncrowned Queen of Fashion.

The peak of her career (1867) came when Prince Napoleon installed her in a mansion from where she observed: "Why! The Tweeleries is my lumber room!" It was rumoured that she also became mistress of Napoleon III himself.

In her early days she called herself an actress, much the same as every other girl in the news these days calls herself a model, but there is little evidence that she played many parts other than a high-class prostitute.

Cora Pearl died of cancer in 1886 and a bitter obituary notice read:

She is dead, and she died in destitution, though she was the mistress of a prince and the paramour of a millionaire. Yet Cora Pearl, as she called herself, possessed neither beauty, wit or culture.

What was the secret of the fatal influence she exercised over men?

There is no clue to the mystery in the dreary pages which record the history of her miserable life.

She was not only vile and vulgar, but vain and vapid. Perhaps the papers she left behind her, which it is said will be published, may throw some light upon the secret of her fleeting success.

Thus passed Emma Couch from Stonehouse. The full story of her conquests (and how she was the first to provide the basis of those Hollywood legends of extravagances by being served up naked on a silver dish in front of admiring guests) can be found in W. R. Holden's fascinating book *The Pearl from Plymouth*.

Getting starry-eyed over actresses is by no means a modern complaint. In 1815 theatregoer Ourry Treby revealed his delight in Eliza O'Neill (later to become Lady Becher), a player of high reputation. She was often looked upon as a worthy successor to Mrs Siddons, but she possessed sweetness and charm in place of the great nobility of Siddons.

Sept 15. I saw the beautiful actress Miss O'Neill as Juliet. She is in my opinion superior to any performer I ever saw in the character. She is, to use a hackneyed phrase, all that painting can express or youthful poets fancy when they love.

Sept 19. I saw her as Mrs Beverley in "The Gamester" . . . she outdid Mrs Siddons. So much for the darling, most elegant Miss O'Neill, it requires the pen of a seraph to give her praises due.

Even the great William Charles Macready was touched and said of Eliza:

It is not altogether the matchless beauty of form and face, but the spirit of perfect innocence and purity that seemed to glisten in her speaking eyes.

But before leaving the first part of the nineteenth century there is a glimpse of life from the other side of the curtain which has come to light in the form of journals kept by ordinary actors. They tell of their trials and tribulations and of the everyday life of the touring player in the West Country.

One of the actors who appeared in theatres throughout Devon was Francis Courtney Wemyss, and his *Theatrical Biography* written in 1820 gives a revealing account of the precarious, rough and ready conditions which he encountered during his stay of some eight months in the county.

Wemyss eventually left England for the United States where he earned a high place in the American theatre as a pleasant, courtly and cultured player.

In the month of January, 1820, I started from Bristol in a snow storm on my journey to Exeter, where I arrived in safety and found myself underlined for Rover on Wednesday evening.

I found the whole city in a state of commotion in consequence of the death of the Duke of Kent [the father of Queen Victoria] for whose reception a box had been splendidly fitted up, and to which he was to have visited on Monday evening.

By the advice of the mayor the theatre was closed for the week as a mark of respect, thus the managers not only lost the profits of an overflowing house, but the actors lost their week's salary.

On the following Monday I appeared in Rover, and my first appearance was pronounced most satisfactory both to the audience and to the managers, but scarcely had I played one week but the death of the King [George III] again closed the theatre for a period of three weeks' general mourning.

About one o'clock in the morning I was aroused by a violent knocking at my bedroom door, it was the general Manager Mr Bennett who was much afflicted with asthma.

He shouted "For God's sake take the key and run as fast as possible to the theatre—it's on fire!"

I was the first actor to reach the spot just in time to see the roof fall in, and all hope of rescuing anything from the theatre was out of the question.

The morning dawned on a heap of smouldering ruins and a company of actors out of employment. This is the first theatre I have ever belonged to which was destroyed by fire.

The people of Exeter with a praiseworthy spirit set up a subscription for the relief of the actors and in less than 48 hours the sum of £170 was received which was distributed among the actors who had lost their theatrical property by this fatal occurrence.

The directors of the New Assembly building leading on to the Northernhay, at that time only roofed in, granted the use

[99]

of the building to Bennett and Hughes, and with magical rapidity we played in an entire new theatre on Monday.

The scenery was brought from Dock, the dresses made up by the local assistance of countless volunteers, and we had a most successful run.

This season was a most disastrous one for the actors who lost six weeks' salary in four months. It is true the managers also have been great sufferers, but they possess many resources —they had a theatre in Plymouth, in Dock, besides Weymouth and Totnes, besides a theatre in the Isle of Guernsey, any one of which they could have repaired to with an assurance of success.

It was with feelings of surprise therefore that we saw a notice posted in the Green room that salaries would be reduced during the ensuing season at Plymouth, a proposition that was illiberal and unjust.

The actors had borne patiently the deprivations of the season which had curtailed more than one third of their income.

A meeting of the company was called to take into consideration this proposition of the managers, and passed a resolution that rather than submit to the terms of the offer, we would form a strolling expedition on our own account and take on the Plymouth theatre on our own responsibility as a commonwealth.

This last proposition was rejected by Bennett and Hughes and the alternative presented was either to accept their terms or to close the theatre altogether.

Apparently the management's proposals were not accepted by the actors and F. C. Wemyss and his fellow players went off on their own through Devon and Cornwall playing anywhere that would offer suitable premises in an endeavour to recoup their losses.

We commenced our new arrangements at Great Torrington in Devonshire, a romantic little town about thirty miles from Exeter.

Our plan was to pay one pound sterling per week to each individual, the overplus to be appropriated to the general fund to provide against reverses.

We remained in Torrington three months, at the expiration of which we had neither added to or diminished our funds, we had paid our way and no more.

Having secured the waggons to transport our baggage to Liskeard in Cornwall, J. Dawson, Butler and myself decided to walk to Launceston where we intended to sleep and proceed leisurely next day to Liskeard.

But before I proceeded two thirds of the distance I found myself unequal to the task and had to avail myself of a conveyance for a few miles in a lime cart which overtook me. However dearly did I pay for this luxury, a drizzling rain saturated my back with unslaked lime, and literally burnt my coat off my back which fell to pieces at the touch.

In Liskeard we remained five weeks under the management of Mr Dawson and added a few pounds to our common stock. We then made an arrangement with Bennett and Hughes for the Plymouth and Dock Theatres in which to pass the winter of 1820.

Plymouth and Dock, although only two miles apart, have each their own peculiar audiences.

The Plymouth theatre enjoys the privilege of a patent, is elegantly built and as capacious as Drury Lane or Covent Garden being capable of holding at country prices of admission from 3–400 pounds sterling, yet rarely yielding in its nightly receipt more than thirty pounds and frequently falling below five pounds.

From its size and beauty and being so seldom filled, it had acquired the significant title of "The Theatre of Splendid Misery".

The Dock Theatre on the other hand is one of the most inconvenient in England but for the fact of possessing a regularly built stage and an excellent stock of good scenery, it is more like a country barn furnished up for theatrical representation than a theatre situated in a large and flourishing town.

When full it will hold about £80, but throughout a long season you can calculate on an average of £20, the inhabitants being partial to theatrical amusement and they have garrison and Dock-yard to assist in filling the house.

Here both Mr Booth and Clara Fisher [this must have been Junius Brutus Booth head of the family of actors which included the one that shot President Lincoln, and Clare Fisher, another infant progidy who showed her precocious talents in *Richard III* and other adult roles] played to good houses in comparison to their receipts at Plymouth and by a strange perversion of taste, the inhabitants of Plymouth would ride over to this inconvenient theatre at Dock to see a play when their own Place with the same attraction would be utterly deserted.

Thus it appears that the still peculiar habit of present-day Plymothians in forsaking their own theatre and going to others outside the vicinity and beating the path to Torquay, is part of a pattern which was firmly set 150 years ago.

In Plymouth and Dock we passed four months very agreeably, and it was in Plymouth that I received the first offer of a London engagement by no less a person than Mr Robert Elliston.

Elliston was indeed a man to be reckoned with, extravagant and eccentric and a brilliant personality. He took over the Surrey Theatre in 1809, and ten years later became lessee of Drury Lane, opening with Kean in *Lear*. He became bankrupt in 1826 and a year later retrieved his position with *Black Eyed Susan* starring T. P. Cooke, a success which made him once more solvent.

Charles Lamb gave him an epitaph that any actor would envy: "Wherever Elliston walked, sat or stood still, there was theatre." Wemyss' description of backstage theatrical life in the provinces is amplified and illuminated by *Nine Years of an Actor's Life* written in 1833 by a Plymothian, one Robert Dyer of 74 Whimple Street, who first appeared as a professional player at Dartmouth in *The Heir at Law*.

He played the role of Dick Dowlas, which was not a very auspicious beginning as the first performance was cancelled owing to lack of support; later he says: "The inhabitants of Dartmouth are not liberal supporters of the Drama for Dowton who joined us during the first fortnight had only £7 for his benefit."

It was at this time that many of the smaller towns of Devon and Cornwall were beginning to provide (albeit primitive) theatres to satisfy the growing public demand for entertainment and amusement, and Launceston, which previously had only the White Hart Inn as its theatre, now had another, as it had become "a centre of county society" and a good stopping place for touring companies, as Dyer records:

My second year began in the stable of the Kings Arms at Launceston which having undergone sundry alterations was named a theatre, and surely such a theatre had never before had existence. Its breadth [the stage] might have been eight feet, its depth the same, its height not more than six feet five inches, for on our opening night the nodding plumes I wore as Aranza absolutely were hid in the flies.

The entrance behind the scenes passed over a large granite water trough, and through a window about one yard square. The gentlemen had access to their dressing room by a common ladder, while everything was conducted with the strictest regard to economy, and the duties of prompter, scene shifter, property man and candlesnuffer were performed by Mr Dawson Sr. I have seen him speak the tag of a piece in the corner of the stage, whilst with one hand off stage he rang the bell and lowered the curtain when the play had ended.

The business in Launceston was worse than bad.

One supposes that conditions at the White Hart theatre were a little better than this, it having been mentioned as far back as 1759 when the Plymouth manager visited it to engage players.

It was also in that year that a daughter was born to a Launceston baker called Harvey, who later as Mrs Davenport was to prove the finest character actress of old women roles that the English stage had seen. She appeared at Covent Garden on 24th September 1794, and continued to play there for thirty-six years.

The Exeter Comedians had appeared at Launceston in May and June of 1772 at "The New Theatre at the White Hart" in *The Celebrated Tragedy of The Orphan* or *The Unhappy Marriage* with a farce called *The Jubilee*, and at the end of the play *A Facetious dialogue between Sir Toby Belch and Sir Andrew Aguecheek*.

The prices of admission were Pit 1s. 6d. Gallery 1s., Second gallery 6d. The building in which these performances were given stood at the back of the White Hart, abutting on Madford Wall and were also used as assembly rooms.

Travelling on through Cornwall, Dyer had even less praise when he arrived at the Theatre Royal in Bodmin:

"The Theatre Rural", Bodmin, stood in Back Lane, and when the players were gone was converted into a stable. The dressing rooms were in the hay loft. On the second season we had better accommodation in a pig-sty, but of which I did not avail, as a chandler friend allowed me to dress in his melting shop.

Our stage had a little depth, and less breadth, while the room behind was proportionately less and I remember that in *Falstaff* Manager Dawson was obliged to unpad, as with his artificial corporation he could not pass between the wings and the wall.

Dyer next went to Penzance and his journey is worth recalling:

Never can I forget the truly Thespian mode of journeying to the west. As an especial favour, Manager Dawson invited me to join his family party.

We started in a wagon, the back part of which received the extensive scenery, machinery, dresses, decorations, etc. of the erratic company and on the whole lay the inebriated body of Mr —— and the huge carcase of Triton a mixed Newfoundland dog.

In front sat Mr and Mrs Dawson with Phillis, a fat little goggle-eyed lap dog in her lap; next to these were seated Mr and Mrs James Dawson jr and their infant son; Mr and Mrs Sally Scholey sat next and in the background I jolted on, and this load of sin and scenery was drawn by a pair of half starved horses.

We had a plentiful supply of provisions, the manager was facetious and with an eye to business examined every barn we passed on its convertible capabilities should he ever be tempted to open a theatre there.

Of his eventual arrival at Penzance, Dyer has little to say as the local dramatic magazine gave him a slating, comparing his head to a mop, his mouth to a vast cavern and his attempts at Corinthian elegance to an Irish Watchman.

At Penzance he must have played at the theatre known locally as "The Stable" which was situated above the stables of the Ship and Castle Hotel (later called the Union). This theatre had existed since 1787 and was eventually dismantled in 1839.

Dyer also appeared with John Brunton of the Plymouth and Exeter theatres at Teignmouth where they played *Othello* for one night, after which it was withdrawn as, according to Brunton, "it was no go".

[104]

After a rumpus with the Plymouth management Dyer struck out on his own and played a season at Tavistock where he advertised his coming:

> So many years have passed since a regular dramatic establishment made its appearance here, there can be no doubt that Mr Dyer's campaign will prove at least a profitable one, and we hope that from the boards of a Theatre, even so obscure as that of Tavistock, it is possible a wreath may be bound around his brow.

Despite his bravado in advertising his own talents "obscure Tavistock" did not want him, and he left after a two-month season with a profit of only £8.

He records playing in *Lover's Vows* when Frederick enquired, "Is there a doctor in the village?", and an old countryman in the audience called out, "Oh yes surr. There's Old Parfit the horse doctor lives up'n town."

A slightly more refined version of "Theatre Rural" was to be found in Liskeard where the Town Hall was used for such entertainments and which was well known to itinerant players during their Cornish tours. One such example is found on a playbill advertising an earlier visit in 1828 of W. R. Grossmith, on his own this time, and then aged nine and a half. He was billed to perform:

> An old schoolmaster getting up the play of Richard III. As Richard and Lady Anne. An Old Welsh Lady, a judge and a Doctor.
> He will sing all the most admired songs "The Cats Meat Man" "The Flower Girl" and "Buy a Broom"
> Part II
> He will appear as Hamlet—Soliloquy
> Macbeth—Dagger Scene
> Four fresh scenes from Richard III and the Dying scene. The whole to conclude with musical glasses and Farewell Address. Afterwards at St. Astle and Truro.

Master Grossmith must have been quite a boy!
Dyer found the Redruth theatre:

> A spacious loft erected over an eight stalled stable, two of which were apportioned as dressing rooms for the company,

and we had access to the stage by a step ladder through a trap door.

Every motion of the horses and every neigh was heard, and while the tent scene of Richard was made more illusive by the actual sound when Richard said "Steed threatens steed with high and boastful neighings" yet these confounded interruptions occasionally disturbed our solemnities.

Dyer's manager, James Dawson, had a better one, for he records the playing of Hamlet over the stables at Penzance:

> The aroma made our ghost sneeze and one evening when Hamlet conjures Horatio and Marcellus to "Swear by my sword" the ostler underneath roared to his horse "Come up you boogger, or I'll scat the brains out of tha!"
>
> This unexpected salutation acted like an electric shock on the nerves of Hamlet who rushed off the stage exclaiming "Oh Day and Night, this is wondrous strange!"

A few years later another visitor to Cornwall was to find the Redruth Theatre and give in some detail what it is like from the audience's point of view.

The novelist Wilkie Collins recorded in his book, *Notes on Cornwall taken A-foot*, his finding at Redruth the grandiose-sounding "The Sans Pareil Theatre" where, on a rainbow-coloured playbill, was announced a performance of *The Beautiful Drama of the Curate's Daughter*:

> The Sans Pareil Theatre was not of that order of architecture in which outward ornament is studied. There was nothing florid about it; canvas, ropes, scaffolding poles and old boards, threw an air of Saxon simplicity over the whole structure. On each side of the proscenium boards was painted a knight in full armour, with powerful calves, weak knees and an immense spear.
>
> Tallow candles stuck around two hoops threw a mysterious light on the green curtain, in front of which sat an orchestra of four musicians playing a trombone, an ophicleide, a clarinet and a fiddle as loudly as they could.
>
> Every now and then great excitement was created among the expectant audience by the vehement ringing of a bell behind the scenes, and by the occasional appearance of a youth who gravely snuffed the candles all around.
>
> At last the bell was rung furiously for the twentieth time;

the curtain drew up, and the drama of "The Curate's Daughter"
began. We beheld a ladylike woman who answered to the name
of "Grace" and an old gentleman dressed in dingy black, who
personated her fat father, the Curate, and who was, on this
occasion, neither more nor less than—drunk.

It appeared from the opening dialogue that a pending law suit
and the absence of his daughter Fanny in London combined
to make him uneasy in his mind just at present. But he was by
no means clear on this subject—in fact he spoke through his
nose, put in and left out his H's in the wrong place and involved
the dialogue in a long labyrinth of parentheses whenever he
expressed himself at any length.

It was not until the entrance of his daughter Fanny (just
arrived from London; nobody knows why or wherefore) that he
grew more emphatic and intelligible.

We now observed with pleasure that he gave his children
his blessing and embraced them both at once; and we were
additionally gratified by hearing from his own lips that his
"daughters were h'all upon which his h'all depended—and that
they would watch h'over his h'ale autumn; and that whatever
happened the whole party must invariably trust in 'eabben's
obdipotent power".

Grateful for this clerical advice, Fanny retired into the
garden to gather her parent some flowers; but immediately
returned shrieking, followed by a Highwayman with cocked hat,
moustachios, bandit's ringlets, a scarlet hunting coat and buff
boots.

From this juncture the plot thickens rapidly with the
entrance of "the Good Adam Marle" a teacher at the village
school, and a waggoner with an offer of a situation for Fanny
in London.

The waggoner is revealed as a depraved villain in disguise
commissioned to lure Fanny from virtue and the country to
the metropolis, and the profligate and notorious Colonel
Chartress.

Tragedy befalls her in London where she is picked up in the
street by a benevolent washerwoman and where she dies with
"frightful rapidity in an armchair enveloped from head to
foot in clouds of white muslin". Wilkie Collins sums up his
visit to the hilarious production of The Curate's Daughter at
Redruth with a glimpse at the last act.

With slow and funereal steps, the Curate, Miss Grace, H'Adam, the Highwayman and the "venomous and voluptuous liar Chartress" approached the coffin to weep over it. The Curate had gone raving mad since we last saw him. His wig was set on the wrong side foremost, the ends of his clerical cravat floated wildly, a yard long at least over his shoulders, his eyes rolled in frenzy, he swooned at the sight of the coffin, recovered convulsively, placed Marle's hand in that of Miss Grace, and then fell flat on his back with a thump that shook the stage and made the audience start unanimously. The Tableau thus formed was completed by the Highwayman, the coffin and the defunct Curate, and the curtain fell to slow music.

Such was the Vincent Crummles fare that beguiled audiences in the more remote provincial towns of the far west in those days—places which players of repute declined to visit. So this theatrically unexplored and unexploited country had to be content with such fourth rate rubbish for many years to come.

Francis Courtney Wemyss, although never reaching the top rank of English actors during his time in Britain, did play with Macready whom he first met in Bristol in 1820.

Paying tribute to this great actor, he described him as a gentleman who deservedly ranks high as one of the most finished actors of the stage.

"He is a polished scholar and a gentleman, although an irascible one." Of Macready's first appearance at Covent Garden he records that his performance "wanted but one laugh to have turned all the laboured efforts of the actor into ridicule. Had the tittering which commenced on the first bench of the pit extended a little further, this gentleman, who justly prides himself on having placed the plays of Shakespeare before his countrymen in their proper garb, would have returned to the country a broken-hearted and rejected actor!"

Macready played in Exeter and Plymouth on a number of occasions and he included in his small circle of friends George Wightwick, the architect, amateur actor and sometimes playwright, who together with Foulston designed a number of Plymouth buildings. Son of the fierce old William Macready from the Birmingham theatre, William Charles was educated at Rugby. Honest and dedicated to his art, he was impatient

FIG. 18.—William Charles Macready (1793–1873). Son of a provincial actor-manager, Macready was an earnest and cultured man
who earned a great reputation as an actor, equalled only by
Garrick and Kean. He was also renowned for his outspoken and
disparaging remarks about his fellow actors, and not the least
about the Plymouth and Exeter managements. (Picture by courtesy
of the National Portrait Gallery from the painting by Maclise.)

with any kind of incompetence among his fellow actors. To
them he became a dour, forbidding, growling creature, but
he had his place in West Country theatre history by virtue
of the vivid impressions he left of the local actors and conditions of the day.

He was certainly one of the finest tragedians that the
British stage has ever seen. Being a perfectionist he criticised

himself continually, worrying at a part, studying a character endlessly—he worked on Richard III for some three years before he would admit to himself that he was ready to perform the role in front of the public. In his meticulously-kept diary, he revealed his intense objection to actors, their and his way of life, and the common business of the theatre in general, only tolerating himself as a player when on rare occasions he would admit to giving "a successful performance".

He certainly could not tolerate slackness in others, inveighing with venom against local actors and against the peculiar set-up of the stock company then in vogue. But when one considers the prevailing situation in nineteenth-century provincial towns one can have sympathy with both sides.

The stock company had been a feature of most theatres for a considerable time. Indeed, it dated back to the end of the seventeenth century when it became the nucleus of the Restoration theatre in London. By 1750, when the strolling players had settled, however tenuously, in other towns, the system of a resident group of actors with a stock of plays ready to hand gradually became accepted as a pattern for all provincial theatres. This system existed in some cases up to 1850, although it was abandoned in London some years before.

Robert Dyer pointed out in his biography:

Any person who is in possession of sundry scenes and dresses calls himself a manager and fits up a theatre. He then collects his adventurers and the probable receipts are agreed to be shared amongst them.

Out of each night's receipts the expense of rent, printing and lighting is first taken, and the remainder is divided in equal shares. Six of which go to the liquidation of the Stock Debt, four to the manager, and one each to the company.

This Stock Debt incurred for the original outlay is never acknowledged to be paid by the manager, and in fact constitutes his authority, for a contumacious actor is made obedient when the Stock Debt is advanced as a justifiable reason for withholding supplies.

Everything is shared after the performance, the very candle ends are objects of competition, and many a luckless player has gone to bed in darkness when a long production has burnt down the candles to a wick.

The main difference between repertory and stock was that in the first the play was discarded after its run and seldom repeated, whereas in the second a number of plays were always kept in hand and could be given at the shortest notice.

With the erection of permanent theatre buildings in the early nineteenth century, the stock companies consisted of groups of actors and actresses, each existing on a pittance, and each restricted to performing certain roles (the beginning of the type-casting system). Charles Dickens caricatures them brilliantly in *Nicholas Nickleby* with Vincent Crummles, Mrs Crummles, Mr Folair and the Infant Phenomenon (based, so it is believed, on Jean Davenport, daughter of T. D. Davenport the touring manager 1792–1851).

A typical stock company from a theatre of good standing would consist of a round dozen players in the following order of seniority.

1. The star.
2. The leading man.
3. The heavy.
4. First old man.
5. Second old man.
6. Comedian.
7. Light comedian.
8. Low comedian.
9. The villain.
10. Juvenile.
11. The walking gentleman.
12. The walking lady.

To these may be added utility men and supernumeraries.

It is interesting to note that some of these are still retained in stage parlance, notably the "leading man" and "light" and "low" comedians. Right up to the 1930s advertisements in the profession's newspaper *The Stage* contained requests for heavies, juveniles and utilities.

Each member of the company would be expected to know by heart the regular round of stock plays and so be able to change a production at a moment's notice and fit in with any visiting star that came to swell their ranks.

At least that was the theory, but with small intellect, little incentive and complete self-confidence in their ability to "carry on", the resulting role was more often than not a fiasco, being but a rough outline of the character with lines left out, "made up" and interpolated according to the whim and condition of the actor.

Thus lines and whole parts were often forgotten or deliberately left out. With the more popular plays the audience was often quick to notice such omissions and would shout their disapproval. To these criticisms the actor has been known to stop midway in a speech and apologise with a polite "we wish to give every satisfaction to such a genteel and appreciative assemblage", and continue unperturbed.

In the case of a new or rarely performed play, there was no suggestion of each actor having a book of the play from which to con his lines. Instead the words of each character were copied out separately by hand, with only the barest cues shown as to where in the play the actor was required to enter.

In the rural stock companies some of the old players still gave the name "sides", which had been used by the Elizabethan players, to these slips of paper, written in two columns on one sheet.

Thus an actor with two "sides" or more considered himself having a fat part.

There was no such person as director or producer; rehearsals were rare and then only quickly run through "to see if they have got the words"; and the only guidance given was the "instruction" handed out by the prompter or sometimes the theatre manager some few hours before the performance was due to begin.

Visiting stars considered that only a perfunctory rehearsal with the company was necessary (sometimes half an hour would suffice to give them the star player's "special business"), because the pieces were familiar, the stage groupings stereotyped and freedom of movement was allowed to the supporting cast so long as it did not interfere with the effects of the visiting actor.

This was the situation that Macready and other visiting stars found when they left London and toured the provinces, and such also were the prevailing conditions at the Exeter and Plymouth theatres in the 1830s and 1840s.

# CHAPTER VIII

# Noble Thoughts, Sin and Scenery

The new Victorian age found the theatre giving a moral and uplifting push to the public who were exhorted to look to it for its educative values rather than for pure entertainment.

Enlightenment was the watchword of the day, and these lofty ideals were firmly upheld by Macready who set the tone of moral dignity both in front and backstage. The result was that the actors became fearful of his abrasive tongue and his stern attitudes to their calling, while the more earthy members of the audience who craved low comedy did not much look forward to being educated and uplifted—and stayed away.

But the British people like acting and they like actors to be actors, and despite his dour visage and stern ways, Macready possessed that great gift of being able to command audiences.

By 1841 Macready had established himself at the head of his profession and was known as an intolerant personality with an ungovernable temper.

While he was acclaimed by the public and was to be decribed in an ode by Tennyson as "moral, grave, sublime", to his fellow actors backstage he lacked completely the Bohemian flavour of their calling and in consequence was feared. But they might have had cause, as his diary for that year shows: "23 April, 1841, Exeter. Acted Cardinal Richelieu as well as the wretched murdering of the other characters would let me."

The following day he travelled by stagecoach down to Plymouth where he was to appear on his third tour, to play Macbeth at the Theatre Royal.

26 April, 1841, Plymouth. Acted Macbeth in my very best manner, positively improving several passages, but sustaining

the character in a most satisfactory manner. . . . Wightwick came here to tea with me and sat late. . . . I have improved Macbeth. The general tone of the character was lofty, manly, or indeed as it should be, heroic, that of one living to command. The whole view of the character was constantly in sight; the grief, the care, the doubt was not that of a weak person, but of a strong mind and of a strong man.

The manner of executing the command to the witches, and the effect upon myself of their vanishing was justly hit off. I marked the cause. The energy was more clackened—the great secret.

The banquet was improved in its forced hilarity of tone; the scene with the physician very much so. It was one of the most successful performances of Macbeth I ever gave.

Acknowledging that this performance by Macready was a *tour de force* and fully deserving of his own assessment, *Macbeth* is by no means a one-man play and in this his diary entry must be seen (even if grudgingly by omission) an admission by the star that the Plymouth Stock Company were at least capable of giving him every support.

However, five years later on his fourth tour, Macready was to lambast the Plymouth players with a vengeance.

12 January, 1846, Plymouth. Went to rehearsal (at the Theatre Royal) where I was much annoyed by the manifest indifference of these persons who call themselves actors, in the scenes which I have several times rehearsed with them on Saturday.

They made the very same mistakes, proving that they had never looked at their books, had made no memoranda, nor in fact, ever thought upon the business for which they received the price of their daily bread.

It is not to be wondered at—I must acknowledge—it is not to be wondered at that the Drama is deserted. Who would see such ignorant, such offensive beings obtruding themselves in the creations of Shakespeare?

13 January, 1846, Plymouth. Acted Cardinal Richelieu, not at all to please myself; was cut up, root and branch, by these horrid players—but the audience chose to be satisfied. Wightwick came to my room, walked with me to the hotel and supped. Gave me some very salutary criticism.

15 January, 1846, Plymouth. Acted Othello pretty well considering the disadvantage under which I stood with an in-

accurate Iago, shocking Desdemona, bad Emilia and wretched Cassio.

Oh, such a company for Shakespeare.

With one or two exceptions, this was the stock company that had been in residence at the Theatre Royal for some six months and included a Mr W. H. Maddocks who would have played Iago, Miss Connor (Desdemona), Mrs Fels (Emilia) and Mr Dosworth (Cassio); while others in the company were Messrs Woulds, Davidge, Mulford, Montague, Mr and Mrs Wood and Mr Wyndham, who was afterwards to achieve fame as manager of the Edinburgh theatre.

Having suffered all this one would have thought Macready would have removed the dust of the Plymouth theatre from his shoes altogether, but he was a glutton for punishment and was back again in November the same year at the same theatre with the same complaints.

23 November, 1846, Plymouth. Went to rehearsal, found the company most wretched; some not arrived and Mr Newcombe [the manager] utterly ignorant of his business.

The rehearsal was one of the most hopeless exhibitions I have almost ever seen. Rested and thought on Hamlet, resolving not to let the inaccuracy and incompetency of these wretches— they are no better!—disturb me.

But we began with waiting twenty minutes for Marcellus, who, when on the stage, stunk of tobacco and a public house to sicken the stomach—Oh! and all this I might have avoided had I been prudent in taking care of the money I have earned. Bitter, bitter reflection!

26 November, 1846, Plymouth. Acted King Lear—trying— but with such a company would sink a navy!

28 November, 1846, Plymouth. Wightwick called with his wife and took me in a carriage to Flete, the seat of Lady Elizabeth Bulteel [daughter of the 2nd Earl Grey the Whig premier]. I was introduced to her, admired her; really a most engaging woman. Lady Morley was with her and Mrs Courtney also. I went over the house, which is a monument of the feeling, taste and talent of the deceased proprietor and builder.

30 November, 1846, Plymouth. Rehearsed Richelieu, disgusted with the actors. Scarcely any of them better than my own servant and several not so good.

1 December, 1846, Plymouth. Acted King Lear with much

care for I saw old Colonel Hamilton-Smith in the boxes, who had come on purpose to see it and I wished to give him all the pleasure I could.

The house was really awful! Not six people beside his party in the boxes! It is hard to know what to do against the advice of persons on the spot; but I ought to have ended last night.

Alas, poor Macready was to act in Plymouth only once more. He went on that same year to play in Canterbury where he treated the local actors there in much the same fashion. Referring to his Hamlet, he entered in his diary: "The Horatio and Marcellus were infinitely worse than the disgraceful promise of their rehearsal."

He came back to Plymouth to play in 1849 and in 1852 for a holiday which was marred by the death of his wife, and again in 1869 to meet Katie his 34-year-old daughter. Once again tragedy struck him, for when the ship arrived he learned that Katie had died on the homeward voyage and had been buried at sea.

But Macready's affinity with the West Country was strong. In 1860 he married again, and his second wife, Cécile Louise Spencer, then aged thirty-three, was the sister of the Rev. James Spencer, Headmaster of Tavistock Grammar School, with whom he kept up a regular correspondence.

Spencer was very proud of his connection with the distinguished actor and kept a bust of him in his study. Upon his death it was given to the Tavistock Council where it stood on a shelf for many years in the public library (to the great curiosity of countless people who have wondered why a bust of Macready as Virginius should have a place of honour in the small Devon town).

Whether Macready ever imparted his secret diary thoughts in words to "the utterly ignorant" theatre manager is a matter for conjecture, but from that time onwards Newcombe learned fast and was eventually to inaugurate the most prolific period of Plymouth theatrical history.

John Reilly Newcombe, born 20th March 1803 in Bath, gained his theatrical experience first in Swansea and later at the Bath Theatre before coming to the Theatre Royal a few months before Macready's rebuke.

He could not have arrived at a worse time (or perhaps a

FIG. 19.—The *Thunderbolt's* cartoon of the ebullient John Riley Newcombe, manager of Plymouth Theatre Royal for forty-two years, during which time he raised it from being "the Theatre of Splendid Misery" to become one of the most successful and versatile provincial theatres in the country. The spelling "Riley" instead of his real second name "Reilly" was adopted in print throughout his lifetime in theatrical circles.

better one) for he described Foulston's theatre as "positively disgraceful, dilapidations everywhere, comfort of the most ordinary kind nowhere; scenery, machinery, wardrobe, nothing of either worthy of the name, and, to crown it all, its standing in the eyes of the theatrical world I cannot better describe than simply as a refuge for the destitute." Certainly every inch a "Theatre of Splendid Misery".

For the first few years Newcombe tried desperately hard to bring back some of the glories of Brunton's time. He engaged big names. Taglioni, the celebrated ballerina whose father Filippo composed the great romantic ballet *La Sylphide* for her, came to Plymouth for £100 a night. He brought John Buckstone, one of London's most popular comedians with his bluff style and roaring laugh; a return visit was made by Macready in *Hamlet* and *Richelieu*, and plays from the Bath Company were interspersed by "fillers" from his own stock company. But business was bad.

The price of a seat in the circle was 4s., and during the first six weeks of Newcombe's reign one man arrived—at the reduced price of half a crown. In spite of his efforts he had five years of shocking returns, he contemplated bankruptcy and talked of retiring from the theatrical business entirely. There seemed no end to disaster.

During those five years theatregoing was the last thing that Plymothians desired—for the cholera epidemic was again at its full height. There were 946 cases in Plymouth in 1849, with 517 deaths, while in the surrounding countryside there were five at Bere Alston, two at Okehampton, with others at Ashburton, Buckfastleigh, Redruth and Callington. But the tide of despondency was to turn. Industrial strife hit the West Country at this time, and war—the Crimea conflict of 1854— was once again to prove the saviour of the theatre.

Massive projects were undertaken at Devonport with the enlargement of the dockyard and the building of "The Keyham Steam Yard". Brunel's South Devon Railway arrived at Laira in 1848, to Plymouth centre in 1849 and carried on over Brunel's Royal Albert Bridge to Cornwall in 1850. In that year Plymouth's population had swollen to 39,266.

Fleeting competition with the railways came from the steamship companies who, in a final fling, advertised "to London in 18 hours". Sailing from the Cattewater the British and Irish Company was the "Splendid and Powerful Steamship 'The Devonshire', Cdr. John Moppett. Fares . . . Chief Cabin £1 3s. od. 2nd Cabin 15/- Deck 7/6".—and there were many other advertisements for emigration to Canada, New Zealand, Natal and California for those who wanted to get away from it all.

Moral uplift was the theme of the day. *Heaven's antidote to the Curse of Labour* was one of the many published titles, while *The Pearl of Days* or *The Advantages of the Sabbath to the Working Classes* was recommended by Prince Albert who was quoted as saying that "it had entertained both the Queen and myself exceedingly".

Respectability coupled with pleasure was reflected in the number of fringe halls—calling themselves theatres with grandiose titles—which opened in the cities at that time.

There was the Pantheon in Plymouth, which was a going concern in Vauxhall Street, and which performed, to quote the bills, "by permission of the Worshipful the Mayor". That this was a ruse to get around the licensing laws was proved further down the bill which warned that "the performance is for Private amusement only, and that no person shall be admitted but by ticket as no money will be taken".

The Pantheon was later taken over by J. Telfourd who renamed it the Vauxhall Theatre and who "threw himself with the utmost confidence on the kindness of the indulgent public at boxes 2/-, pit 1/- with constables in attendance to preserve the strictest order".

Another was the Lyceum in Westwell Street run by Walker and Poole. It charged 3/- for stalls and 2/- for central seats for a "Series of Operatic Vaudeville and Novel Entertainments, Tableaux Vivants, Vocal and Instrumental Performances etc., presented with new and splendid machinery to the nobility and gentry." It is believed that this building, which stood at the corner of Westwell Street and Princess Square (later to be called the Princess Hall and then the Mechanic's Institute), was destined to become the site of the Plymouth Repertory Theatre a century later.

Competition with the Theatre Royal was also to be found in Devonport to and from which place many of the low-life players would fluctuate in a theatre world of near fairground conditions where coarse living and poverty were the ingredients of the actor's lot even though they now had solid buildings in which to perform.

Newcombe gradually cleaned up the Royal, sacked some of the hardened drinkers and old hands of the stock company, appeared himself, wrote or adapted plays and pantomimes to include many local references and developed a character of *bonhomie* that fitted in with the patrons' idea of what a real theatre manager ought to be.

He brought down Charles Kean to appear in *The Wife's Secret* and *The Merchant of Venice* with his wife, Ellen Tree, as Portia; and for a one-night stand engaged Alfred Bunn, "the ubiquitous Bunn", from Drury Lane and Covent Garden to dilate on Kean, Cobbett, George Colman and Shakespeare, giving advice on "The Qualifications of Public Speakers" and the odd-sounding "The Longest Pause on Record", which might have been a dig at his old antagonist Macready or an early version of a Goon show.

On 29th October 1859, Newcombe presented a drama based on the 1788 murder of a Dockyard clerk in the Five Fields near Stoke Church and called it *The Five Fields Tragedy* or *The Assassin's Bridge* (as Millbridge was to be known for a long time thereafter). For the first time he was able to announce that the play "was received last night with the greatest Applause and Approbation by a house crowded to the ceiling, and will be repeated this evening", and indeed it was repeated many times in the following years.

With his imaginative ideas and an insight into just what the Plymouth public would stand, Newcombe was becoming a legend as a character and a fighter of officialdom and as an energetic and sporting gentleman who rode to hounds and owned racehorses. He soon became beloved of the populace of both Plymouth and Exeter, and in Barnstaple where he leased the theatres on many occasions. He was one of the first to combine the touring system of package shows from the metropolis with productions by the local stock company, each playing alternately at different theatres—a practice which existed in the West Country right up to the last decade of the nineteenth century when stock companies became extinct.

His first impact on the national scene was the engagement in 1856 of Miss Percy Knowles, "the celebrated American tragedian", and Miss Ambrose to play in *Othello*, *Hamlet* and *Virginius*, after their appearance in London at the East End Royalty Theatre where she had earned the report of the press as "a debutante stated to have become a celebrated actress in America but who was a novice and claimed the usual indulgence accorded to unprotected candidates".

This should have been enough to warn Newcombe, but they appeared in Plymouth on 17th December 1856, with Miss Knowles as Othello and Miss Ambrose as Desdemona to a full and expectant house.

After a long wait the curtain eventually rose with Iago

ready, but no Othello—so after a painful pause, the curtain was lowered, to rise again later showing a black-faced Othello with blonde hair.

Her wig had not arrived. It came for the next scene when Desdemona seemed to run mad and began to pull Othello about, frantically clutching at her partner's false beard, moustache and wig. According to the local press, "the character of the noble-minded Moor was brought to the level of an angry nigger" and another critic came out with the vitriolic "Miss Knowles has no conception of the part and Miss Ambrose was still worse, being an attempt on the part of a novice to enact a character of which she knew nothing. It was one of the worst attempts we have ever witnessed."

The following day Newcombe acted, and issued a specially printed public announcement which from a theatre manager dedicated to publicity and sustaining business is unique, for he stated:

## NOTICE TO THE PUBLIC

Mr J. R. Newcombe presents his respectful compliments to the patrons of the theatre, and earnestly entreats them *not* to come during the remainder of the above named artists; as, if they do, they will only witness the crude efforts of two ladies who have everything to learn and have not yet attained even the most rudimentary knowledge of their profession.

This was posted across the face of all the playbills advertising that week's show on the town hoardings.

The two ladies insisted on finishing their week with *Hamlet* and *Virginius*, and there was a remarkable reticence on the part of the press who referred only to their costumes. On the last night Miss Ambrose failed to appear at all.

But by now Newcombe's action had spread to the national papers who all made laudatory comments on his swift move against mediocrity in the theatre.

*Punch* had a skit on the subject with a sketch of Newcombe in a boat fishing for a mermaid; the editor, then Mark Lemon, applauded Newcombe's stand, saying of the Plymouth manager: "A name that deserves to be written in the very brightest footlights, for it is not often that the anxious caterers for public amusement exhibit such touching truthfulness, such affecting sincerity as enhance the character of Newcombe."

The Puritan element raised their heads again in 1861 when Newcombe had his rent raised by the Plymouth Council (they were the landlords of the Theatre Royal and he the lessee) and he rightly asked that they should contribute half the expense of renovation as "the theatre has not been touched by a brush or repaired within a decade".

The Mayor, Mr Alfred Rooker (an apt name for a landlord who declined to spend money on the maintenance of the town's own property), while agreeing that Newcombe "was a respectable inhabitant of Plymouth", went on to argue against the grant for repairs and said: "There was such a strong opinion or prejudice inside and outside the council against theatres that they should only deal out to the lessee that which was strictly right."

But the press of the day was on Newcombe's side and came out strongly in his favour. "The Gentleman is a model manager. No-one can lodge a single complaint against the professional decorum of Mr Newcombe; not even those anti-believers in the virtues, the users, the glories of the Drama, the maiden aunt with two cats and forty pounds a year, and the elderly lady with a weakness for Mr Spurgeon [The English Baptist leader and preacher] and a profound reliance on the Book of Revelation."

Newcombe was a man fiercely jealous of his rights as a theatre manager. In 1869 Mark Twain came to Plymouth and appeared at the unlicensed Assembly Rooms to give his presentation of *Falstaff*. He was summoned by Newcombe who stated that while *he* had to fight hard for his licence from a none-too-friendly Bench, the great humorist had got away for nothing. The writer was duly hauled before the magistrates, fined and admonished.

The same year Newcombe staged one of his many pantomimes and, as usual, included a variety of topical allusions. One backfired when a too sensitive Colonel Penrose of the Royal Marines took umbrage at what he considered "an insult to the Force". Looking back it is as if the present-day navy were upset at the antics of "the Gallant Captain of the Pinafore" so innocent was "the insult".

The objection was to a scene with a backdrop of the Royal Marines Barracks at Stonehouse, where the Clown as part of his "business" put on the cap and greatcoat of the sentry. A big box was brought in, labelled "best red sealing wax", and at the stroke of Harlequin's wand this changed to a sentry box with a marine inside, and a flap fell from the top with the inscription "Warranted to stand as long as the whacks last".

To such childish antics the gallant colonel replied by issuing an order forbidding officers, non-commissioned officers and men of the corps from entering the theatre until further notice.

The trouble came when it affected some of the stage staff who were marines by day and stage hands by night. Also many of the principal marine musicians were in the theatre orchestra. However, Newcombe used it as an advertising stunt, calling it "Martial Law". Business looked up and the silly order was withdrawn in a few days.

Noncomformist consciences awoke in 1873 when it was reported to the Plymouth Council that the Theatre Royal was including in its programme the terribly decadent "can-can" which had shocked the susceptibilities of those fortunate ones who had seen it in Paris.

A full and solemn debate, full of high-sounding speeches denouncing the theatre as a breeding ground for sin, was held to discuss this vile encroachment on the lives of the pure Plymothians.

So incensed were the councillors that Newcombe's licence was challenged when he applied to the magistrates for re-newal, and he was publicly warned not to permit any such performance again. But the controversy while it lasted caused great mirth to the local theatregoers who saw no objection to a girl wearing a calf-length skirt, long Victorian drawers and giving a decorus high kick. One broad-minded councillor suggested the objectors should write to the War Office re-questing that the Highlanders be prohibted from wearing kilts!

Yet another illustration of thin-skinned councillors and their Victorian attitude to the theatre was seen in 1874 when, at a pantomime, characters dressed in the robes of the Mayor,

Town Clerk and Police Chief danced a sedate saraband followed by an Indian dance—an item which was loudly cheered and encored by packed houses every night.

This caricature of local bigwigs, when compared with some of the devastating satirical jests at prime ministers and politicians on television today, seems a trivial "much ado about nothing". Today public figures just grin and bear it if they are lucky enough to be singled out for this sort of thing at a theatre.

But in those days the city fathers considered it a despicable outrage that the lessee of the theatre should burlesque his own landlords. Again there was a full-dress debate and the victims proposed several measures including an appeal to the law. This last threat appealed enormously to Newcombe who replied that if the corporation prosecuted him, he would insist in the interests of justice that the three characters should not only appear in the witness box in their robes, but also perform the two dances so that the jury might ascertain whether his presentation of them was really a burlesque or not!

However after many acrimonious squabbles and jubilant advertising of the show from the national press (who enjoyed this silly scrap) the council solemnly passed a resolution in their minute book. It stands there to this day as follows:

Resolved, that this Council desires to express its disapprobation of the exhibits which have recently taken place at the Plymouth Theatre, representing individuals in public positions in this town in a grotesque and unbecoming manner; and that such a representation of the Chief Magistrates of the Borough is especially deserving of public censure and reprobation. That a copy of this letter be sent to the Manager of the Theatre.

True to his calling, Newcombe replied in fighting fashion:

The stage is intended to hold the mirror up to nature, and if the members of the Town Council were to support their establishment more than they do, they would occasionally receive a lesson that would, I have no doubt, tend to make them better men. Like myself, they are servants of the public and must expect to have their deeds criticised.
I am their tenant—but not their menial.

Such words on the lack of support for the theatre by local councillors and their descendants were to echo down the future years.

This stand by a theatre manager typifies the commencement of the belated revolution that was to eventually make the theatre in the West not only "respectable" but a force to be reckoned with. For while the heyday of provincial theatre in many parts of the country came about between 1750 and 1820, its arival in Plymouth was delayed by some fifty years—mainly by bigotry, caution and the intermittent industrial development in the town.

It thus came about that Plymouth's golden age coincided with the second half of Victoria's reign when the rapidly increasing population (80,000) in Devonport and Plymouth initiated a desire for rousing and romantic entertainment with only a modicum of moral and cultural uplift.

The industrious, overworked and underpaid people were eager for an escape to a more spectacular world for a few short hours—a world where a latent Celtic imagination could identify with the flamboyance of the actor and the highly-coloured illusions of the stage.

From 1860 to 1900 no less than 2,500 different bills were staged at the Theatre Royal, Plymouth, alone, with many of the earlier programmes consisting of the main play (usually, although not always, a tragedy or melodrama) followed by, as afterpiece, a comedy or farce, developing only in later years into one main attraction.

This avid desire for entertainment and enlightenment could not be satisfied by just the two theatres at Devonport and Plymouth alone, and it was during this period that a phenomenal expansion took place—culminating in the city sustaining no less than five major theatres by the end of the century, plus a number of lesser halls and establishments devoted to variety, circus and "scientific lectures with moving pictures" as well as the seedy penny gaffs.

That J. R. Newcombe was, in some measure, responsible for this huge demand cannot be denied, for there is no doubt that his ebullient Bohemian image, sharp business acumen and a remarkable talent for advertising even the smallest detail by surprisingly modern methods paid such dividends that he became an honoured public figure and one of the few who in those austere times could stand up to a rather sour-minded corporation.

But like most of his theatre manager successors, benevolence to the actors he employed was not his best feature.

After his early admonition from Macready over inefficiency of the stock company, he had tried to tighten up their conditions of servitude, and ruled like a martinet. However, actors are notoriously averse to changing their accepted mode of life and, on occasion, they still strayed back to the easy going old ways.

A stickler for discipline, Newcombe then established a written code, still extant, of backstage conduct which considering the dire state of the maudlin company which he inherited, was a long overdue reformation.

Undated, but possibly around 1850, it contains:

*The Lessee and General Manager's Regulations for Actors and Stage Staff, and Rules for Benefits.*
Salaries are not to be paid when the performances are suspended on account of any public calamity, on Ash Wednesday, or other Feast Day etc. nor during the illness of the performer whereby the manager is deprived of his services.

Every vocal performer to go on the stage and assist in all the processions and choruses where it has been customary for principals to be engaged as in "Macbeth", "Pizarro", "Juliet's Dirge", "Alexander the Great" etc. Non compliance with this regulation subjects the party to a fine of 10s.

Every performer is required to go on to the stage, if in the theatre or within call, whenever it is deemed expedient to sing the National Airs, or forfeit 10s.

For using improper language in the dressing rooms or any part of the theatre to forfeit 5s.

The actor shall, if required, perform in other theatres without further remuneration other than the payment of railway fares (third class) and the sum of 2s. 6d. per night for lodgings.
*Rules for rehearsal.*

For missing the first entrance to forfeit 1s. For every subsequent one 6d.

For standing on, or walking across the stage during rehearsal when not engaged in the scene. . . 1s.

For not being reasonably perfect at the last rehearsal (sufficient time being given for study). . . 10s.

For keeping the Prompter's book beyond the appointed time of the piece being rehearsed. . . 2/6d.

*Rules during performance.*

For not being ready to begin at the time announced on the bill. . . 5s.

For keeping the stage waiting. . . 2/6d.

For standing within the chalked lines at the first entrance or sitting at any of the wings. . . 2/6d.

For being obviously intoxicated when engaged in the performance to forfeit one week's salary, or to be discharged at the option of the manager.

The same forfeit to any actor who persists in addressing the audience or replying to any of their observations, or if they introduce any friend or stranger behind the scenes or within the stage door without permission.

The Prompter to be the judge of any violation of the rules and to collect the fines numerated.

The Prompter neglecting to make a just and impartial weekly return of any breach of duty, to forfeit for each neglect, Double the stated sum.

*Benefit regulations.*

Previous to the benefits, a notice will be posted in the green room that the performers who intend to take benefits or ticket nights may make their conditions known to the manager; and those performers who do not give notice to that effect in writing by the appointed time will be considered as having declined the privilege.

No Star allowed to play for a benefit without the special permission of the manager.

No Comic Pantomime allowed but to Harlequin, Columbine and Clown. Performers are not allowed to curtail pieces, but any piece that has been compressed in either of the London Patent Theatres may be acted from the same copy.

*Rules for the property man.*

Not having the properties ready at rehearsal or at night, for each omission to forfeit 6d.

If the stage be not set properly or the properties set out of order for each offence 1s.

*Carpenters and scene shifters.*

The Stage not being ready and properly set for any part of the rehearsal or evening performance to forfeit 1s.

These harsh disciplines, while necessary to raise the stock company member from his lethargy, were contained within a "salary" range of 10s. to 30s. per working week, dependent on the calibre of the player, and had to cover his total existence as well as being expected to provide a good part of his wardrobe. The female members had to supply everything.

The inclusion of benefits as part of the actor's income was a pernicious system, and whereas it died out in London and other places in the middle of the nineteenth century, it was still operating at the Plymouth Theatre Royal in 1897. At the Devonport Alhambra "benefits" were even being given in 1920.

In Doran's *Their Majesties Servants*, it appears that the first benefit was given for the scandalous Mrs Barry on James II's orders as a passing compliment, but the idea of making actors work at "ticket touting" in their spare time was too good to miss by money-grubbing managers, and it soon caught on and became a custom.

A perfect example of the workings of this vicious system of payment is seen in Dickens' *Nicholas Nickleby* when Miss Snevellicci and the Infant Phenomenon went the rounds of the Portsmouth gentry to solicit patronage.

Benefits in Plymouth, Exeter and other major towns in the early 1800s were given two or three times a year, but from 1870 onward were confined to annual events. "The Benefit of the Manager" took pride of place on the list and was invariably fixed for the commencement of the Christmas pantomime when full houses were assured.

Lesser mortals had theirs later in the year or the tail-end of the pantomime season, and one sees advertised "Benefit of Abanazar and the Stage Manager" or "For the Clown and Harlequin" or "For Widow Twankey", while at intervals throughout the year benefits were solicited for "The Band", "The Working Staff" and "The Money and Check Takers".

What they actually received after all the house and production expenses were paid and the manager had advised them of what he considered "their share" was the only addition they were likely to receive to their miserable salary. On some sad occasions it might involve them in a loss.

Another of Newcombe's gambits was to appear himself on

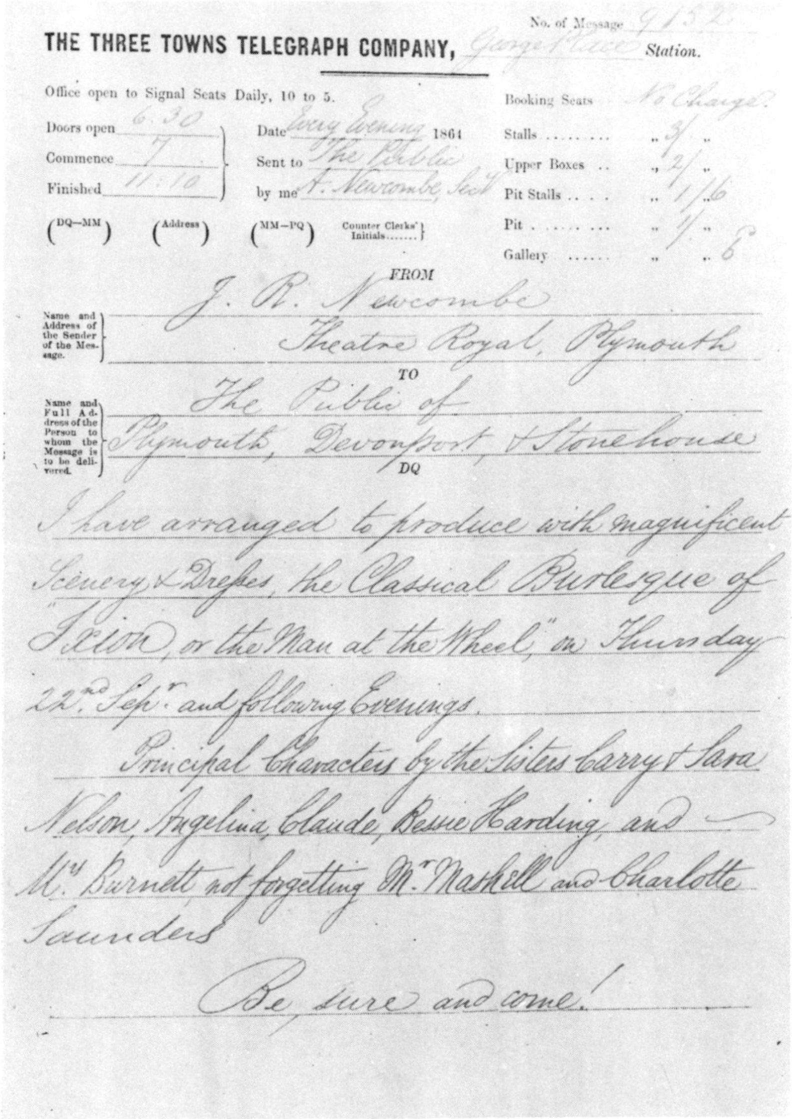

No. of Message 9152

THE THREE TOWNS TELEGRAPH COMPANY, George Place Station.

Office open to Signal Seats Daily, 10 to 5.

Doors open 6.30
Commence 7
Finished 11.10

Date Every Evening 1864
Sent to The Public
by me A. Newcombe, Secy

(DQ—MM) (Address) (MM—PQ) Counter Clerks' Initials.......

Booking Seats No Charge.
Stalls ........ „ 3/ „
Upper Boxes .. „ 2/ „
Pit Stalls .... „ 1/6
Pit ........ „ 1/ „
Gallery ...... „ „ 6

FROM

Name and Address of the Sender of the Message. J. R. Newcombe
Theatre Royal, Plymouth

TO

Name and Full Address of the Person to whom the Message is to be delivered. The Public of
Plymouth, Devonport, & Stonehouse

DQ

I have arranged to produce with magnificent Scenery & Dresses, the Classical Burlesque of "Ixion, or the Man at the Wheel," on Thursday 22nd Sepr. and following Evenings.

Principal Characters by the Sisters Carry & Sara Nelson, Angelina Claude, Bessie Harding, and Mr. Burnett not forgetting Mr. Maskell and Charlotte Saunders

Be sure and come!

FIG. 20.—One of Newcombe's advertising ideas was to send fake telegrams to selected regular patrons. Note the generous amount of time (from 7 p.m. to 11.10 p.m.) given to public entertainment in 1864 in comparison with the prices charged.

occasions, thus saving the expenses of an actor, and his name appears dozens of times on playbills throughout the years in roles ranging from light comedian in pantomime and burlesque, to acting with James Doel in a number of farces laced with topical and local allusions. This was a feature which always went down well with the inhabitants and was perhaps a precursor of "Regional Theatre".

His advertising stunts became a byword among the citizens for he would use every opportunity to create further business for his theatre at a time when competition from others was strong.

One of his favourite ideas was to send fake telegrams to selected patrons addressed to "The Public of Plymouth", with a text reading:

I have arranged to produce with magnificent scenery and dresses the classical burlesque of Ixion or the Man at the Wheel on Thurs. 22 Sept.

Principal Characters by the sisters Carry and Sara Nelson, Bessie Harding and Mrs Burnett, not forgetting Mr Marshall and Charlotte Saunders.

Be sure and come!

Individually addressed, and signed J. R. Newcombe, these telegrams with their personal touch had their effect and business was bolstered.

Another was to capitalise on such items of technical equipment which made news in those days of Victorian invention, and he advertised in large letters on posters around the town: "The Apparatus for the Lime Light has not yet arrived, but will astonish everyone when positively installed."

This was followed a couple of days afterwards with:

Engagement of Mr Brook.
The First Experiment with the New Lime Light in a new and highly interesting drama "Holly Bush Hall".

Another of Newcombe's notices stated in 1882: "Wanted 80 Respectable Good Figured Girls about 20 years of age for the Pantomime—Terms Two Pounds each".

It does not state whether the £2 was for the week or the

run of the pantomime, but the playbill of the same show reveals only twelve girls named in the chorus. Perhaps Plymouth ladies were not so starry-eyed in those days.

Newcombe's turnover of plays at the Theatre was prodigious, and in his own collection of playbills now preserved in the Plymouth Central Library there is a great panorama of nineteenth-century entertainment in lurid colours and flamboyant text.

They range from the primitive beginnings of melodrama in the city through the days of Blood and Thunder, the classics, Virtue Rewarded and the favourite subject of the Unmarried mother with the Baby in the snow, to Pantomime, Burlesque and Shakespearean revivals.

Taking as an example the Victorian taste in fiction with its strictly moral tones, its tearful novelettes and benign teachings of "a greater Power than ourselves", the absence in the theatre of that time of Shakespeare's peaceful pastoral comedies seems surprising.

Instead theatregoers always demanded the most bloody and melodramatic plots containing death and drama (*Macbeth, Hamlet, Othello, Julius Caesar* etc.) with nary a mention of *Twelfth Night* or the comicalities of Bottom in *A Midsummer Night's Dream*.

The niceties of comedy, unless delivered with a heavy hand, were less appreciated. Even a critic of Leigh Hunt's standing dismissed *Twelfth Night* as of little moment, with this paragraph in *The Examiner*:

> Though it has passages of exquisite delicacy and two scenes of irresistible humour, it is perhaps last in the ranks of Shakespeare's more popular dramas.
>
> Inferior to Falstaff pieces in invention, to "Much Ado About Nothing" in wit, and to "The Taming of the Shrew" in effect and completeness of design.

Perhaps he was influenced by Dr Johnson who remarked: "The Character of Aguecheek though drawn with great Propriety is in great measure that of natural fatuity and therefore not the proper prey of the satirist."

The repetition year after year of tried and trusted dramas is a noticeable feature of those Victorian days, especially those

plays which include utterances of good and noble thoughts. William Barrymore's *El Hyder—The Chief of the Ghaut Mountains* is typical, having as its main character a midshipman (always good for business in Naval Plymouth) who gets mixed up in a war with rival Indian chiefs. When he declaimed: "We British lads espouse the cause of all who are oppressed and each true born Briton echoes forth the cry of Freedom!" the house resounded to the cheers.

Local colour was always near to Newcombe's heart and in 1860 he adapted Scott's *Kenilworth* and entitled it *The Fair Maid of Devon*. After a number of successful performances he took it up to Barnstaple and Exeter where it also played to excellent business.

Tragedy and plays of the innocent and oppressed poor were meat and drink to the Victorians, and one of the most oft-repeated works was *The Beggar's Petition* with its tear-jerking playbills. Written by George Dibdin Pitt—an adept at driving home morals—it was subtitled *A Father's love for a Mother's Care*. It dealt with the heart-rending situation of Sir Edgar who, after making Jane his mistress orders the parents to be arrested for theft with the words: "You have my fiat—marriage tomorrow, riches for your child, or beggary for both." Later, when the heroine arrives at the Lodge Gates with her child in her arms (in the snow of course), the audience would bring the house down with roars of disapproval.

Another was the lurid *A Betting Boy's Career from his Home to the Hulks* which was revived many times, always "owing to great demand". There would be added information on the bills—"Cheap tickets on the Railway from Liskeard at 1/9d. in covered carriages."

The tallest actor in the business at that time, Sir William Don, together with his wife, came on regular visits over many years with Shakespearean productions; and Charles Pitt of

---

FIG. 21 *(facing page)*.—The destitute old father being forced to beg at the rich man's gate and the casting out of the unmarried mother with baby in the snow were popular themes of Victorian melodrama. George Dibdin Pitt's *The Beggar's Petition* was revived again and again over the years and audiences never seemed to tire of its harrowing message.

[133]

Covent Garden and Drury Lane came with *Richard III, Lear*
and *Hamlet*, with W. S. Branson as Laertes, and Emily Osmund
as Ophelia. Pitt stayed on for further performances of *The
Lady of Lyons*, Bulwer Lytton's classic.

In 1861 Newcombe took over the lease of the Devonport
Theatre and staged *Hamlet* there with Henry Loydall as the
Dane, Annie Ness as Ophelia and the old-stager James Doel
as First Gravedigger.

An unusual revival was that of *Coriolanus* which Charles
Dillon acted in 1872. He also appeared in *Othello* and *Hamlet*
with Annie Manners as Ophelia. Another unusual production
was that of *King John*—"Not enacted these 16 years"—with

FIG. 22.—Dramatised moral teaching, so beloved of Victorian
England, is epitomised in the "Dreadful Warning" of *The Betting
Boy's Career from his home to the Hulks.*

the tragedian T. Swinburn as the king. He also later appeared as Macbeth and in *Julius Caesar* and *Henry IV*.

The 1870s saw melodrama in full spate with Tom Taylor's *The Ticket of Leave Man*; Boucicault's *Colleen Bawn* and *The Octoroon* or *Life in Louisiana*; Reade's *It's Never too late to Mend*; Bulwer Lytton's play *Money* and a long run of the comic *Have you seen the Shah?*, taken from F. C. Burnand's *Kissi, Kissi*, with music by Offenbach. This gave the Victorians that popular song:

> I love to go out shopping . . .
> Twinkle twinkle little Shah . . .
> Have you seen the Shah? Smoking his cigar.

It was in this decade that Plymouth fortunes were again at a low ebb. Smallpox plagued the town in 1872 and particularly hit its worse slums, which were in Looe Street, Octagon, Bath Lane and King Street. Even so two years later the city fathers, ignoring the infested surrounding back streets, built the Guildhall and Municipal buildings which were opened by the Prince of Wales, later Edward VII.

At this time rail fares from Penzance to Plymouth were 4s. 6d. (1st class 9s.); "Real Kid gloves" were advertised from Whitby's in Fore Street at 1s. 11½d. a pair, and a silver watch could be had for £1 7s. 6d.

Thomas's Hotel in Devonport proudly stated that "Naval and Military Gents and Private Families will find this Establishment replete with every comfort"; the *Lady's Newspaper* advertised: "The most fashionable Bathing costumes are made of dark blue flannell—seven yards will be sufficient"; and Jimmy Doel took his last benefit performance and retired from the stage in 1876.

In 1878 Newcombe's brother Albert was walking away from the theatre after the performance when he saw clouds of smoke issuing from the upper windows. Flames soon followed and within a couple of hours the interior had been completely gutted, leaving only the walls.

Newcombe could not be without a theatre so he temporarily took over St. James' Hall in Union Street until the rebuilding was completed in 1879. The Bancrofts were the first to appear

# THEATRE ROYAL

Lessee and Manager · · · PLYMOUTH. Mr. J. R. NEWCOMBE. 1868.

## FREE LIST ENTIRELY SUSPENDED, THE PRESS EXCEPTED.
### NO HALF-PRICE.
#### DOORS OPEN AT SEVEN O'CLOCK; TO COMMENCE AT HALF-PAST.

PRICES:—Orchestra and Dress Balcony Stalls · · 4s. Upper Boxes · · 2s. 6d. Pit Stalls · · 1s. 6d.
Pit - 1s. Gallery - 6d. Private Boxes, One Guinea and a Half, and One Guinea.
Tickets and Places secured for the Orchestra and Dress Balcony Stalls at Mrs. P. E. ROWE'S, George Street, Plymouth.

### THE EMINENT COMEDIAN, MR.

# SOTHERN

## FOR FIVE NIGHTS,

It being his FAREWELL VISIT previous to his departure for the UNITED STATES;—assisted by

# MISS ADA CAVENDISH,

### FROM THE THEATRE ROYAL, HAYMARKET.

## On TUESDAY, WEDNESDAY, and THURSDAY,

SEPTEMBER 1st, 2nd, and 3rd,

The NEW PLAY, with a Prologue, and in Four Tableaux, from the French of M. OCTAVE FEUILLET, revised by Dr. WESTLAND MARSTON, and performed at the Theatre Royal, Haymarket, with the greatest success for over 100 Nights, entitled A

# HERO
## OF
# ROMANCE.

### The New Scenery and Effects by Mr. BROWNING.

The Part Song of "The Reapers," sung in the 3rd Act, composed by Mr. WALLERSTEIN, is published by E. HENRY & Co., St. Ann's Square, Manchester.

| | | |
|---|---|---|
| Victor Marquis de Tourville | | Mr SOTHERN |
| Doctor Lafitte | (formerly of the French Army) | Mr T. A. PALMER |
| M. de Vaudrey | (a wealthy middle-aged Bachelor, and a man of the world) | Mr C. SEYMOUR |
| Gervais Dumont | (a very old man, formerly Captain of a Privateer) | Mr J. G. SWANTON |
| Antoine | (a Confidential Domestic) | Mr R. HORN |
| M. Jourdain | (a Notary) | Mr BOLTON |
| Michel | (a Breton Shepherd) | Mr HAMBLIN |
| Pierre } Reapers | | Mr NEEDHAM |
| Jaque } | | Mr PEARCE |
| Madame Dumont | (Daughter-in-law to Gervais) | Miss WALLIS |
| Blanche | (her Daughter, aged 19) | Miss ADA CAVENDISH |
| Mdlle. Buzigny | (a Governess) | Miss M. BEINHARDT |
| Madame Borage | (a relative of the Dumont family) | Miss AMY FAWSITT |
| Ursule Beaudrou | (formerly Nurse to Victor, now keeper of a Lodging-house) | Mrs PALMER |
| Ninon | (a Breton Peasant Girl) | Miss NELLIE THOMPSON |
| Marie | (a Reaper) | Miss FINDLAND |
| | Guests, Servants, Peasantry, &c. | |

### SCENE DURING THE FIRST TABLEAUX, PARIS; AFTERWARDS THE PROVINCE OF BRITTANY.
(A lapse of a Week is supposed to take place between the First and Second Tableaux: Three Months between the Second and Third Tableaux.)

PROLOGUE.—Scene
## VICTOR'S LODGINGS IN PARIS.
TABLEAU 1.—Scene
## A SALON IN THE CHATEAU DUMONT.
TABLEAU 2.—Scene
## THE PARK OF THE CHATEAU DUMONT.
TABLEAU 3.—Scene
## RUINS OF THE TOWER OF ELFEN !
TABLEAU 4.—Scene
## A SALON IN THE CHATEAU DUMONT.

The Intervals necessary for the rendering of the Scenic Effects are between the Prologue and 1st Tableau, 10 minutes; between 1st and 2nd Tableaux, 14 minutes; between 2nd and 3rd Tableaux, 13 minutes; between 3rd and 4th Tableaux, 13 minutes,

To conclude with the laughable Farce called

# MY WIFE'S MAID

Mr Lysimachus Toozles, a young man with romantic tendencies ............ Mr C. SEYMOUR    Mr Toozles, sen., his father ............ Mr T. A. PALMER
Capt. Crackthorpe Cruncher ............ Mr J. G. SWANTON    Mast. Sprouts, a Greengrocer's boy, hired as a Page ............ Master DELAFIELD
Mrs Whiffleton ............ Mrs WALLIS    Lucinda, her daughter ............ Miss NELLIE THOMPSON
Barbara Perkins, a sentimental maid servant, with a firm faith in destiny ............ Miss EMILY VINING
Scene - - - Mrs. Whiffleton's Drawing Room.    Time - - - Present Day.

I. W. N. KEYS and SON, Printers, Booksellers, Stationers, &c., Bedford Street, PLYMOUTH.

in the newly-decorated edifice in *Diplomacy*, to be followed by the Gilbert and Sullivan opera *H.M.S. Pinafore* with W. S. Penley as Capt. Corcoran, William Hogarth as Ralph and Ethel Pearson as Josephine.

The following years saw the coming of many of the touring companies from the London successes with Mrs Langtry appearing as Lady Teazle in *The School for Scandal*; Lewis Waller in J. Comyns Carr's play *Dark Days*; Wilson Barrett in *The Silver King* and Kate Santley in *Vetah* a musical play with Robert Courtneidge in the cast.

John Reilly Newcombe died on 18th July 1887, at the age of eighty-four, having been in the theatre business for over half a century, forty-two years of which had gone to the building up of theatre in Plymouth from almost nothing to one of the most well-known and popular places in the West.

Tributes to his work came from all over the country. Actors who had worked for him, the general public and the corporation all mourned the passing of the great character of the Plymouth Victorian age.

He left the theatre in the hands of his son-in-law Henry Reed, leader of the band in the orchestra pit at the Royal, who eventually took over the lease from the corporation and held it until 1889. It then passed to Rollo Balmain until 1892, to be followed by C. F. Williams up to 1903.

It is pleasant to record that as late as 1937 a Plymothian of the sporting fraternity, Harry Jenkins, remembered Newcombe, and made an appeal through the press of that time for the preservation of the monument over his grave in Plymouth Old Cemetery. Jenkins, who was the proprietor of the Cosmo boxing hall in Mill Street, wrote: "The memorial was erected by his many friends as a token of esteem and respect. I well remember people flocking to the cemetery on Sundays to view the monument when it was first erected. I

FIG. 23 *(facing page)*.—Edward Askew Sothern (1826–81), an English actor, first toured the provinces for a number of years before going as an eccentric comedian to America, where he made his name in *Our American Cousin*. In it he created the role of the imbecile Lord Dundreary, and his long side whiskers thereafter became internationally known as "dundrearies".

also remember him singing in panto his old song "Gentlemen were Gentlemen some Fifty years Ago." Cannot we be gentlemen now?"

Sufficient money to renovate the monument was raised from people who still remembered the gay old hunting theatre manager.

The last years of the nineteenth century saw many changes in the city with competition from other theatres and halls, hitting the old Theatre Royal where it hurt most—in the box-office. Henry Reed, following Newcombe's example, took over the lease of his main competitor, the Grand Theatre in Union Street, and worked them both for some years.

That great Madam—Violet Melnotte—came to the Theatre Royal in 1888 to appear in *The Barrister*.

Known to the profession as "Mad Melnotte" because of her independent views and fondness for litigation, she was the first to build her own theatre in London's St. Martins Lane, then despised, but today the centre of the theatre world.

Pinero was the vogue and his farces, *Dandy Dick* and *The Magistrate*, both received a good welcome in the city in 1889; while the D'Oyly Carte Company were beginning to make regular visits to the city, finding it a lucrative provincial date at a time when, for some inexplicable reason, they had lost their London drawing power.

The "gay nineties" which hit London in the last decade began to have their effect on Plymothians in a remarkable fashion, for, while paying cautious lip-service to culture and the drama and covertly preferring the more rumbustious burlesque, the comedies and the pantomimes, they fell hook, line and sinker for musical comedy in such proportions as to influence the taste of generations yet to be born.

CHAPTER IX

# Disaster at Exeter

While the Plymouth theatre was in the throes of establishing itself into the daily lives of the people of the nineteenth century, the Theatre Royal at Exeter, which had had a much earlier and firmer start, was consolidating its position as a "good date" for players of all shades.

Being fifty miles nearer to the metropolis and more easily accessible on the stagecoach highway, it became the centre for all actors and companies touring westward. From Exeter they could visit Bristol, Bath, Weymouth, Barnstaple and Plymouth, if the fancy and the promise of patronage took them.

Through the late Georgian and early Victorian years it had seen on its boards most of the great actors of the times, for it had the added advantage of a more or less static population loyal to their theatre and for whom the theatre formed part of life.

It, too, had its troubles with dwindling audiences in the early part of the century caused by the fluctuating times, the plague, war and crises. Its worst enemy, however, was fire. It had three in the space of sixty-five years, the last to culminate in a horrific tragedy.

The first occurred in 1820 after gas had been installed, and a huge chandelier, 21ft. in circumference and 6ft. high, had been added to the auditorium. At 2 a.m. on 8th March 1820 flames burst through the roof and the whole place was soon ablaze. By next morning it was completely gutted, and thus ended thirty-three years of the first theatre in Bedford Circus.

But the enterprising Hughes and Bennett moved with astounding rapidity and arranged for the construction of a

new building on the same site. Incredibly it opened with a
performance of *Macbeth* and *A Roland for an Oliver* within
nine months, on 10th January 1821.

The new theatre seated just under 1,000 and the main
entrance under a colonnade gave direct access to a circle of
boxes set around the pit. A second circle had a separate
entrance and a further one was proscribed for "servants and
the gallery".

Having a circular dome in the centre, the theatre was lit
by a Georgian bronze chandelier with twenty-four gas lamps
on its circumference. The opening advertisement read:

> The interior of the theatre has been lined with wood that no
> apprehension might be felt from damp. Fires have been con-
> stantly kept going night and day during the progress of building.

The management's concern for the health of their public
was to no avail, for the audience stayed away. Within only a
few months of the opening one company played to £3 a night.
In 1823 a notice appeared:

> In consequence of the theatre being almost deserted and the
> newspapers ascribing it to the inadequacies of the new mem-
> bers of the company, the manager is (very reluctantly) obliged
> to close the theatre.

However, Brunton came over from Plymouth and gradually
revived the theatre's flagging spirits with tried favourites,
re-engaging Kean and Macready with many others, thus beating out the familiar path of the West Country circuit.

Exeter, too, had its share of rough-houses. Even the press
complained bitterly of unruly behaviour at the theatre. Bottles,
orangepeel and other missiles were flung into the pit from
the gallery, and in 1823 two constables were specially sworn
in to take over duty at all performances. They hauled before
the magistrates a boy charged with pouring beer onto the
heads of the pittites below, the offender being fined 5s. and
given two days imprisonment.

The ever-present fear of fire was again roused one night
when an explosion took place in the gallery. The management
issued a notice on the gas supply which said: "At no time

was there any danger. The cause being from leaden pipes which were improperly placed."

However, Brunton was not taking any more chances and decided to remove gas from the front of the house entirely. Lights in the lobbies were replaced with patent oil lamps and the interior of the theatre reverted to wax candles.

After Brunton the Exeter theatre had an uneasy time, especially in 1847 when there came a demand from the patrons for reduced ticket prices in view of the bad times of commercial panic and the bread riots. Money was even shorter than normal and would-be patrons boycotted the theatre for so long that on some occasions admission money paid at the door was returned before the performance was due to start as there were only two or three in the house.

But from 1850 onwards the theatre settled down to a period of increasing business, often working in conjunction with Newcombe of Plymouth who leased the Exeter house on occasions for considerable periods. Thus he was able to engage players on more favourable terms and interchange his own stock company between the two places.

A frequent date at both theatres was a show described as Hengler's Circus; but apart from one or two horses and bareback riders in a very restricted arena the rest of the programme resembled a variety show interspersed with a performing bear or monkey amid jugglers, conjurors and singing clowns.

One of the early touring companies from Drury Lane was the English Opera Company, which came to the West Country in the 1850s playing at Exeter, Plymouth, Teignmouth and Barnstaple with the English tenor Henri Corri, Fanny Reeves and Julia Harland, "with an efficient London Chorus".

Charles Pitt, grandson of Charles Dibdin, appeared in 1854 at Exeter as King Lear, Richard III, Othello and Hamlet, with W. S. Branson as Laertes and Miss Errington Mills from the Plymouth company as Ophelia.

In 1864 there was a more ambitious forerunner of the moving pictures with *A Moving Panorama and Diorama of the Great American War*, described in flowery terms as "painted by an American artist covering 30,000 feet of canvas." This, in reality, was the old hand-driven roll of pictures which Poole's Myrriorama had been hawking around Devon's towns and villages for many years.

J. L. Toole, famous for farce and burlesque on his regular summer tours of the provinces, visited both Exeter and Plymouth in the 1870s and there was the usual run of repeats of the old favourites, *East Lynne*, *The Octoroon*, *The Beggar's Petition* and *Called Back* interlaced with regular productions of Shakespearean tragedies in sympathy with the 'self-improvement" mood of those Victorian times.

In the early hours of 7th February 1885, a fire was discovered by a passing policeman. In spite of the efforts of three private fire brigades, "the Sun, Norwich and West of England", the building was gutted, leaving for the second time four walls of what was once described as "one of the prettiest and oldest provincial theatres in the south of England." Rebuilding this time took place at a much later date and the one-time theatre became the Drill hall, standing firm until it was destroyed in 1942.

With the usual Victorian speed and energy in business matters plans were prepared almost immediately for a brand new theatre on another site.

The Exeter Theatre Company was formed with a capital of 1,000 shares of £10 each, and the site chosen and purchased for £3,000 was at the junction of Longbrook Street and North Road.

The estimated cost of the theatre was £6,500 complete with fittings, the chairman of the company being William Cotton. He later became an authority on the Exeter theatre and published a booklet *Story of the Drama in Exeter*. It was Cotton who laid the foundation stone on 12th May 1886.

The stage was 50ft. by 35ft. and the auditorium (comprising dress circle 166, pit 650, upper circle 150, boxes 24 and gallery 550) sat 1,540. With a fearsome disregard of former fires the entire building was covered with a wooden roof overlaid with zinc sheeting. The corridors, workrooms etc. were also timber-lined.

An innovation was the placing of the gallery as a continuation of the upper circle, with a 3ft. wooden partition keeping them apart. This not only served as a canopy over the pit but prevented the usual horseplay whereby the pittites were showered with missiles from the exuberant occupants of "the gods".

The new Theatre Royal was managed by Sidney Herberte Basing and on the opening night—attended by the mayor and prominent citizens—the packed house saw Pinero's *The Magistrate*, followed by T. W. Robertson's *The Breach of Promise*.

The manager delivered the prologue customary on such occasions and included the following doggerel lines which were to prove prophetic:

> If faults there are, and faults there are no doubt,
> We'll rectify them as we find out.

Business continued to be good at a time when the railway fare for playgoers from Exmouth was 1s. Patrons flocked from all sides to see the new theatre which presented such dramas as *The Guvnor, Formosa* and the musical *Les Cloches de Cornville*, to be followed by Milton Rays in the comedy *Kindred Souls*, of which it was said that the plot was so involved and rambling that it was almost impossible to follow.

The new theatre flourished and a good house assembled on Monday 5th September 1887, to see the first performance of George R. Sims' romantic drama *Romany Rye*, which was to begin a long tour of the country after its Exeter opening.

Scenery had been specially made in London for the tour and despite a few minor hitches the first four acts went well. But at about 10.10 p.m., just after the "second price" patrons had arrived, the scene was changed to Ratcliffe Highway by two panels being slid on from the sides of the stage. There was a pause and the two villains in the play returned to gag in front of the scene while the panels were being adjusted. There was a loud bang. The audience tittered, and there followed that uneasy silence which audiences adopt when unsure of whether what goes on is a stage stunt or is for real. At that moment the canvas act drop fell heavily on to the stage directly in front of the two actors and began to billow out towards the audience who were horrified to see that flames were leaping just behind it.

The orchestra began to play but had not proceeded with more than eight bars when a cry of "Fire" was raised, and almost as one the audience rose from their seats and rushed for the exits.

The occupants of the stalls and the dress circle managed to struggle through the side door; some jumped from the circle and some went through the side windows to escape the blaze. But the pittites and those in the gallery were less fortunate.

In a few minutes the place was a dreadful scene. Smoke and flame climbed to the wooden ceiling and the gallery, which was the most crowded part of the theatre. Here there was a horrible panic when it was found that there was only one exit and that this was past the obstruction of the pay box half way down the zigzagging stone stairs.

Those who managed to escape through the lower doors assembled outside the theatre until a large frightened crowd had formed, supplemented by those who had seen the flames from afar and had come to watch.

The building was by then a complete mass of flames and it was not until after the arrival of the private and commercial fire brigades that it was realised that a particularly horrible tragedy had occurred. Rescue work began at once when it was reported that some forty or fifty people had been seen lying at the top of the gallery stairs.

Further engines and the military arrived and rescue work was redoubled; some heroic attempts were made by sailors, soldiers and civilians who dashed through the fire and smoke to drag out half-mutilated bodies.

The next day was one of the grimmest in Exeter's history. The work of recovering bodies went on all day and into the next. It was found that the death toll had reached the appalling figure of 186, out of which only 68 were recognisable. Most of the dead were from the poorer western part of the city.

The cause of the fire, which seems incomprehensible to modern ears, was due to the much vaunted use of gas which was used to light the back stage—the naked fish-tail jets covered with a wire cage flared from gas pipes, battens of which were set in between the hanging canvas scenes.

Wires were strung in between the battens and the scenery

to prevent them flapping against the flame; but in order to obtain different colours in the lighting a dyed calico gauze was often draped in front of the fish-tail burners. These, called "mediums", started the fire high up in the flies.

When the flyman had first seen the flame ignite the gauze he had acted promptly and, in accordance with custom in an emergency, had slashed the ropes of the act drop with an axe. This was the falling scene that had dropped so dramatically during the show. But the fire had too strong a hold and raced swiftly through the flies to the wooden roof in a matter of minutes.

The inquest took eight days and sitting with the Coroner was the fabled Captain Shaw, Chief of the Metropolitan Fire Brigade who was immortalised in *Iolanthe*.

Evidence was given by the actors, members of the audience, the architect of the theatre and the managers, and it emerged that Home Office regulations had been thought only to apply to London theatres and not to those in the provinces. The licensing magistrates had not fulfilled their proper function when inspecting the place before it was officially opened, and the architect had been at fault for producing a building with so many structural defects.

When the real horror of the disaster became known throughout the country, and indeed throughout the world, messages of sympathy came from far and near. A subscription list was opened and these soon totalled £20,776, which included £700 from the theatrical profession with £100 from Henry Irving and a further £100 from Queen Victoria.

Columns and columns of newsprint were devoted to the calamity in all the national and local papers for a number of weeks. Many were the criticisms levelled at almost everyone connected with the theatre. One cannot omit to mention the harsh words spoken just afterwards by the Rev. J. Tremelling, pastor of the Zion Bible Christian Chapel in Torre, who preached the following Sunday and referred to the disaster from a text which dealt with the destruction of Sodom and Gomorrah. He said:

The painful calamity was one which ought to have been averted or which would not have occurred had not something been wrong in the management or morals, or both. To allow two or three thousand people to place their lives in the hands of a few vain, drunken, ignorant, thoughtless stage players was a mistake. It was the morality of the question and the theatre-going tendency that lay at the bottom of the mischief, for if the tone of morality which governed the numerous spectators was of a higher order the probability was that they would have been alive today.

No collection was made in aid of the relief fund.

Such was the hard and cruel line taken by the strict non-conformists of the day, and it amply illustrates the prevailing atmosphere which overshadowed any theatrical enterprise.

It was as a direct result of the Exeter disaster that Home Office Regulations for theatres and places of amusement were drastically overhauled and made to apply to every building in the land.

From those regulations—and springing directly from the Exeter fire—are the present-day rules that: "all exits in sight of the audience shall be indicated by the word 'Exit', that all other doors leading from the auditorium shall be labelled 'No Thoroughfare', that doors shall be unlocked and open out-wards; and that in premises seating over 400 persons in which scenery is employed, a stage roof or side vents opening direct to the open air shall be provided."

It was shortly after this legislation that safety curtains, such as those operated at Drury Lane, were made compulsory in all theatres.

From the remains of this terrible tragedy there is now only one grim reminder—the pin fire six-chamber pistol used as a prop in the drama of *Romany Rye*. It now rests in the Royal Albert Museum in Exeter.

The shock of this major disaster took two years to recede into a painful memory, and it was not until March 1889 that a contract was placed with a Mr Dart, a Crediton builder, to reconstruct the theatre using the remaining four burnt walls as a shell.

Working under a penalty clause of six months the building was finished in September. One of the more modern innova-tions was the installation of electricity. A proviso was made that gas should be retained as an alternative in case of sudden

FIG. 24.—The Theatre Royal, Exeter, built after the disastrous fire of 1887 and which was known locally as "the Irving Safety Theatre".

failure—a reminder of which can still be seen in some theatres today where the "Exit" sign is lit by gas.

The directors of the company appointed S. L. Gifford, an actor-manager, as sole manager of the theatre, and with the Coroner's and Capt. Shaw's stinging criticism of the magistrates' inspection still in mind, invited all and sundry to examine in detail the new construction. Not the least of these was Henry Irving, who had taken an intense interest in the rebuilding and the plans—particularly the backstage facilities and safety precautions (even though he retained for himself those dreadful fishtail burners right up to 1902)—and so much was his influence felt that the place became known locally as "The Irving Safety Theatre".

Accommodating 900, with room for an extra 400 if required, the theatre reopened on 7th October 1889, with a gala performance of *The Yeomen of the Guard*, then just one year old. The *Evening Post* commented:

The event which took place in Exeter on Monday night would doubtless be received by the theatregoing world as one of

National interest and of vast importance to every civilised community, not only in Europe, but over the larger part of the Globe.

The interest lies in the fact that an entirely new departure is shown in the handsome temple which was that night the scene of such a brilliant assemblage; and the importance which attaches to the occasion is but due to the fact that it is plain to all who are competent to judge of matters appertaining to building construction that the Theatre Company have at last adopted a plan which will give not only the maximum in comfort to those who may visit the theatre, but will also enable the public to be assured of their absolute safety during any performance they may be witnessing.

The events leading up to this latest in the long line of Exeter's theatres are faithfully recorded in Eric Delderfield's fascinating book *Cavalcade by Candlelight*, and he also records that at this opening performance the Mayor was presented with a handsome silver medal to serve as a free pass in perpetuity for the holder of that office.

Such mayoral passes (one is also surviving for the Plymouth Theatre Royal) were the usual civic offering in those days when much depended on the continuing goodwill of the local council. This one of solid silver, some 3 in. in diameter, bears the image of Queen Victoria on one side, on the reverse an engraving of the city's coat of arms and an inscription around the edge: "Theatre Rebuilt and re-opened 7 October, 1889. W. Peters, Mayor. E. J. Domville, Chairman."

While the general pattern of productions presented at the Exeter Theatre during the last decade of the nineteenth century followed that of Plymouth, there was now a noticeable divergence from the more lurid transpontine melodramas to a more genteel choice, giving a hint of the changes in taste that the two cities were to adopt in the coming years.

Interleaved with the conventional dramas of the day, *The Lights of London, The Ticket of Leave Man* and *Harbour Lights* there was an increasing number of slightly more advanced productions brought by some of the No. 1 touring companies.

Yet this step forward to a higher standard was not reached without a struggle, as historian George Gissing recorded in

[148]

1891. "It is curious that the people of Exeter will not support anything good in drama or music—the place is intellectually dull," he wrote.

One of these more advanced productions was *The Silver King*, which received great acclaim at Exeter. The author, Henry Arthur Jones, began his early career in the city as a commercial traveller and West Country representative for a firm of textile manufacturers.

Indeed, his first play, *It's Only Round the Corner*, was first seen in Exeter, having been offered to Wybert Rousby, a legitimate actor of the old school who was playing the South West circuit at the time. He offered to produce it and play the lead —if in return Jones would undertake to purchase half the seats in the dearest part of the house, the dress circle. The bargain was struck and the piece, retitled *Harmony*, was later produced by Wilson Barrett with his own company at the Leeds Theatre.

It was around this time that the Rev. Prebendary Reginald Barnes of Exeter and his wife were bringing up a remarkable family that was destined to influence a wide spectrum of the theatre world.

First was the distinguished actress Violet Vanbrugh (born 1867) who joined Sara Thorne at Margate, where she appeared as Ophelia and in many other roles. In London she played Anne Boleyn to Irving's Henry VIII at the Lyceum, understudied Ellen Terry, and in 1894 married Arthur Bourchier the actor manager and became his leading lady for many years, earning a reputation as a great and respected actress.

Her younger sister Irene also appeared with the Margate Company and played many parts afterwards with such distinguished actors as Toole, Tree, Alexander, Bourchier and Wyndham. She appeared in Henry Arthur Jones' *The Liars* as Lady Rosamund in 1897 and was the original Rose in *Trelawny of the Wells* in 1898. She was married to the actor-director Dion Boucicault, the dramatist's son, and, incidentally, the original Sir William in *Trelawny of the Wells*.

Prebendary Barnes' son Kenneth was to become director of the Royal Academy of Dramatic Art in 1909 and to be knighted in 1938 for his services to the English stage.

# CHAPTER X

# Victorian Heyday

So far we have traced the story of the Theatre Royal in the two main centres of public entertainment in Exeter and Plymouth, both of which had maintained stable theatre companies, in spite of setbacks, for 100 years or more.

But there were many other places in the South West peninsula which were forced to rely on the very occasional visits by touring groups for their pleasure.

Their main drawback was the lack of proper accommodation, for many had only the local Town Hall, which in a large number of cases was entirely unsuitable for theatrical performances.

So it was during this bustling Victorian period that these towns felt the need to provide for themselves the high life and entertainment only obtainable until then in the big cities. They began to build or to convert suitable premises, especially in those centres which were drawing increasing numbers of visitors for the holiday seasons, like Torquay and Teignmouth in the South and Barnstaple and Ilfracombe in the north.

Barnstaple's claim to have had the rare visit from William Shakespeare may be legendary; but there is a strong local tradition that its theatrical history goes back to Elizabethan times, when a theatre of sorts existed on Barnstaple Strand (still called Theatre Lane). The site is at the rear of what is now the Regal Cinema, so it is still used for its old purpose of entertainment.

Some sort of theatre was certainly operating in the early part of the nineteenth century, for in 1813 Edmund Kean played at Barnstaple in Henry Lee's company from September until November, when the company moved on to Dorchester.

But a regular place for players did not appear in the oldest borough until 1832 when the Grecian Hall was built. Later to become known as The Barnstaple Theatre, the hall presented many of the touring shows that travelled the West Country circuit.

The lease of this theatre was taken in 1854 by J. R. New-combe, and he brought Jimmy Doel, the comedian, who appeared as the comic character Captain Copp in a play

FIG. 25.—An old photograph of the Theatre Royal, once the Grecian Hall in Boutport Street, Barnstaple. It was demolished in the 1930s to make way for a cinema.

[151]

called *Charles II*. This was part of the celebration to commemorate the opening of the North Devon Railway on 12th July 1854.

The same year Newcombe also staged *Uncle Tom's Cabin*, with 12-year-old "Miss Clara Cass—Possessed of Intelligence and Artistic Powers far beyond her Age", as well as a number of plays and operatic concerts in which his son-in-law, Henry Reed, and other notable Plymouth artists took part.

In the late 1870s the theatre fell into disuse and at one time was used as a Salvation Army barracks. Remodelled in the 1890s it became known as the Theatre Royal and was billed as: "One of the smartest and best equipped theatres in the Provinces".

Theatrical productions were also presented in the Barnstaple Music Hall, erected under the powers of the Markets Act in 1855, and later renamed the Albert Hall. This building continued to be used as a theatre, concert hall and later as a cinema, until the Second World War when it was gutted by fire.

It was eventually rebuilt, with 800 seats, in 1951 as part of Barnstaple's celebration of the Festival of Britain, and now, municipally run, it is called the Queens Hall.

There have been many famous names on its stage over the years and it has the distinction of presenting the first-ever production in this country of Brecht's *Mother Courage* which was directed by Joan Littlewood with Harry H. Corbett playing a leading role.

Benjamin Britten conducted his version of *The Beggar's Opera* in John Gay's home town—with Peter Pears as Macheath—and Shakespeare plays were staged at the Queens under the direction of Peter Hall.

From 1940 to 1953 Barnstaple was the smallest town in England to support its own weekly rep. It started in the town with the coming of George Wood's Little Theatre Company which was established in a converted warehouse and came to be called the John Gay Theatre.

In mid-Victorian times the West of England became fashionable for the well-to-do and middle classes. As a holiday resort no place was in greater demand than Torquay, which was among the first to enjoy a large number of visitors in the summer months. They found the sub-tropical climate so agreeable that many of them decided to take up residence.

The Union Hall, Torquay, became the first place to house any sort of public show, when, in 1864, a travelling showman presented his "30,000 feet of canvas depicting the Great American Civil War". This was followed by small touring companies who found that the growing summer audiences would accept their fare uncritically unlike the more discerning citizens of the larger towns.

The old Victorian Winter Gardens were converted in 1879 to yet another Theatre Royal. A gilt-and-plush affair with boxes, stalls and circle, it served to present select productions for both summer visitors and local citizens up to the late 1920s, when light comedies and musicals were the rage (two of its last were *No, No Nanette!* and *Tons of Money*) plus, of course, the regular Christmas Pantomimes without which no theatre of any stature could exist in those days.

It was finally engulfed by the films and converted after some very extensive alterations in 1930 into the present-day Odeon cinema.

In fact the Theatre Royal, Torquay, had already been superseded, for in 1912 the resort had become so popular with visitors from all over the South of England that a new theatre was opened on the seafront. This was the Pavilion, built by the Corporation, with Mr and Mrs Wiltshire as joint managers.

Its elegant Edwardian-style façade belied the interior, which, being widely spread and with little height, was more like a concert hall than a theatre, and gave the impression of a comfortable lounge.

This was no doubt intentional, for during the most part of its early life this was exactly what it was used for—to beguile the visitors in luxurious surroundings with genteel entertainment.

Celebrity concerts were a regular feature all the year round—with such singers as Clara Butt, Harry Dearth, John McCormack—while world-renowned pianists appeared in between genteel concert parties and informative lectures on all sorts of subjects.

The world famous ballet dancer Pavlova appeared at the Pavilion during her provincial tour of Great Britain, as did the great Russian pianist Vladimir Pachmann, who was then approaching his eighties.

The most astounding stories are revived about this great little man; how he crawled under the piano in search of Chopin, and how he was always followed around by a keeper.

That he dazzled the audience on that occasion with his magical perfection at the piano is recollected by a member of the audience who was present at the performance. The eccentric Pachmann had a habit of keeping his audience waiting, and when he eventually appeared on the stage he just sat down, frowned, got up and walked off.

He came back, sat down and again faced the piano, and at last said "Pachmann not play", and walked off again.

Two attendants then came on, adjusted the piano stool an inch, and Pachmann was at last persuaded to perform—which he did brilliantly.

After the 1914–18 war the Pavilion became established as the main theatre in Torquay, for, with its entrance on the road and the fact that it was bordered on the other side by flower gardens and the sea, it became the perfect attraction for the holidaymaker's amusement.

The 1920s and 1930s saw the Torquay Council taking full advantage of the desire for something new in summer entertainment, and the Pavilion became the centre in the South West for all that was best in concert party—then the most fashionable type of holiday show.

During the out of season months there were plays, musicals and recitals given by high class artists, which combined to build the town into what was to become for the profession "A No. 1 date".

One of the most unusual, and surely the smallest, of West Country theatres was the tiny Bijou Theatre in Paignton which earned lasting fame as being the first ever to stage a performance of the Gilbert and Sullivan opera *The Pirates of Penzance*.

This took place in 1879 when the two collaborators were having trouble with pirated versions of their operas, which had proved such a tremendous success all over the world, particularly in the U.S.A.

In order to establish the law of copyright for *The Pirates*, which was due to go to America in 1880, Rupert D'Oyly Carte arranged for a "one-off" performance to be given in this country, and the company, then appearing in neighbouring Torquay, took over for one night (30th December 1879) a large room in a Paignton hotel. Before a specially-selected audience they read through the lines of the opera, dressed in the naval costumes of *Pinafore* which they had just finished playing at the Pavilion.

The Bijou Theatre, as it came to be called, is still in existence and forms part of the Gerston Hotel in Paignton; its part played in Gilbert and Sullivan history is marked by a plaque on the outside.

In 1883 the North Devon resort of Ilfracombe had its Oxford Hall which presented its share of Blood and Thunder to the citizens and holidaymakers.

The Holt and Wilmot Company staged a whole series of Adelphi dramas for a number of seasons, including an early Western, *Daniel Bartlett—a Drama of the Wild West*.

Ilfracombe now has two theatres. The Alexandra in Market Street was formerly the old town market and became the garrison theatre for thousands of British and American troops during the D-Day build-up. The Victoria Pavilion on the seafront has been built into the rock of Capstone, Ilfracombe's most celebrated cliff. It was badly damaged by fire in the 1940s and has been rebuilt. On the small side, seating 600, it is now, together with the Alexandra, mainly used for summer shows.

That great burst of Victorian energy which came about in the second half of the nineteenth century not only made its impact on industry and communications, but also brought with it a great demand in the towns for a diversification of entertainment.

While culture and morals might be the watchword of some of the plays and melodramas at the legitimate theatre, the English Music Hall had come into its own in London and parts of the North, bringing with it a desire for broad laughter and raucous song.

Pantomimes, with elaborate scenes and fantastically long scripts and cast lists, were to run for three months or even more; families were beginning to frequent places of amusement, and "all round theatres" were springing up everywhere.

[155]

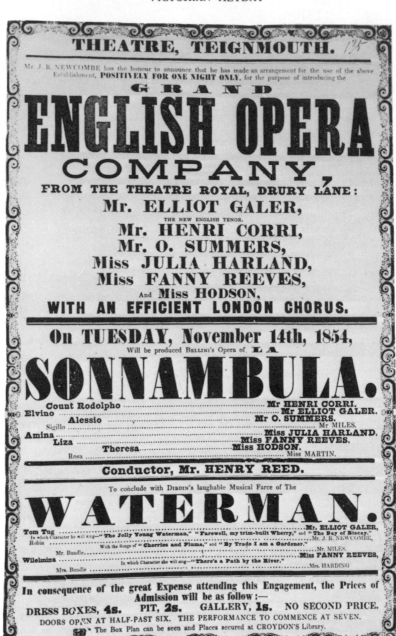

Falmouth converted an old chapel into a theatre, while Truro and Bodmin had theirs too.

St. Austell's theatre was in a brewery, which might have been the reason for that old theatre manager James Dawson saying: "In Plymouth they only laugh occasionally, but we always got louder laughs in Cornwall."

Newton Abbot had its Empire Theatre, and the more sedate part of Exeter went in for its Royal Public Rooms in London Inn Square where regular operatic concerts, musical soirées and recitals were held.

The place was used by the D'Oyly Carte Company when the theatre was closed, and it was at the Public Rooms that Sir Charles Hallé and his wife came to give a piano and violin recital to the ever-increasing number of Exonians who appreciated classical music.

But with the advance of laughter, the delicate tears and refined applause in the Public Rooms declined, and they made way for the Hippodrome which catered for the new style variety shows.

It was the son of an Exeter cabinet maker named Westcott who put the Hippodrome on to the theatrical map. He was none other than Fred Karno, himself born in the city and who later worked in a Nottingham factory and as a plumber's boy.

Fred Karno, synonymous with knockabout and crazy comedy, first learned the business in the North as one of an acrobatic turn who called themselves the Karno Trio.

Later he went in for "sketches" or "wordless playets in which the characters set out with one determination—to get laughs". His *Jail Birds* and *Mumming Birds* not only provided these in plenty and in doing so gave to the world the expression "Fred Karno's" to describe disorganised chaos, but they also proved the training ground for many well-known stars.

These included Charlie Chaplin who began his career with

FIG. 26 *(facing page)*.—Teignmouth, Devon, in 1854, was on a par with nearby Torquay as a select seaside resort and its attractions were socially undefiled by some of the baser theatrical fare seen at other places.

[157]

Fred Karno in *Mumming Birds*; Stan Laurel of Laurel and Hardy fame and those two lovable comedians of the music hall, Fred Kitchen and Harry Weldon.

It was Fred Karno who, returning to his home town, secured the lease of the Exeter Hippodrome and spent a great deal of money on the place including entire reseating and redecoration.

He also built a completely new stage and opened the refurbished building with the most famous of all his comic sketches, *Mumming Birds*.

Thereafter the Hippodrome became the place Exonians went to see Eugene Stratton, Hetty King, Little Tich, Ada Reeve and Marie Lloyd, and that great host of Music Hall talent that was to tour the provinces in between their London appearances.

The Hippodrome lasted for a number of years but eventually went the way of many small theatres—it took to the films. The Plaza Cinema occupied its site only to be demolished in turn by a bomb in 1942.

In contrast, Plymouth, with its three towns—the main one the shopkeeper's city, the respectable residential town of Stonehouse and the overcrowded shipbuilding town of Devonport—as if making up for being a late starter, became the combined home of no less than seven theatres at one time varying from the classical columns of the Royal and the ornate Grand, to the earthy Metropole and Hippodrome, the Palace, the St. James' Hall and later the Repertory Theatre. Lesser halls and penny gaffs added to the number.

The old Dock Theatre in Devonport degenerated badly towards the 1890s and the stage which had once housed Jimmy Doel, James Dawson and Timothy Quaint (the comics who invariably brought the house down with raucous laughter) was given over to nothing more than penny gaff material and ended its days in 1899 when it was closed and the site cleared.

Today nothing is left to remind the passer-by of its existence except for a tiny lane with the legend "Theatre Ope" and a pub called "The Shakespeare".

Its death was hastened by the building of the Hippodrome and the Metropole, both within 500 yards of each other.

The Metropole in Tavistock Street (the site is now within

the walls of H.M. Naval Base and that of the Hippodrome behind Marlborough Street) was renamed the Alhambra in 1928 and was the more successful of the two. It was taken over in 1901 by Arthur Carlton, the same man who became the lessee of the Theatre Royal in 1903.

The old Metropole did good business in the early days, providing a venue for No. 2 tours and variety; it has the distinction of being the only theatre to continue to hold right up to the 1920s "Benefit Nights" for the actors appearing in pantomime.

Dramas were also part of its life and this was continued in the 1920s when the Dorothy Mullord Company took up residence there for some time as a repertory group. The theatre continued afterwards with variety and its death came one Tuesday evening in the Spring of 1941. Bransby Williams was topping the bill, but he did not arrive for the first house as the place was obliterated by a bomb just after six o'clock.

The Hippodrome, under the managership of Guy Prance, presented revues, musicals and, of course, variety. Gracie Fields made a very early appearance there when she was completely unknown, and so did the young Jack Train. Talent concerts were the vogue and in the early days of the Hippodrome the legendary long hook was pushed forward from the prompt side to pull off those who did not please the patrons in front.

But the biggest threat to the business of the Theatre Royal was the existence of the Grand Theatre in Union Street. This was solely brought about by a wily city council who, after Newcombe's death in 1887, had put the lease of the Royal up for tender. Newcombe's son-in-law Henry Reed, who had expected to inherit the tenancy, lost to Rollo Balmain.

An incensed Reed decided to fight and cash in on the flourishing times and on the goodwill of his father-in-law, so he negotiated for a completely new theatre of modern design to be built in Union Street, then the hub of the three towns.

Completed in the quick time of sixteen weeks at a cost of £7,000, it was christened the Grand Theatre, Stonehouse, and opened on Boxing Day, 1889, with the pantomime *Cinderella*. "Grand" it was, having a fine stage—one of the largest in the West Country—a spacious auditorium seating 1,300 people

# THEATRE ROYAL, 44ᵃ
## DEVONPORT.

Lessee · · Mr J. R. NEWCOMBE
UNDER THE MANAGEMENT OF

# MR. HENRY REED & MR. JAMES O'SULLIVAN.

OPEN FOR

# SIX NIGHTS ONLY

## On MONDAY, March 14,

The Entertainments will commence with the favourite Drama, of intense interest, in Three Acts, entitled

# BELPHEGOR
## THE MOUNTEBANK,
## OR THE PRIDE OF BIRTH

| | |
|---|---|
| Guillaume, surnamed Belphegor .. .. .. | Mr JAMES O'SULLIVAN |
| Fanfarronade .. .. .. .. .. .. | Mr H. BARFOOT |
| Henri, Belphegor's Son .. .. .. .. .. | Miss QUICK |
| Madelaine .. .. .. .. .. | Miss ELISE GORDON |

To conclude with DOUGLAS JERROLD'S celebrated Nautical Drama, entitled

# BLACK-EYED
# SUSAN,
## OR ALL IN THE DOWNS.

| | |
|---|---|
| William .. .. .. .. .. .. .. | Mr JAMES O'SULLIVAN |

In which he will sing "All in the Downs" and dance the NAUTICAL HORNPIPE.

| | |
|---|---|
| Black-eyed Susan .. .. .. .. .. | Miss ELISE GORDON |

To-Morrow, TUESDAY—"The Lady of Lyons" and "The Gipsy Farmer."

Musical Director....Mr. WILLIAM REED     Stage Manager....Mr. JAMES O'SULLIVAN

**Doors open at half-past Six; to commence at Seven o'clock.**

Centre Boxes .. 2s. 6d.     Side Boxes .. 1s. 6d.     Pit .. 1s.     Gallery .. 6d.
Children under Five Years of Age Not Admitted.
Second Price at Nine o'clock, or as near as possible to prevent interruption to the Performances.
Centre Boxes .. .. 1s. 6d.     Side Boxes .. .. 1s.     Pit .. .. 6d.
Children under Twelve Years of Age admitted to the Boxes and Pit at Second Prices from the Commencement.

ISAIAH W. N. KEYS, Printer, &c., Bedford Street, PLYMOUTH.

and decorations in the flamboyant Victorian style. Around its lanterns were painted voluptuous cupids and generously-proportioned ladies representing the Arts. Written large for all the world to see was "all the world's a stage", latinised to read "*Totus mundus agit histronem*", as befitted Victorian higher education.

Its safety curtain, ornately painted with a picture of Shakespeare at the court of Elizabeth, was a later addition coming (after renovation) from the Theatre Royal in the 1930s.

These were surroundings that suited the patrons, citizens from the three towns and the ever-changing naval personnel —a backcloth of a garish, florid and comfortable kind that Union Street had made its own.

For the first ten years or so it paid its way, very soon settling its competitive difficulties and running amicably side by side with its rival the Royal. It perhaps concentrated more on melodrama and comedy than musical shows, and competed strongly every Christmas with what came to be known as "The Grand Pantomime at the Grand".

Osmond Tearle's Hamlet was seen on its boards in 1890, and in 1892 Louis Calvert appeared in *The Corsican Brothers* and as Shylock. In the same year the young Frank Benson played in *The Shrew*, *Hamlet* and *The Rivals*, with a cast that included Alfred Brydone, Jessie Bateman, Ada Ferrar, E. Lyall Swete and the young O. B. Clarence. They came again the following year, but with the addition of the slim and youthful Oscar Asche as "An Officer" in *Twelfth Night*.

In 1904 Sydney Fairbrother appeared in the Adelphi drama *Lost Paradise* and the following year two opposites were featured—*The Royal Divorce* (with J. H. Clyndes as Napoleon) and Shaw's *Arms and the Man* with A. E. Drinkwater as Captain Bluntschli and Ethel Verne as Raina.

But the demand for more musicals could no longer be denied and at the turn of the century they came in increasing num-

Fig. 27 *(facing page)*.—One of the last programmes at the decaying Devonport Theatre was the double bill of *Belphegor*, an emotional drama which had played at the Surrey and Adelphi theatres in London regularly, and Douglas Jerrold's hoary nautical drama *Black Eyed Susan* taken from *Sweet Poll of Plymouth* in the early part of the nineteenth century.

bers alternating with the ever-popular *The Silver King* and the eternal *East Lynne* and *Lights of London*. There came the George Edwarde's musical comedies from the Gaiety Theatre, *Florodora* in 1903, *Veronique* (1905), *The Arcadians* (1906), interspersed by the Moore and Burgess Minstrels, *Charley's Aunt*, *The Private Secretary* and the tear-jerking *Peg O' My Heart*, as well as a much welcomed production of *The Sign of the Cross*, the Wilson Barrett religious spectacular which appealed greatly to the emotions of the Plymouth citizens.

John M. East, of the renowned theatrical family, recalls, in his fascinating book *Neath the Mask*, how his grandfather, Charles A. East, played the villain in a Red Indian story *On the Frontier* at the Grand Theatre in 1891 and at one stage in the proceedings had to strike the heroine.

> The house was in uproar. He snarled at them in character "Curse you! Curse you again!" A man tried to climb on to the stage and when the play was over, Charles East had to leave by a side door to avoid the angry crowd waiting for him outside.

Another John M. East (his father) was responsible for many of the Grand Theatre Pantomimes which every year became the talking feature of the town. In 1909 he produced the record-breaking *Robinson Crusoe*, setting a pattern for long spectacular pantos with corny gags and doggerel rhyming scripts which were the accepted style of the times and beloved by the audience. The pattern continued until the early 1920s when he wrote, and appeared in, *Jack and the Beanstalk*.

It is strange that Cornwall's greatest theatrical son, Henry Irving, should only have played in his own West Country during the last two years of his life. He appeared at the Grand (a theatre which he favoured more than the Royal) in 1903 in *Becket*, *The Bells* and as Shylock in *The Merchant of Venice*, and some eight months before his death in 1905 appeared in the same plays at Exeter's Theatre Royal.

A true Westcountryman by birth and upbringing, he was born at Kenton Mandeville in Somerset to Mary Behenna from Cornwall and Samuel Brodribb from Somerton. When his father decided to move away to Bristol which offered better opportunities at a time of industrial slump, the young four-year-old John Henry Brodribb, as he then was, was taken by his mother to live with her sister Sarah Behenna in Halsetown near St. Ives, where he stayed until he was ten to be nurtured in true Cornish surroundings.

FIG. 28.—Sir Henry Irving, a picture taken in the last decade before his death in 1905. The magnetic and compelling pose reflects the hypnotic power of the "Great Actor" so beloved of Victorian and Edwardian audiences.

The ghostly pile of Ghew tin mine at the top of the hill looks down still upon Halsetown, a dour grey stone village that has hardly changed, with its chapel, shop and two-storey houses typical of so many rather grim-looking communities to be found in stannary Cornwall. It was here in his formative years at the time of the great religious revival in Cornwall, with his aunt, a Methodist and teetotaller, and her husband, a dominating quick-tempered mine manager, that John Henry acquired his Celtic temperament. Brought up amid pagan legends, the strange and ancient folklore of deepest Cornwall with its long-remembered history of the primitive Rounds and *Guary* and touched by the histrionic fire of Wesley's followers, his emotions were roused and he began to assume that mystic look; so that at one time he was seriously considered by his aunt to show suitable promise for the church.

At the age of ten the boy was sent back to his parents, now living in the City of London, where he was sent to the City Commercial School under headmaster Dr Pinches.

He had a stammer; and yet it was at school that speech became his forte and his predilection for recitations (the more dramatic the better) was encouraged. When he was twelve his father took him to see his first play at Sadler's Wells, where his imagination was fired when he saw another Westcountry-man, the great Samuel Phelps, as Hamlet.

After leaving school, it was during his years as a drudge clerk in a lawyer's office that his obsession for the theatre took root, and despite the long hours, working until seven at night, he found time and money to study plays, indeed to learn them by heart, before seeing them performed live upon a stage.

At nineteen, with a bequest of £100 from his uncle Thomas Brodribb, he went to Sunderland to begin a precarious acting career and changed his name to Henry Irving (after the American writer Washington Irving) so that his mother might not be embarrassed among the Cornish chapel-goers when seeing the name "Brodribb" connected with the despised stage folk.

The first words Irving ever spoke upon the professional stage were "Here's to our enterprise", in Bulwer Lytton's play *Richelieu*; and these were fumbled, for, as he afterwards admitted, he had all the disadvantages for an actor—a bad gait, a face that did not fit the part, a stammer and a voice which still held traces of his Cornish origin.

The rest is an integral part of theatrical history. Henry Irving rose to become one of the greatest of all British actors and the first ever player to be honoured with a knighthood by Queen Victoria, thus at long last breaking the bonds that for centuries past had branded all actors as rogues and vagabonds.

Indeed Irving achieved more than this, for his acting style and conduct marked the transition from the early spouters, the stompers and ranters to a much more enlightened and intellectual approach appealing to people's emotions as well as their minds; but still retaining the high drama so beloved of the Victorian period to such an extent that even "bad" plays were made to appear sublime.

His acting performances have become legendary, and none more so than those in the provinces where audiences revered his name and would travel from miles around to see him, and afterwards, even in their dotage, would tell, and retell, every detail of his style. A quarter of a century after Irving's death, the late Dr W. H. Waterfield, physician and surgeon to the profession and a great authority on matters theatrical in Plymouth, reminisced on the great actor's Shylock. He told of how, seeing Irving at the Grand Theatre, he was "struck by the delicate yet confident manner in which he held the knife —just like a surgeon would handle it."

As late as 1960, one octogenarian from Exeter could still recount in vivid detail the entrance of Mathias in *The Bells*— how, when the scene opened with the snow falling outside the window of the inn, the noisy talk of the customers was stilled into an almost uncanny awed silence by the commanding presence of the figure in the doorway.

He walked slowly to a seat, bent down and began, with such mesmeric slowness, to unlace his boots that a hushed house looked on enraptured by the great actor's presence. When the first tinklings of the sleigh bells were heard, Mathias turned his head slightly and listened, bringing at once—even though the curtain had been up no more than five minutes—a sense of great dramatic force and tension.

With the coming of "natural acting" from the plays of Ibsen and Shaw, through the style of Gerald Du Maurier in the 1920s and 1930s to John Osborne and beyond, it became the custom among instant actors fresh from drama school to theorise and look down their noses at men of Irving's stature, belittling such performances as "corny" and their delivery as "ham".

Of course by present-day television standards, where performers seem incapable of raising their voices louder than front-parlour conversational tones, and where in public places they are classed as top entertainers and singers if they can muster a whisper into a microphone, then Irving's style, by comparison, might seem flamboyant and embarrassing to watch.

The theatre world of playwrights and actors has of course changed, and the pendulum has swung from the stilted de-clamatory speech of Macready, Phelps and Charles Kean into the opposite direction of the confidential, quiet approach that outlaws emotion, colour, romance and excitement, and creates comparatively little reaction in the audience. The result is that today, in spite of the ever-present microphone, words often fail to cross the footlights to the stalls, let alone the pit and gallery, and if this is the case, the actor's effect fails completely.

It is of course absurd to expect that an outworn style of acting would fit in with a Pinter or Joe Orton play of today, audiences having been indoctrinated over the past half-century with the casual "throw-away" approach, but is the day of the bravura performance really over?

Theatregoers remember with reverence Robert Lorraine's great performance in the 1930s in the title role of *Cyrano de Bergerac*; Ernest Milton's electrifying portrayal of the intellec-tual in *Rope*, and the effect of half a dozen lines given to Esme Percy as the one-eyed drunken tinker in *The Lady's Not for Burning* in the 1950s, who brought the house down in the last act in spite of competition from the others in the cast—John Gielgud, Pamela Brown, Harcourt Williams and Richard Burton.

That the bravura performance can still command respect was revealed in an unexpected quarter in 1973, when, at the Royal Command Variety Performance, Ron Moody, who had been an enormous success in *Oliver*, earned terrific applause for his eloquent and broad interpretation of the old actor-manager, spoken in rolling, ringing tones that completely cap-tivated a highly critical and fashionable audience at the London Palladium.

Such performances are still the meat and drink of theatre to many provincial playgoers, who, although they may be labelled well behind the times in the view of their sophisticated London counterparts, remember them with affection.

Allowing for the fact that Devon and Cornwall have a larger population of retired folk than most other counties, it has been surprising, during the research for this book, how many octogenarians have mentioned Henry Irving and other old time actors, and how many, who although by virtue of their age never saw him can remember the great impression made upon their parents.

The turn of the present century saw the Grand Theatre still running in conjunction with the Royal under J. Langdon Lee who was lessee of both theatres.

But fiercer competition came from just across the road when the New Palace Theatre of Varieties, which had opened in 1899, began to attract patrons, and the delights of the Grand slowly began to wane.

It also had another competitor, for just along the street opposite the Palace was the St. James' Hall, at one time operated by the zealous Henry Reed and by the renowned Jimmy Glover. Formerly it had been the home of the Lion Comique, the popular Christy Minstrels, the circus and the wonder of the age, the Myrriorama, yet another primitive edition of the moving picture.

Emma Santley appeared there in 1871 in "a Musical, Dramatic and Ventriloquial Entertainment of 36 distinct voices in Two Hours", followed by a Christmas pantomime *The Yellow Dwarf—or Harlequin and the Queen of the Fairy Blondes*, an apt choice for Union Street. This included Professor Anderson—Wizard of the North, who stayed for weeks afterwards giving one-night stands with a seemingly never-ending change of programme.

"General" Tom Thumb, with whom Queen Victoria had been so "taken" in 1865, came to the St. James' Hall in 1877 (admission 6d.) with "Songs, Burlesques, Comic Acts and Eccentricities"; and a few years later the comic vocalist Harry Clifton entertained Plymouth audiences with his immortal *Polly Perkins of Paddington Green* and *Paddle your own Canoe*.

Another odd place in Plymouth was the inappropriately named "Royal Albert Hall" in Eldad, which had existed in

# BEHOLD!

A

# HAUNTED MAN

## AT THE
## NEW HALL, TAVISTOCK.

### IMMENSE SUCCESS! CROWDED & DELIGHTED AUDIENCES.

# FIVE NIGHTS LONGER

## Entire Change of Entertainment.

NOTICE.—Messrs. POOLE & YOUNG beg to announce that, at the request of numerous influential parties, and in consequence of the immense success of their Entertainment, they have made arrangements to remain in Tavistock for **FIVE NIGHTS LONGER**, commencing on **MONDAY MAY 9; POSITIVELY CLOSING ON FRIDAY**, as the Exhibition opens in Devonport on the 16th instant.

By Authority, the wondrous Spectral Illusion, THE

# GHOST

With all the recent Scientific Improvements.

## On MONDAY EVENING, MAY 9th,
### AND FOUR FOLLOWING NIGHTS,

Mr. J. C. HORETON will introduce (First Time in Tavistock) WASHINGTON DAVIS's new adaptation of "**A HAUNTED MAN**," pronounced by the Press to be unequalled as a vehicle for the production of Spectral Effects, and is certainly the most beautiful Metaphysical Ghost Sketch yet produced.

### "HE LOOKED LIKE A HAUNTED MAN."—*Charles Dickens.*

#### THE ARGUMENT.

The Chemist is a haunted man—haunted by his memories of wrong, of sorrow, and of care—brooding deeply—the canker worm gnawing at his heart. His imagination breeds Spectres, which take shapes connected with his thoughts—his second self. The embodiment of his cares is a metaphysical creation—a reflection of his inner mind, of whose presence he would fain be quit. The Spectre warns him that, dreadful though his companionship is, it yet exercises a beneficial influence on his destiny—so himself a vic-tim to wrong-doing, it creates in him a sympathy for those that suffer wrong. The Spectre cannot convince the Chemist by reasoning, so it causes to pass before him the shades of those long departed, through whom he had suffered; his Sister first and then her betrayer —his false Friend. Their dialogue teaches the Chemist a lesson—he sees his error, and commands the Phantoms that had disturbed his peace, but which he now welcomes back as the source of all his pleasures.

NOTE.—*In this sketch will be introduced an effect never before succeeded in by any Scientific Illusionist,—that of projecting*

# THREE SPECTRES ON THE STAGE AT ONE TIME.
## SCENE.—THE CHEMIST'S CHAMBER.
AIR.—' THE HEART BOWED DOWN.'  THE CHEMIST SURROUNDED BY BOOKS AND APPARATUS—MEDITATION—A

# HAUNTED MAN

Thoughts on Life—Misery—Wrong—Sorrow—Love—Emotion—Ingratitude. No peace—" Take away from me the dread remem-brance of wrong." "**The Second Self**" in the rustling of trees, in the sighing wind—The Compact—The Fall of Destiny o'er the inner life—The Disappearance—" Give me Oblivion, give me Oblivion." **The Sister**—Upbraiding—Sorrowful Memories—Misery and Wrong—Away, away—The Wanderer—The Outcast—Mystery—**The Wrong-doer**—Excitement of the Chemist—The Lesson—In effects—The old, old Tale—Forgiveness—Pleasures derived from Pain—" Keep my Memory Green."—The Pleasures of Memory. AIR.—" Sweet Spirit, hear my Prayer."

1872, but no other record remains except an old playbill advertising the famous Blondin and a visit from a circus the same year.

Whitfeld mentions a building constructed in Wyndham Square to which the name of Eldad (the favoured of God) was given in the religious controversies of 1825; it is generally supposed that this same structure fell into disuse and later became the venue for travelling circus companies and equestrian performances with occasional concerts and other entertainments.

Penny gaffs had been a feature of Plymouth life for a number of years and continued up to the early Edwardian times. The earliest was Brown's Amphitheatre in Plymouth Market where, emblazoned on its canopy, were the words "Amphitheatre Negrand Mercardo de Plymouth"; while, inside, a huge man with debauched face did his act balancing swords, tobacco pipes and plates on his chin.

Another, close-by, proclaimed itself "A respectable place of Entertainment" where a "Mrs Chaff rode at full speed with or without saddle or bridle and Mrs Wells demonstrated her skill on the slack wire with a modesty of dress".

Samuels Theatre presented a tragedy, a comedy and a harlequinade with several songs—all in double quick time, for the show only lasted a bare hour.

Within living memory there was the penny gaff in old Frankfort Street run by Bill Linsdell with Fred Cavendish. It catered for the crowds which assembled when the fishing boats arrived, and performed such things as *Convict 99*, *Sweeney Todd* and *Maria Marten*; all, of course, in the space of thirty minutes because shows were repeated *ad nauseam* all the evening whenever there was custom.

Among others, there was one in Martin Street cockily calling itself "St. Martin's Hall"; Poole's Myrriorama in Fore Street, Devonport, opposite Aggie Weston's Royal Sailors Rest; Wallser's Waxworks at the Octagon and "Hales Tours of the

FIG. 29 *(facing page)*.—Charles Poole, who was just a cut above the "penny gaff" proprietor of Victorian times, travelled his shows over a wide area of the West country, purveying "Fashionable Entertainment" even to the smallest communities.

[169]

World" in Old Town Street, where one walked in at one end of a supposed railway carriage and looked out of the window at the swiftly-passing scenic beauties operated manually by a sliding roll of pictures from a handle turned by the man outside.

These gaffs, which flourished in the poorer quarters of all large towns, were a feature of night life and were generally situated in empty double-fronted shops or houses. Upon an improvised stage a foot or so off the floor and some 6–8 ft. wide, severely truncated, bloodthirsty melodramas were performed in gory and crude detail. Their presentation was contrived to last the shortest possible time in order that those who were waiting for the next performance should be able to pay their pennies at the door.

In the case of Lindsell's the gaff was a private house, the audience entering by the front door. They either stood or sat on rough benches in the front room facing the stage which was in the back room. The exit was through a window.

Generally the audience had to stand, although one or two rickety chairs or forms were sometimes provided. At the more elaborate establishments the admission fee was 2d.

The gaffs became a bit of a nuisance to the authorities at times, and in December 1895 the chief constable of Plymouth had to issue warnings against their unlicensed performances; but, like their more salubrious theatrical brethren in the past where licences were concerned, they somehow slid around the law. The penny gaff survived until the first decade of the twentieth century, leaving, regretfully, the old Penny Plain and Tuppence Coloured Plymouth scene one of drab uniform grey respectability.

# CHAPTER XI

# The "Not-so-roaring" Twenties

The end of the long Victorian period and the dawn of the twentieth century which brought such a vast change in the national outlook and habits of the people, their way of life and communication, also brought to the entertainment world the Edwardian euphoria of the graceful, romantic approach where laughter was more highly valued than tears and elegance more than fustian.

Almost forgotten were the creaky melodramas with messages of moral guidance and righteous indignation at the state of the oppressed poor; and whereas patriotism still remained a firm favourite ingredient of popular plays the taste for more robust romance, spectacle and glamour replaced the stilted twitterings of Victorian heroines, while Shaw, Strindberg and Ibsen were altering theatrical fare in drastic fashion.

Although this trend had been obvious in London for a decade or more, the far West Country did not fully feel its liberating breeze until well on into the new age. It was then that the great wave of musical comedy and actor-managers' productions began to arrive at regular weekly intervals at the provincial theatres, and, in the case of Plymouth and Exeter, were to continue for almost fifty-two weeks in the year over the next quarter of a century. Such was their influence that the impression they left was to remain for many decades in the future.

Devon memories are long, and with a population nowadays composed of a larger proportion of longer-lasting folk than in most counties, nostalgia plays a prominent part. Remembrances of those halcyon days of the theatre are still recalled, and when today "theatre" is mentioned in Plymouth one almost automatically hears references to "those days at the Royal" (or the Palace or the Grand) as the epitome of good entertainment. But alas, nostalgia does not pay at the box-office for long, as the years to come were to prove.

The effects of the touring companies of George Edwardes, Tom Arnold, Macdonald and Young and the rest, with their provincial editions of the latest London musical comedy successes, on the people of Plymouth, Exeter and the surrounding districts were remarkable, as were the equally eagerly awaited visits of stars like the Terrys, Seymour Hicks and Ellaline Terriss, Matheson Lang and Charles Macdona. Together with many others they all found a rich source of patronage and hero worship among the audiences of the Devon theatres.

Perhaps the chief amongst these was Sir John Martin Harvey, who with his company and wife Nina de Silva, paid a number of visits to the Theatre Royal with his almost unchanging repertoire of *The Only Way*, *A Cigarette Maker's Romance*, *The Corsican Brothers* and, of course, *The Bells*. The last two plays were among those he inherited from his old master when the mantle of Irving fell on him after the great actor's death.

The diligent Dr Waterfield saw Martin Harvey's Mathias together with W. G. Lennox, a teacher of elocution in the city, who also knew Martin Harvey personally. He related that the actor-manager always instructed his cast to look in the direction of the speaker. Even a dominant character was told to look towards the conversation of a minor character, as it focused attention: "He had eyes like a hawk, and would notice any irregularity on the stage, even when seemingly engaged in a major declamation, and the defaulter would be admonished after the performance."

While Martin Harvey did, to a great extent, perpetuate the lives of the older melodramas into the twentieth century, he did add much to the stage and gave us his unforgettable *Oedipus Rex* (Sophocles) which demanded this style of acting.

Whatever the faults of the old actor-manager system, the fact remains that players of Martin Harvey's calibre did possess great personalities as well as great talent. In every sense a "star", he gave those great emotional performances that the public adored, a state of affairs nowadays considered very old fashioned and anti-Brecht, who proclaimed that: "The modern theatre should prompt the audience to make decisions, and not like the traditionalists arouse their emotions."

But the public like their emotions roused, and still go to the theatre to see "stars".

This was also the time when the D'Oyly Carte Company was all the rage in the provinces, bringing a fresh taste to musical theatre that even the most Puritan-minded could not find objectionable. However, many had reservations about the arrival of the rows of chorus girls who came in with the vogue of popular musical comedies.

Paramount amongst these were the Gaiety Girls, so called from the highly successful George Edwardes' shows at the Gaiety Theatre in London, and their provincial counterparts generally consisted of girls chosen more for their looks than their talent. They were to be the first of a long line of dancers and chorus girls destined to become a permanent feature of any musical show worth mentioning.

To the West Country audience's huge delight, ladies of the chorus appeared in such tuneful shows as *The Shop Girl*, *The Runaway Girl* and *The Circus Girl*, while others were seen in *The Arcadians* and *The Belle of New York*.

Thousands of West Country hearts were captured by the lilt of Lionel Monckton's music for *The Quaker Girl* and *Our Miss Gibbs* ("I'm such a silly when the Moon comes out"); by the skipping *Veronique*; by the romance of "Come, Come! . . . I Love you Only" from the Oscar Straus musical *The Chocolate Soldier* (loosely based on Shaw's *Arms and the Man*, for which he refused to accept payment); by Lehar's *Merry Widow* (complete with Hetty the Hen, now banished from the modern edition) and by many others from that golden age of light opera.

Edna May was the toast of Plymouth when she appeared in *The Belle of New York* as was Zena Dare when she starred in musical comedy for a week at the Royal in 1910.

The legitimate side of the profession in Plymouth's pre-1914 days were mainly housed in the Theatre Royal, the Grand and the Devonport Theatres who were trying out all sorts, from such plays as Hall Caine's *The Christian* to Shaw's

[173]

*Fanny's First Play*, both of which were staged in 1912, and Robertson's *Caste* was still acceptable fare. Frank Benson faithfully appeared again in the city and in 1913 brought Baliol Holloway, F. Randle-Ayrton and Eve Titheradge to play in *Antony and Cleopatra* and *The Merry Wives of Windsor*. Close behind came Johnston Forbes Robertson, with his wife Gertrude Elliott, in *The Light that failed*, *Hamlet* and *The Passing of the Third Floor Back*, thus creating in those peaceful years a wealth of top-class productions that inspired many a Devon theatregoer.

Foreshadowing the concert party vogue, Pellissier's Follies made many repeat visits to both Exeter and Plymouth, but the smoulderings of the coming world conflict could be seen in the plays of 1913–14 with *A Military Drama called Tommy Atkins*, *Our British Empire—A Scottish Military Drama* and Louis N. Parker's spectacular *Drake*, which had been the tercentenary production at Drury Lane under the direction of Augustus Harris, so stirring local patriotism.

The Grand and the Alhambra carried on through the 1914–18 years with similar patriotic offerings, revues, plays and variety programmes purveying Kaiser Wilhelm jokes and urging the boys to "join up" with: "On Saturday I'm willing/ If you'll only take the shilling/To make a man of every one of you." Those poignant popular songs of the day, "Keep the Home Fires Burning", "Tipperary" and "A Long, Long Trail a-winding" were performed by companies thin in ranks due to the demands of the armed forces on man and woman power.

But at the end of hostilities in 1918 all their days were numbered. The year of victory saw Seymour Hicks and Ellaline Terriss in *Cash on Delivery*; Matheson Lang in *The Purple Mask*; Albert Chevalier in *My Old Dutch* and the musical revue *The Bing Boys*, and a visit from Vesta Tilley.

The beginning of the "roaring twenties" saw the Royal trying to hold its position as the premier West Country theatre; but, as always, it remained far too large for the town now largely bereft of the military, and failed to attract full houses for plays, however attractive the cast and inspiring the play.

Imagine what a crowd would rush to fill a theatre today with Charles Doran's Shakespeare Company of the 1920s which came to the Royal with a number of then unknown actors—Ralph Richardson, Donald Wolfit, Neil Porter, Abraham Sofaer, Edith Sharpe and Norman Shelley!

West Country theatregoers could hardly complain that they were being served up with second best when on another occasion the mellifluous-voiced Ernest Milton came to play his controversial Hamlet and to appear as Oberon in *A Midsummer Night's Dream* and as Macbeth.

These were unforgettable performances for those privileged to see him act. He was, in turn, followed by Seymour Hicks—this time in French farce—and Russell Thorndike, who was in one of the first performances of *Dr Syn*. Thus a variety of plays which should have satisfied even the most jaded of appetites was on offer.

The late 1920s and early 1930s saw Phyllis Monkman, Jack Buchanan, Olive Groves and Gilbert Childs in a Charlot Revue *Wild Geese*; Phyllis Neilson Terry in George Du Maurier's *Trilby*; Connie Ediss in *Lord Richard in the Pantry*; Viola Tree in *The Eleventh Commandment* and Iris Hoey in *The Man from Toronto*, plus a gathering host of popular musical comedy shows.

The Grand Theatre struggled on mainly with dramas and a continuance of its famous pantomimes, notably those featuring the popular Randolph Sutton, much beloved of Union Street audiences.

He was one of the first to appear as principal boy in tights half a century before Danny La Rue in drag, and never failed to include in his own spot "Mother Kelly's Doorstep", the song which became his signature tune. The "sob stuff" was also maintained for a while at the Alhambra which presented such tear-jerkers as *The Price she Paid* and the unforgettable *No Mother to Guide Her*. In later years it turned wholly to variety.

The West Country drama in the inter-war years was, as in the rest of the country, declining; 2LO was calling on the radio in 1926 that *Paddy the Next Best Thing* was on "the wireless"—a popular play that had been seen at the Royal a few weeks before. Competition from the air was beginning to be felt.

But this was nothing compared with the onslaught of

Hollywood with its talking films which in the 1930s caused havoc in the live theatre, putting talented artists out of work, making musicians two a penny and causing theatres either to close completely or to install projectors instead of actors.

The slump, as it was called, was not confined to the theatre, for this was the period of "Buddy, can you spare a dime?", when Britain and America, indeed the whole world, was struggling to achieve order out of the industrial holocaust.

Life in the provinces was hard everywhere, especially so in the rural West Country. Money was hard to come by and not easily spent on entertainment for although prices were comparatively cheap, wages and the dole were dreadfully low.

Spooners in Plymouth were selling dining-room suites for £15; cream cakes were four for 3½d. and Hylda Baker was appearing at the Palace Theatre for £12 a week.

The red trams (pre-1914 they were brown for Devonport and green for Plymouth) trundled their rattling, swaying way in and around the tightly-packed streets of old Plymouth up-hill to Mutley and along to Peverell. George Street was the social hub of the city and Union Street the great gay highway with shops open until 10 p.m., pubs galore and milling crowds liberally sprinkled with blue uniforms denoting that Plymouth was still the great naval base. Putty Philpott, with his ukulele and rosy face dominating his rotund figure, was entertaining his customers in his pub at the Union Street end of the "Ha'penny Bridge" and making his annual appearance as King Carnival.

That well-known personality Jimmy Glover was manager of the Theatre Royal, and with his connection with Drury Lane was able to book a number of new London productions to be tried out in Plymouth. His transformation scenes in the Christmas pantomimes, obviously constructed on past Drury Lane shows, were masterpieces and miracles to West Country audiences.

Mrs Patrick Campbell appeared in *Voodoo*, described as "a play founded on a negro superstition", and one who saw her performance called it "hammy, handsome and elegant, with beautiful gestures". Right down at the bottom of the bill of this Theatre Royal show is the part of "a travelling negro minstrel" played (in small type) by Paul Robeson. Mrs Pat.

came again to Plymouth later to appear in Ibsen's *Hedda Gabler* at the same theatre.

The late 1920s and early 1930s saw the weekly programmes designed to appeal to popular tastes of the times, for these were the days of the thrillers, and Edgar Wallace was then uppermost in spine-chilling plays, with such productions as *The Terror* and *The Squeaker*. The Aldwych farces were favourites and among these came *Rookery Nook*, with Harold Warrender and Ralph Truman playing the leads. Others included *The Constant Nymph*, with Sebastian Shaw as Lewis Dodd, Edward Chapman as Birnbaum, plus Henry Cass, Pauline Lacy and Andre Van Gysegmhem in the cast.

The Royal also saw the highly successful war play *Journey's End* with local man Jack Train appearing in the small part of "A German soldier". Adelaide and Eden Philpott's own Devon play *Yellow Sands* came more than once, as did *The Farmer's Wife*. Both were much appreciated—and criticised for the difference of the Devon dialect as uttered by the actors from "the smoke".

As with Shakespeare, Shaw was becoming more popular with Plymouth audiences and the Macdona Players came bringing *Man and Superman*, *Pygmalion*, *Mrs Warren's Profession* and *Candida* all in the same week. They came again years later with *The Apple Cart* which followed a highly popular week of the Naval comedy by Ian Hay *The Middle Watch*, one of the first to get humour rather than drama out of the Royal Navy.

Noël Coward's plays were not far behind Shaw in popularity, and there soon followed touring editions of *Private Lives* then considered daring and, perhaps, too outspoken for many provincial audiences. As if to soften the effect, soon afterwards there came Alan Wilkie and Miss Hunter-Watson in a season of Shakespeare and Sheridan, and another of *Hamlet*, *Macbeth* and *The Merchant of Venice* with the young Dickie Meadows-White appearing in a minor role.

Martin Harvey came again this time in *The King's Messenger* with actor Huntley Gordon playing a small part, and a large number of lesser-calibre companies (mainly musical) brought a deluge of No. 2 touring shows without "names" but having, nevertheless, the tunes of the times. There came *Rose Marie*,

FIG. 30.—"Rising in column'd pride and Attic grace. . . ." The portals
of the old Theatre Royal, Plymouth, pictured a few weeks before
they were brought down by the demolition gang in April 1937.
(Photograph by courtesy of The Western Morning News Co. Ltd.)

*Mercenary Mary, The Vagabond King, The Desert Song, Bitter Sweet* and *The Student Prince* (with Thorpe Bates) which were sufficient to give the citizens something to sing about and to inspire local amateur operatic societies, thus continuing the long line of repeat productions which have flourished ever since.

The end of the Theatre Royal came slowly over two or three years. Audiences dwindled and theatregoers only patronised the odd show they wanted to see—be it Shakespeare or musicals—not caring that theatres must remain alive for fifty-two weeks every year in order to exist. Even the Royal's rare film shows were largely left unattended by those who (rightly so) could see them in greater comfort at the new, modern, super cinemas.

Then, for some inexplicable reason, the Plymouth Council, which in truth had seldom given much of a thought to their own theatre, ordered its destruction so that a cinema could be erected in its place, and on 11th April 1937 an insensible and callous council looked on while Foulston's famous pillars came tumbling down at the breaker's hand.

It was reported at the time with sanctimonious platitudes that "the theatrical atmosphere would be preserved", that live shows would be presented there at intervals in order not to lose the aura of "The Theatre Royal" and that with this in mind proper facilities were to be provided for the stage.

But after those graceful Ionic columns and the auditorium were razed to the ground, there rose a bland-fronted super cinema, having a stage lined on three sides with a brick wall, leaving no space for scenery, not even a piano, but just enough room for the descending screen.

Perhaps it was a sign of some heavenly reproach from Foulston's ghost that when the bombs fell in 1941 the rest of Foulston's Georgian Leisure Complex, the Royal Hotel and Assembly Rooms, were completely destroyed, but the cinema was left standing—and still is today.

The general impression of the older playgoers who remember with affection and nostalgia the days of the old Theatre Royal is that council action in pulling down their theatre was an act of vandalism and sheer destruction. But are such criticisms strictly true, or just crocodile tears over the past?

Remember, this was "The Theatre of Splendid Misery", the theatre described as "elegant and as capacious as Drury Lane", yet which, in spite of its size and elegance, was so seldom filled.

This was the theatre that brought financial ruin to Farren and Foote after it was erected; which later caused Manager Hay to say: "It is impossible to make the theatre pay. It is too large for the town—a mere wilderness and a comfortless sight."

Wightwick was to lament in poetic vein its gloomy, tomb-like emptiness while Wemyss pointed out the peculiar Plymothian habit of forsaking their own theatre for others outside the city.

Macready recorded in Plymouth that "the drama was deserted", and there is the sad record of J. R. Newcombe who took the miserly 4s. for six weeks' dress-circle receipts.

Of course it was too big for the city and too expensive to maintain by private enterprise without the assistance of the owners. There were too few managers of Newcombe's calibre to follow in his footsteps and so give what every theatre needs —a life and personality that will not only attract custom, but give people that compulsive urge to see for themselves (and every week of the year at that) what lies behind those magic doors.

As Plymouth theatre critic of that time, J. C. Trewin was later to lament about the city he loved:

In its declining years the Theatre Royal added nothing to stage history. It was certainly (always excepting the musicals) a bad date for the profession.

No-one could have said that Plymouth playgoers were not catered for in the 1920s; they had everything from Hamlet to Frills and Spangles.

It was not so much that the audiences were apathetic, rather they were defiantly low-brow, for there could be no other explanation, rather than a certain obstinate resolve to follow fashion.

Nothing mattered in the arts except the things that were being currently talked of; hence the sudden swing to the talking films that by the mid-thirties left Plymouth culturally dead.

Its nadir came when in quick succession, it lost the Repertory
Theatre and the Royal.
I'm afraid that not many people cared.

This was, indeed, a repeat performance of what happened
to the Plymouth theatre a hundred years before, and it had
persisted on more or less the same lines ever since. In times
of peace the theatre never paid, and left to the local inhabitants it would have died long before.

One cannot help wondering whether had the old Theatre
Royal, Plymouth, (which seated over 1,200 people) survived
the decision of the Council in 1937 and escaped the blitz of
1941 into the days of the Arts Council, it would have been
preserved, and perhaps done for Plymouth what the Bristol
Old Vic has done for Bristol and the Theatre Royal for Bath.
But a theatre building is but nothing if it lacks an audience.

The Grand Theatre, too, was on its last legs. It had lingered
on to the late 1930s with films and cups of afternoon tea for
the patrons, all of which, together with a packet of cigarettes,
could be had for a shilling. Its faded frescoes now had to
compete with such glittering rivals as the Odeon and the
Gaumont as well as many lesser establishments of a similar
kind.

During the Plymouth air raids, fire bombs destroyed part
of the backstage dressing-room accommodation. The stage
trod by Irving, which had seen such diverse characters as Frank
Benson and George Robey, was doomed to lose its last shabby
shreds of theatrical dignity and to become a place where even
the ghosts of those who had once appeared on its great stage
would disdain to walk.

After the 1939–45 war, its grey, dilapidated façade in
Union Street shamefacedly hid its interior for eighteen years.
During this time it was used as a warehouse, a workshop for
making furniture and as a boatyard, until in the bitterly cold
March of 1963 the breakers stepped in and reduced the Grand
Theatre, Plymouth, to a heap of rubble, leaving "not a rack
behind".

Looking back now at those fateful years of 1920 to 1939
through the flamboyant wordy flow of the old playbills still
preserved, one is apt to gain the impression that Plymouth

[181]

FIG. 31.—The sad façade of the derelict Grand Theatre, which stood nearly opposite the Palace Theatre in Union Street, Plymouth, just before it demolition in 1963. (Photograph by courtesy of The Western Morning News Co. Ltd.)

theatre was always thriving and that cultured entertainment of a consistently high standard could be had for the asking.

But this was not always so, for the majority of productions in the commercial theatre of those times were part of a nationwide trend by theatrical managers and impresarios to combat the advance of the "talkies" by delivering a constant stream of London successes. The latter were performed by touring companies of limited ability on a profit-sharing basis, the management of the theatre covering their expense first.

Although it may appear otherwise, the number of "stars" to visit the provinces—when spread over a decade—did not amount to many. Audiences were thin, artists poorly paid (there was no Equity minimum then) and the discerning playgoer would often be offended by "corpsing" among the principals. Matinées were skipped through, and it was an accepted fact that the ladies of the chorus in musical shows had other things on their minds and one would often see them whispering among themselves and giggling while tastefully arranged about the stage awaiting their cue to sing and dance.

But standards remained high in some of the smaller places in the West as we shall see.

# CHAPTER XII

# The Fringe, from Morley to Minack

The past fifty years have seen the rise of "The Commercial Theatre", a name used by some to differentiate between the companies that performed popular plays, musicals and the like with the freely-admitted aim of making money, as opposed to those whose primary ambition is non-profit-making and to provide what is often erroneously called "good theatre". The latter includes productions that are commercially un-economical to stage because of large casts, scenery etc., the classic, experimental plays and those that have a limited appeal.

Like most theatrical innovations this laudable ideal has swung to the other extreme and today we see mini-minority groups producing all sorts of rubbish under the banner of "experimental non-profit-making" productions subsidised with public funds, which might equally be described as "bad theatre".

Mercifully, a number of the more extreme types are becoming extinct in the provinces due to the tightening of national funds, but between these two groups there still exists that large slice of theatrical activity called the Repertory Movement—now, alas, but a shadow of what it used to be in the early part of the century.

Although there were a few odd professional play-producing groups existing in some towns in the late Victorian period, it was left to a Londoner, Miss Annie Horniman, in 1907 to establish the Repertory Movement in Manchester. More than any other person of her time she was responsible for the improvement of English provincial theatre.

Miss Horniman, born in Forest Hill, London, together with B. Iden Payne as her general manager, made the Gaiety Theatre, Manchester, world famous. She financed it privately with the intention of "producing new, good plays, reviving old masterpieces and presenting translations of the best work of foreign authors".

Succeeding beyond all expectations it gave its patrons good drama without the halo of an "Arts Theatre" and in doing so provided the first rungs of the theatrical ladder to such players as Lewis Casson, Basil Dean, Milton Rosmer, Esme Percy and Sybil Thorndike. It also brought Shaw and Galsworthy to the public and was the theatre from which *Hindle Wakes*, Stanley Houghton's play of the Lancashire mill girl, was transferred to London and posterity.

Miss Horniman's example was followed by similar companies all over the country and in the middle of the First World War there was a gallant attempt to install such "good theatre" in Plymouth, when, in 1915, "The Rep" was born.

George King, an exceptional man of the theatre world, held the firm conviction that a public really existed in Plymouth for good well-done plays which did not need the pomp, panoply and expense of circuit theatres. Being an actor with a thorough knowledge of theatrical business he turned his thoughts to establishing a regular play-producing company of his own.

The old Mechanics Institute, in Princess Square at the corner of Westwell Street, had been empty for some time and in 1915 King took it over and turned it into one of the first repertory theatres in the country. It opened on 24th December 1915, with *A Bunch of Violets*, followed by *The Second Mrs Tanqueray* with Marie Robson and Frederick Victor in the leading roles.

A curious building, more suited to offices than a theatre, it had a smallish stage, and even smaller dressing-room accommodation, yet it managed to seat around 400 people. Despite many setbacks and closures King kept it going for twelve years without any official help by letting it to travelling companies for periods at a time. Financial assistance there was none, for there was no Arts Council in those days.

It was in 1921 after "The Rep", as it came to be affectionately called, had one of its worst slumps that George King engaged Bernard Copping, an experienced actor from Miss Horniman's Gaiety Theatre where he had played many parts under the direction of Lewis Casson.

FIG. 32.—Bernard Copping, actor, director and the inspiration of the Plymouth Repertory Theatre in the 1930s.

The opening play of the new season was that torrid drama *Bella-donna* with Bernard Copping, Eric Morden, Noel Morris, Mabel Edwardes, Frances Waring and Peter Godfrey in the cast—the same Peter Godfrey who was later to establish that famous Gate Theatre (first in Floral Street and later transfered to Charing Cross in 1927).

Peter Godfrey brought the Gate Theatre Company to Plymouth in 1926 with *The Race with the Shadow*, acted by

Wilfred Walter, Molly Veness, Ronald Simpson and Godfrey Baxter. A truly exciting event. But Plymothians did not want to know and the theatre was nearly empty.

When King died in 1927, Copping devoted all his energies, time and money to keep the Rep going. He played many roles himself, engaged good and experienced players and put in an astonishing amount of effort into building up the Rep.

From the 1929 season (which opened with Noël Coward's *The Queen was in the Parlour*) he continued to give weekly change of programme with an almost resident company whose names were to become legendary among Plymouth playgoers.

There was Sadie Speight, later to play many roles, to become a playwright and British Drama League adjudicator who was much in demand. One of her great performances was as the pathetic Irish mother in Percy Robinson's attack on capital punishment, *To What Red Hell*.

Then there were the veteran actor W. Davenport Adams, E. Vernon Harris (who left Plymouth to join the Birmingham Repertory Theatre and later still the BBC), Noel Morris, Mabel Edwardes, Margaret McDougall, Leslie Sanders and the young Elspeth Duxbury. Not to be forgotten is Dempster Paul, who in those times did a four-year stint acting juvenile roles and working as stage manager, and was still in the business recently as house manager for the ABC Theatre in Plymouth.

One of the old-stagers was Clifton Earle, who died in 1970. Southcombe Parker (who now lives in Guernsey) remembers him as a typical "Laddie, me Bhoy" old time actor who "thoroughly enjoyed poor health". "On meeting him in the street he would tell of all his aches and pains, indicating the various states of the current troubles and he seldom forgot to mention that his wife had only one kidney!"

Bernard Copping, himself an extremely versatile actor, played Toby Belch in *Twelfth Night*, Shylock, Mr Wu and dozens of other major roles, among a list of plays that over the years proved that if the Rep did nothing else it certainly provided a constant stream of popular and rewarding productions. Even the most plebeian natives of the city could hardly criticise the Rep on the grounds that it was "too highbrow".

Perverse Plymothians did not recognise the merit of the

[187]

# Repertory Theatre.

PRINCESS
SQUARE
PLYMOUTH

(Lessees: Plymouth Repertory Players, Ltd.)

## FOR SIX NIGHTS

Commencing

## MONDAY, SEPT. 3rd.

at 7-45.

FRIDAY AT 8-15.
MATINEE SATURDAY at 2-45.

# THE PLYMOUTH REPERTORY PLAYERS

IN

An Extremely Well Written Comedy,

# 'THE DEVIL A SAINT'

By JAMES R. GREGSON.

with

A. DAVENPORT ADAMS.

| | |
|---|---|
| SADIE SPEIGHT. | MARGARET GIBSON. |
| R. MEADOWS WHITE. | ROY REYNOR. |
| LESLIE SANDERS. | LOUISE LESTER. |

PRODUCER - A. DAVENPORT ADAMS.

## NEXT WEEK

grossly undervalued Copping or the highly talented company of actors, who, had they been situated nearer London, would have earned both praise and support for their great work performed on a shoestring.

The company's energy and devotion in giving the city a wealth of entertainment was enormous, especially when it is considered that they staged real "Weekly Rep".

This meant preparing and rehearsing for the following week and the week after that, while playing at the same time to the public at night.

How much more demanding was this when compared to the modern method of so called "repertoire" which entails rehearsing one play at a time and then performing it for some weeks before tackling the next!

But in spite of all this activity and endeavour, business gradually declined, until the company, its resources exhausted, wound itself up in 1934.

It closed because the Plymothians of that time, in spite of the city's large population, could spare neither time nor effort to sustain even this small theatre, which was one of their greatest theatrical assets.

Whereas the 1930s were bad years for theatre business all over the country, a look at the Exeter scene shows a slightly brighter picture, for its Theatre Royal was to continue uninterrupted. This came about because while it felt keenly the effects of the slump in business, the manager Percy Dunsford had the foresight to use every opportunity and device to make it pay its way.

Percy Dunsford, one of that rare breed of theatre managers who not only knew his job but also where he was heading, carved for himself a name that was to become part and parcel of Exeter's theatrical life. He began as assistant manager to Mr Gault and was appointed manager in 1925, a position

FIG. 33 *(facing page)*.—The Plymouth Rep, one of the earliest repertory theatres in the country, was founded in 1915 in Princess Square, Plymouth. On its "tea-tray stage" were performed a wide variety of shows ranging from historical dramas and tragedies to drawing room plays and comedies, as in this early 1930s production then considered to be highly sophisticated.

[189]

he held until his death in 1940. One of his achievements was to maintain the run of the traditional Exeter pantomime which reached a total of sixty-one consecutive shows in as many years—a world record.

Dunsford realised at an early date that West Country audiences had a penchant for musical comedy and that a tie-up with Plymouth on the South West circuit would be of benefit to both. He booked an almost endless stream of Macdonald and Young's touring shows which brought not only the Edwardian romantic revivals, but also those from the Jazz age—*Lady Luck, Love Lies, Hit the Deck* and many others. His largest operation was the touring version of the then "mammoth show" *The White Horse Inn*, which ran for two weeks at increased prices—6s., 5s., 4s. and 2s.—which did not please the patrons at all.

They stayed away for the first two performances in protest, but filled the theatre to capacity later on in the run as the show became talked about.

When business waned, Dunsford joined the film-show bandwagon and followed the fashion of the London theatres, who were in the same dilemma, by presenting variety acts and Music Hall programmes. So Exonians experienced the delights of Billy Bennett, Nellie Wallace and her feather boa, Ella Shields (who was still going strong as Burlington Bertie), Wee Georgie Wood and his "Ma" Dolly Harmer and other world-famous names.

Variety shows could also be seen at the Exeter Hippodrome which had taken the place of the old Royal Public Rooms in London Inn Square, and which, in its turn, was eventually replaced by the Plaza Cinema, later obliterated by a bomb.

While parts of Exeter were severely damaged during the Blitz of 1941–2, its theatre was luckily spared, and the management were able to book superstars available to the provinces for the first time in years.

Owen Nares came west to appear in Daphne Du Maurier's *Rebecca*; Emlyn Williams and Angela Baddeley appeared in *The Light of Heart*; Robertson Hare and Alfred Drayton starred in *Women Aren't Angels*; Alastair Sim was in *Cottage to Let*, while Jack Buchanan, Elsie Randolph and the exclusive Dame Marie Tempest (too refined to give autographs) all came to the Theatre Royal, Exeter, in those war years, and for a brief period the West Country enjoyed a taste of London's theatrical glory.

The 1930s had their hilarious moments. It is hard to visualise the vast and loquacious Robert Morley saying the line "Pull pudden" in the character of Tim Bobbin in the old melodrama *Maria Marten or the Murder in the Red Barn*, or to imagine a top-flight company of West End superstars playing regularly in a W.I. hut in a remote Cornish village. Yet such was the case in 1935 when the then unknown Robert Morley, Peter Bull, Frith Banbury, Roger and Judith Furse and later Pamela Brown took over the Women's Institute hut at Perranporth for the summer season.

On a stage measuring at the beginning just 6ft. by 12ft. they presented four plays a week for the holidaymakers when the total capacity of the "theatre" was only 200.

After the first season, this cheerful band of players returned every year until 1939, presenting during that time three brand new plays: *Goodness How Sad*, written by Robert Morley, which went on afterwards for a London run for eight months; Noel Langley's *The Walrus and the Carpenter*, with Pamela Brown and Robert Morley in the cast; and Peter Bull's play *To Sea in a Sieve*. Alas September 1939 put an end to this Cornish idyll and they all went back to civilisation to become the stars they are today.

But if Cornwall cannot boast, like its Devon neighbour, of having a number of well-established theatre buildings, it certainly is the proud possessor of the most beautiful open-air theatre in the whole of the British Isles. Thousands of people flock each year to the Minack Theatre at Porthcurno, "nine miles from anywhere", to see the world's classic plays as well as musicals enacted on a stage hewn out of solid Cornish rock and set against the backcloth of the Atlantic Ocean.

Minack has not "been there since the Romans", as one girl from a visiting party told her friends, but is the miraculous result of forty years of hard-slogging, back-breaking manual effort by one indomitable woman, Rowena Cade, assisted by Charles Angove and the rough, faithful Bill Rawlings.

In 1929 Rowena Cade, who lived in Minack House at the

Fig. 34.—The Minack Theatre, Porthcurno. The stone seating, not shown in this picture, is cut into the cliff face and looks out on to the stage with the Atlantic Ocean as a backcloth. (Photograph by Robert Roskrow, Truro.)

top of a steep cliff sweeping down to a tiny beach and the wide ocean, saw an open-air presentation by local amateurs of *A Midsummer Night's Dream* and, inspired by the play itself with its fairy qualities and the magic Cornish landscape, she determined to turn that cliff into an acting arena.

They first began to level the terrace by placing concrete slabs on the rugged rocky Cornish seacoast in 1931, their puny efforts seeming futile. But ceaselessly they laboured at the staggering task of cutting huge granite boulders, of dragging tons of sand up the cliff from the beach below, of digging, moving and building.

A hundred times Miss Cade herself literally hauled a hundredweight bag of sand up that great slope, and her fee for any angler who might ask her permission to fish from the beach below was always the same—that he should bring up a bag or so of sand with him when he had finished.

This was used to mix the concrete and fashion the stone stage, the seating and the columns that have transformed what was an almost inaccessible piece of coastline into an open-air theatre unsurpassed in its beauty and wild, dramatic atmosphere.

The joys, the hazards, and the great attractions of playing at Minack are far greater than those to be experienced at any traditional theatre. They are well cited in Averil Demuth's book on Minack which is a symposium of all who have worked there over the years and enjoyed the countless productions which the summer months bring to Porthcurno.

There is the director who finds his puny play overwhelmed by the vast expanse of "scenery" and has to revise all his preconceived views of the production; and the actor who soon learns that he is always compelled to look up at his audience seated in serried ranks right up above him, and who has to be watchful on making an exit too hurriedly or he may land on the rocks below.

Then there is the electrician who finds the full moon and the sea a combination that makes his manpowered lights look like glow-worm fire and the effects-man who has to combat the roar of the ocean, gales, wind, rain and thunderstorm—for, once started, plays are seldom abandoned at Minack, while an audience still sits there.

[193]

A member of the audience remembers a performance one summer night when a great ocean liner came in close to the shore compelling even the actors to stop and look.

The first performance at Minack was given in 1932 with an amateur production of *The Tempest*—surely the most apposite and natural setting available for this great play. This was followed by more or less annual presentations until 1939 when Violet Vanbrugh (who had celebrated her golden jubilee the year before) brought *Tristan and Isolt* together with *The Count of Monte Cristo*, thus giving the theatre it first professional production.

Minack was taken over by the military during the Second World War and turned into an anti-aircraft post; and its pill-box gun site, which was left after the war, now serves as the box-office at the entrance.

In 1949, Minack opened again with *The Trojan Horse*, this time with many additions to the stage and seating, including some ninety steps up the cliff, for Miss Cade had not been idle.

It was after the Festival of Britain Year (1951) when the Cornwall County Drama Adviser, Frances Collingwood Selby, had arranged a festival of amateur drama that it suddenly became immensely popular. What had been just annual events of a play for one week in the summer, now became weekly from June to September.

Still thriving, it has become known throughout the kingdom, and dates for playing at Minack are eagerly sought each year by universities, local groups and companies of actors from almost every county in Britain. One can now visit it during the summer and see the most incongruous selection of productions ranging from Gilbert and Sullivan, *Othello* and the *Legends of King Arthur* to *War and Peace* and Victorian melodrama.

In one year alone Minack attracted over 25,000 visitors. It stands not only as a monument to Cornish drama, but also to the devotion and imagination of its 80-year-old founder, Rowena Cade.

CHAPTER XIII

# Enter Variety

Contrary to what some people and the Arts Council may think, the variety stage has sometimes more to offer in the way of talent, artistic approach, imagination, personality and a boost for morale than whole heaps of representative classical plays. It sometimes happens that the successful stand-up comedian who relies on his own material, powers, and judgment of an audience may well possess far more artistry than the legitimate actor speaking from a script under the direction of a producer.

It is a strange trait in the British character that because a performer deals with the seamier side of life, creates laughter and sentiment and uses colloquial language rather than lines from Shaw or Shakespeare, his work is somehow considered inferior to the more seriously-minded performances of a play. Even though those characters in the play may be comical, the actor who plays them is always looked upon as having a sense of one-upmanship.

As has been shown, the gulf between the legitimate player from the Patent Houses of the eighteenth century and those common players in the provinces outside the Patent purlieus of London was the main cause of this snobbish outlook, which to a certain extent has been absurdly fostered ever since among the profession. But when one considers that even today, 200 years afterwards, officialdom in the shape of the Arts Council has only very recently recognised the existence of the variety theatre as worthy of very limited support, one is also apt to wonder just how far prejudice must go.

It was a major tragedy that the Music Hall, the one artistic institution born of British people alone, which contained sentiment, song, satire, laughter and a refusal to take politicians and snobs seriously, should have been allowed to die the death it did in the 1930s. While frantic efforts have been made over the past decades to "save" theatres, grant subsidies to dramatic companies and to spend millions on the National Theatre, Ballet and Opera, governments and their advisers have not lifted one finger to save the Music Hall from extinction, preferring to leave it as a museum piece to be exposed every once in a while by the BBC as an example of *The Good Old Days*. In reality the latter is as much akin to traditional Music Hall— which was beery, and had a long programme content comprising 90 per cent comic turns—as it is to the vicar's tea party.

Nowhere has the Music Hall been more appreciated than in the heavily-populated industrial towns where the citizens can suspend their disbelief for a few short hours in their illusion that life is ruled by laughter and song. Nowhere in the West Country has this been catered for more than in the variety theatres.

The British Music Hall originally came from London, swiftly followed by the "Singing Rooms" in the North, and was born out of social history when millions of workers from the Victorian industrial revolution sought more than just beer in the pubs.

It was in the Music Hall that the working man could identify with high life, with "Champagne Charlie" and the Lion Comique, personified by George Leybourne with his puce-coloured jacket, check trousers and gaudy waistcoat.

It provided carefree and raffish entertainment beloved by the masses, for it dealt with understandable everyday themes and humour, ranging from mothers-in-law, the lodger and overdue rent to kippers, beer and the state of being "stony broke".

Patriotism was always present and bathos proliferated, embracing the poor, the errant husband and the innocent lass.

Despite its early rough-house atmosphere it became the place for inverted daydreams, gentle satire, and above all a place where convention could be defied, and a close acquaintance could be publicly claimed with the great in such lines as:

> The Prince of Wales' brother, along with some other,
> Slaps me on the back and says "Come and see Mother".

They could demand equality with the famous in:

I live in Trafalgar Square with four lions to guard me . . .
If it's good enough for Nelson, it's quite good enough for me.

For, as that eminent dramatist T. S. Eliot was to write
prophetically in 1922 after Marie Lloyd's death:

> The lower class still exists; but perhaps it will not exist for long.
> In the Music Hall comedians they find the expression and
> dignity of their own lives; and this is not found in the most
> elaborate and expensive revues. In England at any rate, the revue
> expresses almost nothing. . . . The working man who went to
> the Music Hall and saw Marie Lloyd and joined in the chorus
> was himself performing part of the act; he was engaged in that
> collaboration of the audience with the artist which is necessary
> in all art and most obviously in dramatic art.

From the middle of the nineteenth century pubs and taverns were providing space for comic singers, dancers and
turns of all kinds, and London, with its Gatti's, Collins, Canterbury and the Middlesex (known as the Old Mo after the
Mogul Tavern which once stood on its site), has always been
the foundation and centre of the British Music Hall tradition.
While there were many other houses in the provinces following
this example of presenting single turns to a drinking audience,
it was not until the advent of the Empires and the Hippo-
dromes that variety became acceptable all over the country,
and free to be witnessed by respectable Victorian families.

Exeter, Plymouth and other West Country towns had their
variety theatres in the 1870s and 1880s which they combined
with occasional dramatic presentations, but it was not until
1898 that the first purpose-built theatre was erected in Plymouth for Music Hall acts alone.

The Palace Theatre still stands in Union Street and its
eighty-one years can serve as a classic example of similar
places in the West, for many of the artists appearing on its
boards toured the circuit regularly and became household
words from Torquay and Exeter to Penzance.

It was built at a time when the Victorian expansion was
bursting into the twentieth century and when Plymouth had
become an industrial township, crowded with merchants,
shopkeepers, artisans and service people. Union Street, con-
necting the three towns, was its main artery.

[197]

Designed by William Arber from the London firm of architects, J. T. Wimperis and Arber, of 25, Sackville St., the Palace was indeed "The Talk of the West" with its commanding façade lined with Royal Doulton-tiled panels depicting the sailing and the defeat of the Armada, and with its wrought-iron canopy covering the entrance to the foyer and elegant lounge via a noble marble staircase to the mezzanine floor. If one could see the Palace as it was then, new, and from a vantage point more distant than the present-day width of Union Street, it would have certainly seemed an imposing edifice.

With seating for over 1,900, the interior (which included luxurious stalls and a large grand circle as well as side boxes and gallery) was elaborately carved and gilded. Painted panels around the dome and proscenium were filled with frescoes of naval and military triumphs, unfortunately soon to be destroyed by fire and never replaced.

The scheme to build the Palace, which cost £98,000, was financed by a consortium headed by a London millionaire Henry Pocock together with the Livermore Brothers. The latter also provided the know-how for they themselves had worked in the Christy Minstrel style in the north of England as "the Court Minstrels", and they formed themselves into United Counties Theatres Ltd. Almost immediately Victorian business acumen came into action.

The St. James' Hall, the competitive house opposite, was bought out and a little later so was the Grand Theatre which from then to 1913 only opened fitfully.

The project also included the building of the adjacent hotel, and the total cost to the group was £185,000, the largest amount of money so far invested on any West Country building scheme.

"Three hours Entertainment at the Handsomest Theatre in the World" was the way it was described, when on 5th September 1898 the New Palace of Varieties opened its doors for the first time to the waiting crowds at prices ranging from 2s. 6d. Stalls, Grand Circle 1s. 6d. and Gallery 1s.

The "daybills" proclaimed that there would be no nonsense as that seen at other local theatres, with the following warning to patrons:

New Palace Theatre

Chris Robinson

FIG. 35.—The New Palace Theatre, Plymouth, after its restoration in 1978. (From the original drawing by Chris Robinson.)

Seats not guaranteed.
No Improper characters admitted.
Strict Order will be enforced.
No shouting or whistling allowed, offenders will be immediately expelled.
No Re-admission.
Children in arms 5/- each.

The first ever bill at the Palace on that opening week consisted of: The Marvellous Craggs, a well-known acrobatic act headed by the veteran J. W. Cragg; dancer Emmie Ames; Florador, an eccentric musical quartet that caused great hilarity in the audience; the Cassons and the Sisters Levy, Adele and May; trapeze artists Leopoldines; vocalist Walter Stockwell; Fred Darby a comedian who also did a skating act; Harry Comlin, comedian, and, of course, the band in front.

After a selection of patriotic airs, one of the directors, Horace Livermore, stepped on to the stage "illuminated with fairy electric lights and tastefully decorated with foliage plants", and told the crowded house: "What we have looked for has come at last", and promised them that far more was to come in the future.

The following week he kept his promise. Top of the bill was the most beloved comedian of them all, Dan Leno, supported by the Medoras Marionettes, Will Mitcham, instrumentalist and eccentric comedian, Maud Ross dancer and comedienne, Palles and Cusick—"Yankee Curiosities", and Lalla Yamina, the wirewalker. For such a bill there was a charge of "3d. extra for all parts". Poor little Dan Leno, who a few years later was to be taken to Peckham House asylum and certified insane through overwork, was the first of a long, long line of star names of the Music Hall that were to illumine the Palace bills for many a year, while Will Mitcham and Maud Ross, who appeared with Dan Leno, were destined to become the grandparents of the comedian Max Wall.

There soon followed the inimitable George Robey, who was later to take for himself Dan Leno's eyebrows as a trademark, bringing with him those rich and fruity comments of "honest vulgarity" which in after years brought him the title of the Prime Minister of Mirth.

Billed as "The Pawky Scottish Comedian", Harry Lauder appeared low down on the bill singing, of all things, Irish songs, but he was to return again many times as the star turn. He was followed by "I do like to be beside the Seaside" Mark Sheridan and T. E. Dunville of "I'm Twenty-one Today" fame.

The theatre had not been opened but six months when trouble hit the Palace. A patriotic scene was being presented which included a mimic battle scene where squibs were let off to represent guns firing as part of the finale to the show. The audience had left the theatre, but apparently a spark had lodged in the scenery; because the much-talked-of safety curtain had been left suspended in the flies, fire broke out and destroyed most of the stage and the front of the auditorium. The seating was completely destroyed as were the original murals by H. B. Brewer, and only the main building was left.

The theatre was closed for several months for repairs and redecoration, but it was found too costly to replace the paintings and the empty panels stand there to this day.

Through the courtesy of George Roseman, the last managing director of the Palace before it went over to bingo in the 1960s, the original account books for some of those early years have been made available.

They show in detail the artists engaged from 1907 up to the 1930s, their fees, the state of the house and the manager's comments on the success (or otherwise) of each performance.

It would appear that during the first ten years of its existence the total "take" for the theatre amounted to not much more than £600 per week, out of which artists, band and staff were paid. However, considering the lower standard of living in those days, a profit was generally guaranteed, especially when it is noted that the weekly band bill was never more than £19, the whole staff wages amounted to £40 and the average cost of the bill (which included at least eight artists) seldom exceeded £250 and quite often was less than £200.

Some idea of the great difference in the amounts now paid today to "stars" can be seen in the sums paid to the great names of 1907–8 when the whole of the Casey's Court Company received £50; Harry Clifton £14; Archie Pitt (who found Gracie Fields and Tommy Trinder) £5; Harry Taft £14; Adah Payne, the singer, £6; the great Florrie Forde, the original singer of "Tipperary" and "Hold your hand out you naughty boy", £40; the 18-year-old Gertie Gitana £15; and the favourite comedian of Plymouth citizens, Dusty Rhodes, £25 a week.

That extremely funny comedian Harry Weldon, with his catch phrase "Sno use" and his whistling speech, was paid a bare £15; the star of them all, Marie Lloyd, came in July 1907, while the week's weather was "very hot" and received the top salary of £130. Three extra men had had to be engaged for the early doors at a cost of 30s. to keep the waiting crowds in order.

Many a sober Devonian has happy memories of Marie Lloyd, the superstar—perhaps unjustly renowned for singing *risqué* songs. Even today she is still considered by some to have been far more "blue" than most music hall artists of the times, yet when the printed words of "The Old Cock Linnet", "When You Wink the Other Eye" or "One of the Ruins that Cromwell Knocked About a Bit" and the rest, are considered, they are as inoffensive as a nursery rhyme.

Ernest Short, in his *Fifty Years of Vaudeville*, relates the delightful story of how Marie Lloyd once came up against the licensing authorities over her performance in public of a certain song (that is still quoted today as being typical) of a lady in her vegetable garden. "She Sits Among the Cabbages and Peas".

After their formal objection, Marie altered it, but still they were not satisfied, and in the end she was asked to present herself at a council meeting and run through her repertoire so that they could hear for themselves any objectionable matter.

Their misgivings were overcome and their honour satisfied, for Marie cut out all the nods, winks, looks and leers which she normally interjected to give the songs a dubious significance.

"Thank you," said Marie, when the verdict was announced. "Now you've wasted my morning, I'll sing you a song such as your wives and daughters sing at home."

The councillors very foolishly allowed her request. The pianist began to play "Come into the Garden Maud". Marie sang the words, but this time included the actions. The elderly councillors were stunned, not realising in their innocence of

Music Hall matters that such depravity existed in so innocuous a song.

It is by such ignorance of the ways of the theatre and of audiences that local Watch Committees and, indeed, the Lord Chamberlain when he was the public censor, have many times made fools of themselves in the light of history.

The year 1908 saw Tom Costello at the Palace, the entertainer whose name is now sadly forgotten by all but a few people, but whose songs "At Trinity Church I met my Doom" and "Comrades, every since we were boys" sung while dressed in a soldier's Boer War uniform and leaning on the back of a chair (he had a "gammy" leg), are still hummed and sung by millions who watch *The Good Old Days* on television. It was Tom who was tragically found dead in a Brixton street one night during the London Blitz of 1940.

The Palace, as it became known to its many regulars, with its red plush seats and gilded cupids stood on an equal footing with the Theatre Royal in those days and in terms of nostalgia it has become representative of the heyday of variety.

Many a citizen still remembers those "Palace nights" when he would arrive at the ornate doors, to be welcomed by the resident manager with a smile and greeting, to walk through that cosy, mysterious, delicately-illumined corridor to the stalls, to hear the band in the pit and to receive a nod from the conductor—until that magic moment when the "No. 1" lit up on the sign at the stage side, and the heavy plum-coloured curtain silently swept upwards to reveal the opening act, generally a juggler or acrobat.

Once can still hear the laughter for the ridiculous antics of that flamboyant roisterous character Harry Tate who appeared in 1909 with his "Motoring Sketch", or on the same bill that droll comedian Sam Mayo who would dolefully sing a song to a bottle of whisky delicately poised upon the piano.

For quick-fire humour there came Harry Champion in March 1910 to sing "Any Old Iron" and "Henry VIII", of course, and there was the side-splitting crazy act of The Ten Loonies, and Florrie Forde was to come again just before the First World War with a voice that could be heard in the gods without any assistance from a microphone yet to be invented. She brought with her this time "Down at the Old

Bull and Bush" and "Anybody Here Seen Kelly", songs that have kept their world-wide popularity ever since and for which she was never paid more than £25 for the singing rights.

The 1914 war years came when Plymouth was once again packed with soldiers and sailors, when Union Street pubs were nightly filled and rough-houses commonplace and when the Palace weekly programmes saw a gradually diminishing number of acts by male performers who were soon to join the services. In these years there came the early versions of "The Revue", a new type of entertainment that was to become in the 1920s the sophisticated style of the day.

In 1915 there was Hetty King, a name that conjures up a performer of perfection. There was also Ella Shields, whose husband William Hargreaves wrote a song for her called "Burlington Bertie", which almost alone among Music Hall songs, has her name and personality indelibly stamped upon it years after it had become a classic in itself.

Then there was Little Tich with his great elongated boots; the "not a pretty sight" of that very funny eccentric comedienne Nellie Wallace, to be followed in 1916 by the fading Lillie Langtry in a "speciality act". On the same bill was R. A. Roberts, the protean actor, in *Dick Turpin* in which he took a dozen parts, changing dresses and costumes with miraculous rapidity so that the stage seemed always occupied.

That world-famous master of the concertina, Percy Honri, made a number of appearances in the West and nowhere was he more welcome than at the Palace; for it was in Plymouth that he met the renowned Professor McCann who lived in Union Street.

J. H. McCann had appeared in Music Hall since 1865, billed as "Professor", and was then acknowledged as the "King of the Concertina". But apart from his public appearances he was also a craftsman and inventor, and it was the McCann duet system which he invented and built into the English concertina that captured Percy Honri's notice.

So proficient did Honri become at the instrument that in 1891 McCann presented him with an engraved medal acknowledging him as the master for "his marvellous playing of the duet concertina".

It was Percy Honri's grandson Peter Honri who was to

renew the family's connection with the West when in 1970 he came to Newquay Theatre to appear for a season in the Ronnie Brandon and Dickie Pounds Old Time Music Hall Show.

Another regular visitor to the Palace was that well-known performer Bransby Williams, who would always please with his famous "Characters from Dickens" act, playing Uriah Heep, Peggotty, the dramatic death-cell scene with Fagin, and always remembering to remove his false teeth surreptitiously before tackling the Grandfather in *The Old Curiosity Shop*. Then there was that urbane character, Vivian Foster, billed as "The Vicar of Mirth", caricaturing the clergy with his parish notices and "Yes, I think so" catch phrase; the antics of Old Mother Riley with daughter Kitty, and Charles Austin, with his own comic figure as Parker P.C.

It was early in 1915 that the first revue came to the Palace, called *Sign Please*, a title which reflected the mobilisation fever of the times. It was shortly followed by *Fall In* with Ernie Lotinga, and when victory was in sight a few months before the Armistice of 11th November 1918, the Palace came up with a revue aptly called *All Clear*, the legend then used by the police on placards to tell public that air-raids were over.

Thomas Hoyle, whose proud initials still stand emblazoned over the proscenium arch, first purchased the Palace Theatre in 1912, sold it a few years later, and rebought it in 1922. The Hoyle name was to continue to be associated with "respectable and good entertainment" for the next quarter of a century.

Also landlord of the Golden Lion public house in Old Town Street, Hoyle made such a success of the Palace that he had to increase the seating capacity by doing away with the ground-level boxes, taking away the staircase leading from the stalls to the grand circle and bringing the front of the grand circle forward.

Thomas Hoyle, much respected in the city, was a business-man as well as a man of the theatre, and was very particular about what, who and how things appeared upon the Palace stage. A martinet both in front and backstage, he demanded perfection from his artists and employees alike.

With the advent of the 1920s Hoyle joined the fashion and began to book the "big shows", which included a week of

[205]

ballet with the great Pavlova dancing to full houses every night. This was followed by that most renowned of concert parties, *The Co-Optimists*, those gentle satirists who with song, humour and personality guyed and poked fun at the people of the times.

These were the days when "wireless" was the "in" thing, bringing in its wake the first trickle of radio stars to the West Country, where the people were avid to see in the flesh such stars as Elsie Carlisle, Stanelli with his orchestra of motor horns and those two humorous performers at the piano, Flotsam and Jetsam. Quickly on their heels came topical revues with titles like *Listening In* and *Radio Days* and, mirroring the depressed times, shows called *On the Dole*, *Rations* and *Out of Work*.

That great old comic Dick Henderson (father of the present star Dickie Henderson) was there too, as were Dorothy Ward and Shaun Glenville, with Dorothy, the most glamorous of Principal Boys, being one of the first to sing a love song to a member of the audience coaxed up on to the stage.

"Almost a gentleman" Billy Bennett came in 1925 with his raucous "rec'tootians" which always included "There's a Cock-eyed Yellow Poodle to the North of Waterloo, There's a Little Hot-cross Bun that's Turning Green", thus totally demoralising the fashionable elocutionists of the day.

The same year saw the dapper little dude comedian George Clarke with his very up-to-date sketch which had a brand new yellow Austin Seven car on the stage, in which he would dare his infant daughter to bounce—lest she broke the springs.

The one and only Max Miller captivated the cautious West-countryfolk with his cheeky Cockney chat across the footlights in 1926, appearing then for a fee of only £12. The same year saw Seymour Hicks and Ellaline Terriss, Billy Mayerl and Gwen Farrar (with songs and a piano plus a 1920s Eton crop sophistication), the dithering Robb Wilton, Herschel Henlere (the gaily eccentric pianist who never knew when to close his act and on whom the curtain was invariably lowered on the protesting artist) and the "chocolate-coloured coon" G. H. Elliott singing and soft-shoe shuffling after the pattern of the famous Eugene Stratton from whom he inherited "Lily of Laguna".

While radio became big business in the late 1920s, it was also the time of the Big Bands. Plymouth and Exeter shared in the national thrill of seeing in person the Debroy Somers Band, the Savoy Orpheans and the big spread of musicians in Jack Hylton's Band with the curly-headed figure of "Jack's back" conducting.

The variety theatres of those days saw a different kind of comedian from the old rip-roarers of previous times, for radio brought to the live stage such performers as Gillie Potter, Claude Dampier and John Henry, as well as musicians Albert Sandler with his Palm Court orchestra, and those well-loved coloured duetists Layton and Johnstone.

Each act played for a week in a decade that was to hasten the decline in live entertainment caused by Marconi's invention.

The depression which began in the 1930s had its effect on the Palace Theatre as it did on every other theatre in the land who were all experiencing box-office hardship as mass unemployment spread through the country. Money, besides jobs, was hard to come by even at a time when ordinary things (by today's standards) were cheap. Palace theatre programmes of the day advert:sed Coates Plymouth gin at 11s. 3d. a bottle; ladies' shoes from 10s. 11d. to 21s. a pair, gents' shoes at 12s. 11d. to 25s. and, at Mumford's, a Wolseley Hornet car could be purchased, brand new, for £175.

Not the least of a theatre manager's worries was the imposition of the iniquitous Entertainments Tax which had been fixed by government on all forms of public entertainment from live theatre and films to boxing displays and amateur productions. This was in the form of a sum added to every ticket sold, which thus not only put up the prices of admission, but also gave extra work to the management who had to keep strict records of attendances for each performance. The Palace, like the other theatres, joined the "slump".

But Tommy Hoyle persevered with his policy of providing a mixture of wholesome family shows with all the best names he could muster—all too easily in those days when the acting and variety professions were also at a low financial ebb, with work harder to find every day as more and more theatres turned to the "talkies".

During the uneasy 1930s there came a profusion of bands bringing the radio sounds to the West Country, through such names as Jack Payne, Henry Hall, Billy Cotton, Nat Gonella and Louis Armstrong. Variety bills were topped by Gracie Fields, Naughton and Gold from the Crazy Gang at the Palladium, Stanley Holloway, tenor Richard Tauber and film star Anna May Wong who came for £200 on a bill which included Frederick Harvey. A local boy, Harvey received five guineas and was later to become one of the country's top baritones on the concert platform, radio and on gramophone records which sold by the thousand.

Another local boy was Jack Train from Torpoint who had risen to become Colonel Chinstrap in the radio show *It's That Man Again*. Together with Tommy Handley and Company he appeared for a week at the Palace in the late 1930s.

One of the greatest of variety acts that mystified Plymouth audiences on many occasions was that of Jasper Maskelyne, the illusionist, who was always a welcome visitor. He always cleared the stage staff from the wings, for he would allow no one to watch him perform from the side of the stage. His virtual "miracles" are still topics of speculation on "how was it done" by those who saw him and his immaculate style and presentation have never been equalled.

In the late 1930s the Palace presented an occasional play after the Theatre Royal was pulled down, and Plymothians were introduced to the new play *Love on the Dole*, Walter Greenwood's tragedy of unemployment in Lancashire. In contrast there was Jerry Verno in theatre critic W. A. Darlington's classic comedy of the First World War *Alf's Button*.

Thus the Palace carried on unfalteringly right up to that last uneasy period when the hot summer days of 1939 were overshadowed by the approaching outbreak of war—the third its tiled façade had seen.

Thomas Hoyle had died in 1933, leaving behind him a tradition of high-class management which was faithfully maintained by his wife. She, in turn, kept the theatre alive in the ensuing war years, adopting the same policy of providing all-round entertainment and maintaining the genteel atmosphere of the Palace Theatre.

CHAPTER XIV

# Picking Up the Bits

The declining theatres in Plymouth did not die in the decade commencing 1940. Like many others in the country, they were just killed off.

The air raids on Plymouth, which eventually blasted and burned the heart out of the city and many surrounding districts, began in earnest in 1940 when the population was swollen to three times its normal figure by the vast numbers of service people and civilians, not only from this country, but from the Dominions and the Continent after the French collapse in June of that year.

Performances at any place of amusement and relaxation left standing at that time were well attended by audiences who refused to be dictated to by the enemy raids. The only concession made was that all public performances should cease at 9 p.m., a "curfew" imposed to save petrol and tyres on public transport, so that patrons could catch the last bus home as the use of private cars etc. was prohibited (except for essential services).

Theatregoing in the blacked-out streets was no idle matter in those dreadful times, especially when the whole of the city centre lay in complete ruin. It was a case of picking one's way over rubble and craters along streets that no longer existed and with the prospect of an air raid warning on most evenings at around 6.30 p.m.

But with amazing spirit the population of both civilian and service people refused to be cowed and they were always ready to snatch a moment of relaxation in live entertainment whenever war work and raids allowed.

A few amateur societies bravely kept going, and even the

newly-formed Auxiliary Fire Brigade members got together and gave variety shows all over the district, while Plymouth Arts Centre in Looe Street attracted so many members that it was compelled to draw up a waiting list.

The Pilgrim Players from London stayed in the city for a number of weeks on several occasions presenting popular plays; the West of England Theatre Company from Bristol began their tours with a cast that included a young actress called Joan Greenwood, and, most amazing of all, the Ballet Rambert appeared at the Quaker's Meeting House in Swarthmore Hall in a full programme of ballet. Just how they managed on that tiny stage was nothing short of a miracle.

Apart from the Globe Theatre within the Royal Marine Barracks, the one and only professional theatre left standing in the battered city was the Palace—the home of variety. After a brief closure when things got "a bit too hot", it re-opened with an 8.30 p.m. curfew under Mrs Hoyle's ownership to bring a much-broadened programme to suit changing wartime tastes.

It drew from London companies and artists who were available and, more important, were willing to visit the city, for as Ronald Green, the theatre manager, said at the time of the air raids:

> Some vaudeville stars did not fancy playing in Plymouth. In some cases this may have been due to nervousness, not necessarily about personal safety, but the risk of losing valuable stage wardrobes, equipment or musical instruments, the loss of which might mean temporary "ruin".
>
> While other things that made Plymouth unpopular were the difficulty of finding digs in the bombed city, and such home comforts as plenty of hot water for removing greasepaint, and a well cooked meal to come home to.

In spite of the "lack of comforts" the Palace kept going with many professional stalwarts. These included Joe Loss and his band, who made their first visit to the city in May 1940, and matinée idol Carl Brisson, who appeared in a variety bill, was also the man who "discovered" film star Greta Garbo.

There were a number of revues. Bryan Michie came down with a youthful Tessie O'Shea and Dick Bentley (in small type on the daybills); Tommy Handley came again with ITMA and Jack Train (first discovered by M.P. Leslie Hore-Belisha in an amateur concert party); Tom Walls appeared in Benn Levy's *Springtime for Henry*; and Hugh Wakefield, with Olga Lindo, played in *Good Men Sleep at Home*.

Noël Coward made a personal appearance at the Palace, and at the final curtain recited Clemence Dane's tribute to Plymouth's wartime courage in her poem *Plymouth Hoe*.

Another personal appearance was that of Richard Tauber in *Old Chelsea*; a week of D'Oyly Carte Opera Company, which attracted packed houses all the week as usual, a week of Polish Ballet and a visit from the National Philharmonic Orchestra.

A tribute to Mrs Hoyle and the Palace in wartime was handsomely paid by H. P. Twyford in his book *It Came to our Door*. As an eye-witness he wrote:

> I know Mrs Hoyle went out of her way to secure these great performances, because she knew the tonic effect they would have on a people which had had such a raw deal in the war's holocaust.
>
> If ever there was a doubt as to whether Plymouth was sufficiently classically minded to appreciate such entertainment it was well and truly dispelled by the way in which audiences booked in advance and packed the theatre.
>
> Plymouth can look back with gratitude on what the Palace management did to bring pleasure to the battered life of the city.

Mrs Hoyle placed her theatre at the disposal of the authorities every Sunday night, with the staff giving their services free. Specially arranged "Free Concerts for the Forces" brought into the theatre hundreds of service personnel who were thronging the town after dark.

But even in wartime the voice of protest against the theatre was raised in Plymouth. The combined Free Churches passed a resolution protesting strongly at the opening of the Palace Theatre on a Sunday and added a rider that they were concerned at "the secular nature of the Youth Movement in the city".

Mention has been made of the Globe Theatre inside the

Royal Marines Barracks at Stonehouse, and this delightful little theatre is one of the finest examples of early Victorian theatrical architecture outside Bristol or Bath.

The part covered by the present stage was once used as a hayloft and the auditorium was a racquets court in 1788. Around 1820, after years of disuse, it was turned into a theatre "for the recreation and instruction of the men of the battalion".

In 1864 the Admiralty decided that it should be enlarged to seat 600 persons—a rather wild guess considering its limited space, but the conversion took place and today it seats 182 in the stalls and 70 in the circle. It has a fully-equipped stage containing a "thunder roll" (in which an old-time cannon-ball is rolled along an iron trough running the width of the proscenium arch) and the original timbered stage machinery set up in the flies.

It was at the Globe Theatre that Lt. Vivian Ellis, R.N.V.R. (one of the many thousands of service folk who passed through Plymouth during the war years) wrote his musical *Bless the Bride*, picking out the tunes on the theatre piano. Vivian Ellis also produced a revue called *It's All Yours*, which ran for some three months in that tiny Globe Theatre, with a cast that included local comedian Harry Grose, his niece Pauline East (later to become known as radio's Cherry Lind) and a chorus recruited from Polish midshipmen and cadets from the Royal Naval Engineering College.

It was in 1943, before the end of the war, that a bold effort was made to determine the future of the stricken city of Plymouth; and under the joint design of Sir Patrick Abercrombie, the town planner of the day, and J. Paton Watson, the City Surveyor and Engineer, "A Plan for Plymouth" was evolved.

Eventually accepted by the city council, it was the rehabilitation of Plymouth on new and imaginative lines, with a new layout for the city centre and visionary plans for "a beautiful town" allowing for shopping precincts, public buildings, residential and industrial areas, cultural and entertainment facilities. This last was to be incorporated in "a cultural precinct" and was to include a theatre, concert hall and an open-air theatre.

# REGAL THEATRE

Phone 278    **REDRUTH**    Phone 278

**6.20** | MONDAY, FEBRUARY 23rd.    **SIX DAYS**<br>TWICE NIGHTLY. MATINEE SATURDAY 2.30 | **8.30**

# VARIETY FANFARE

### A Cocktail of Mirth, Melody and Mystery

*Kitty McShane presents*

## OLD
## MOTHER RILEY
*and Company*

# BILLY
# RUSSELL
*On behalf of the*<br>*Working Man*

## DALE WILLIAMS
*with a Golden Voice*

## HARVEY SISTERS
*Dancing Delight*

# Humper
*and*
# Dink
*"The Unhappy Wanderers"*

# CARL AMES
*International Harp Star*

## SCOTT & RAY
*Whirlwind Roller Skaters*

# AL KORAN
### TELEVISION'S SENSATIONAL MIND READER

## At the Organ - JACK LAWTON

Prices: 2/-, 3/-, 4/-      SATURDAY NIGHT ONLY 3/-, 4/-, 5/-<br>All Seats Bookable    Box Office open 10 a.m. to 8 p.m.<br>Reduced prices for Children Monday night and Saturday afternoon<br>**NO MATINEE BOOKING**

FIG. 36.—A post-war variety bill of the 1950s—vastly different from the Sans Pareil, which Wilkie Collins saw at Redruth in Cornwall over 100 years before.

[213]

So much for the hopes and vision of the planners of 1943! They did not take into consideration the vagaries and apathy of succeeding councillors who regularly pushed aside any reference to culture and entertainment, so that nearly thirty years later Plymouth was to become a city with a quarter of a million inhabitants, but without a theatre let alone a concert hall.

The nearest commercial theatres were at Exeter (45 miles distant) and Torquay (30) and after the war it was to Torquay that theatregoers went for their entertainment.

Some went to Exeter, for their theatre had luckily been preserved all through the war. In 1948 they saw that great classic comedy *Worm's Eye View* which defied the London critics' prognostications by running for five years at the Whitehall theatre. Its author was Exmouth playwright R. F. Delderfield.

It was at Exeter that they saw Lupino Lane's highly popular musical *Me and My Girl* which sent the whole world doing the Lambeth Walk; they saw Arthur Askey, Wee Georgie Wood, Sonnie Hale and a fine production of *The Quaker Girl* by Emile Littler's No. 1 company, which drew appreciative audiences from the nostalgic music-loving people of the West Country.

The West of England Theatre Company returned in force after the war to travel all over the area in an endeavour to pick up the bits of the professional theatre, playing in Exeter, Plymouth, Taunton, Barnstaple, Dorchester and Seaton and all places west.

Under the direction of Joyce Worsley, who occasionally appeared on the stage herself, they worked under fit-up conditions in the lean 1950s staging everything from *Puss in Boots* and *Seagulls over Sorento* to Maugham's *The Noble Spaniard* and plays by Tennessee Williams—all on a very low budget against the odds of Entertainment Tax and the wintry weather when on tour.

The pre-war isolated respectability of Torquay was beginning to wear thin, and with the summer visitors arriving by their thousands the town was rapidly on its way to becoming the holiday centre of the West and a top theatre date into the bargain.

[214]

PICKING UP THE BITS

These were the halcyon days of the summer concert parties. Clarkson Rose reigned at the Pavilion with *Twinkle*—"The Best dressed show in the business" with such artists as Billy Burden, Olive Fox and Norman Vaughan.

Then there were "The Magpies" with the eloquent "odd-oder" Cyril Fletcher and Betty Astell, and the fabulously elegant "Fol-de-Rols" with the then lesser-known Leslie Crowther, Rex Newman, Cyril Wells and Kathy West.

An ex-miner from the North Country named Henry Illingsworth thought he would try his hand at something different after the war. He bought a ventriloquist's dummy, rehearsed and became a variety artist appearing as a relatively unknown act at the Pavilion, Torquay, and the Palace, Plymouth, during his round of the variety halls of Great Britain. But he appeared under his new stage name, Harry Worth, in a "vent" act which is still one of the funniest of its kind.

He was to perform part of that act again, when, in 1970, in the Bernard Delfont series of supershows he appeared at Torquay in his own *Harry Worth Show* which had a record-breaking season.

The Pavilion also had Norman Evans as that garrulous lady *Over the Garden Wall*, and in the spring and autumn seasons the Malvern Festival Theatre Company gave such plays as *The Deep Blue Sea*, *Our Town* and *The Seven Year Itch* with Barnard Archard in the cast. These were followed by the Barry O'Brien Company, with a young actress called Sheila Hancock; and these in turn by Joan Knight's company with a well remembered production of *Under Milk Wood*—one of the first occasions in which it was seen in the West Country.

Torquay was indeed growing fast and in 1960 the council decided to build another theatre, again on the seafront. The Princess Theatre was opened by Lord Roborough in June 1961, with a No. 1 bill topped by Joan Regan and supported by Tommy Cooper, Canadian singer Edmund Hockridge, Morecambe and Wise, the Munk Sisters Nancy and Molly, the George Mitchell Four, soubrette Patricia Starke and a chorus line as well, the present-day cost of which would be too prohibitive for one local theatre to meet.

Torquay was to prove the place where Morecambe and Wise began their rapid rise to the top after years as "second spot

PALACE THEATRE
PLYMOUTH
Proprietors: PALACE THEATRE (Plymouth) Ltd.
General Manager: WILLIAM WILLIS
BOX OFFICE OPEN 10 a.m. to 9 p.m.
Managing Director: GERARD HEATH
Advance Bookings Phone: 4383 and 5347/8
NO EXTRA CHARGE FOR BOOKING
6.20
MONDAY, AUGUST 11th
TWICE NIGHTLY
8.35
BACK AGAIN WITH A BRAND NEW SHOW
IN PERSON
CARROLL
LEVIS
BRITAINS STAR-MAKER
AND HIS PLYMOUTH AND
B.B.C. DISCOVERIES
STARRING THE ALL WINNERS FROM THE CARROLL LEVIS B.B.C. DISCOVERY BROADCASTS
THE LOVELY B.B.C. SINGING STAR
MARIA PERILLI
STAR OF A 1,000 BROADCASTS
CYCLO BROS.
DEFYING GRAVITY
CAWALINI AND HIS CANINE COMEDIANS
HAL LENNON AND VAL
THE NEW AUSTRALIAN DUO
DICK EMERY
COMEDIAN
THE DISCOVERIES OF TODAY ARE THE STARS OF TOMORROW
TRIBE BROS. LTD., London & St. Albans

on the bill". It was during that 1961 season that Leslie Grade offered them a series on ATV, which led them to negotiate for a script writer and eventually to branch out from their normal Music Hall turn into those hilarious sketches and individual brand of TV comedy which has made them world-famous.

The rubicund Bob Roberts, who had been appearing with his own band at the Spa Ballroom, became Entertainments Manager. There followed at the Princess a series of summer shows that rivalled those of Bournemouth and Blackpool, with such names as Max Bygraves, Val Doonican, Arthur Askey, Harry Worth and dozens of others, which were to prove by the annual box-office returns that engaging top-class artists paid off handsomely.

But this was not all the Princess had to offer, for in the 1960s it became the place for try-outs and pre-London runs in the autumn and spring seasons. It was in 1966 that West Country audiences saw the first-ever production of *The Prime of Miss Jean Brodie*, with Vanessa Redgrave in a not-too-brilliant first performance of the new play which was drastically altered later in its trial run when it got to Hull.

That same year saw *The Exploits of Tom Jones* with Keith Baron and Virginia Stride in the cast, and a beautiful production of the new comedy *The Owl and the Pussycat* impeccably acted by Anton Rodgers and Diana Sands, and which later proved a great success on the London stage.

In 1967 there came the new play *The Rumpus* by Hubert Gregg in which he appeared with Pat Kirkwood, a good clean-cut comedy, but which was not quite a success. In the same year there was a peculiar play, *What Victor Hugo Saw*, written by Hollywood film star Clive Brook, with Jill Browne, Desmond Carrington and that urbane and talented actor Anthony Roye in the cast. One has vivid memories of sitting until the small hours with Clive Brook in his hotel room rewriting the last act; but, alas, the play which was a mixture

FIG. 37 *(facing page)*.—"The Discoveries of today are the stars of to-morrow" was no idle boast on this daybill of 1953, which shows Dick Emery at the bottom of the bill.

of comedy, farce and the unusual had very little hope of success and eventually drifted into the mass of those countless plays which are never heard of again.

Another first production seen the same year which unfortunately never reached the long runs was *The Deadly Game* with the star cast of Stephen Murray, Leslie Phillips, Wilfred Brambell, Ronald Adam and that great veteran actor Ernest Milton. Friedrich Duerrenmatt's play of the three retired lawyers and their strange game of exercising their wits in a trial for murder, did, however, get to the Savoy Theatre in London.

The following year saw the first production of that amusing comedy *Not Now Darling* which opened later in London for a record run. Starring Donald Sinden, Bernard Cribbins, Pearl Hackney and a former Miss World, Ann Sidney, it was obvious from the start that this was going to be a winner, and the production by Patrick Cargill was among the funniest seen at this theatre.

Neighbouring Paignton, then a separate town which was only taken into the newly-formed Torbay fold in 1974, also decided to go all out to cash in on the big summer influx of visitors and build its own theatre on the seafront. On 9th June 1967, the Festival Theatre was opened with television's most famous musical *The Black and White Minstrel Show* with George Mitchell and George Innes in attendance, as well as that great impresario Robert Luff who was responsible for the stage version.

This kind of production suited the West Country folk down to the ground, for a spectacular show with familiar musical items, plenty of movement, dancing and humour was just the recipe that matched their taste. Repeated visits of this famous company to Paignton in the following years were always highly successful.

But all was not well at the first performance in the new

FIG. 38 *(facing page)*.—Seven years before they were "found" in 1961 at Torquay, Morecambe and Wise were touring the halls in lowly positions on the bills as "the new radio comedians". This Palace Theatre daybill of 1953 also includes Wilson, Keppel and Betty, one of the funniest of the post-war Music Hall acts.

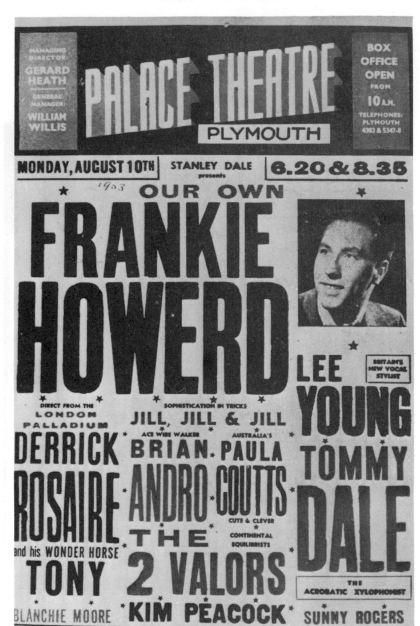

theatre. There were many complaints from the audience, for the place was originally designed as a multi-purpose hall for theatre-cum-conference-cum-dancehall purposes (the sprung floor is still there underneath). It became evident during the run of the show that as a theatre it was just impossible. In a wide auditorium, seating 1,476, only a few seats at the back were raised in tiers, the rest all being on ground level, and only half of the audience could see the show.

So strong was the outcry from patrons that when the show finished in September the Paignton Council decided upon urgent action to rectify the position and within a few months a completely new floor was constructed giving a rake from the back seats. This allowed for ample sight lines from all parts of the house and since then the Festival Theatre has functioned admirably and has staged many return visits of the Minstrels, ballet and similar top-class shows to rival those of its neighbour, the Princess in Torquay.

In the early 1950s Plymouth began to show a semblance of order amid the chaos, when the main part of the population which had lived in and around the centre in the past were resettled some five miles out at Crownhill, and later further still to Whitleigh and Tamerton, leaving the once bustling heart of Plymouth completely dead after the workers had departed each night at 6 p.m.

The garish atmosphere of Union Street with its milling crowds had gone. So had the cosmopolitan night life of the city centre with its cosy, friendly atmosphere where one could be sure of meet'ng at least one acquaintance at Genoni's restaurant or in the long bars of the pubs, much to the regret of the older Plymothians who retained faithful memories of the old city with its higgledy-piggledy streets. For whatever its geographical drawbacks, the old Plymouth had a soul and character of its own and comprised a community that had lived closely together for generations. Industry, citizens and

FIG. 39 *(facing page).*—The power of radio in the early 1950s is shown in this placing of Frankie Howerd at the top of the bill. Less than twelve months before, in 1952, he had appeared at the Palace as an almost unknown comedian, and it was in that year in the radio series *Variety Bandbox*, that he became a star.

administration were interwoven, all within easy reach, with the result that entertainment was near at hand whenever required.

Perhaps it was significant that under the Plan for Plymouth, the first building to be erected in the devastated area was a shop—the first of hundreds that were to engulf the larger proportion of the best part of the town. The rest of the buildings were given over to local government and commercial offices, with the main street, newly named Royal Parade, becoming nothing more than a glorified bus stop for people who were compelled to travel considerable distances from the outlying districts of the new city to seek their leisure pursuits.

Half of Devonport was meekly handed over to the Dockyard which enclosed much of the old town within its walls (including the site of the Alhambra Theatre), and the other half was mainly left as bomb sites—a sad, overgrown derelict area which was sacrificed to the new mercenary zeal and the clean look of the city centre.

The word *"Resurgam"* ("I will rise again") had been printed in large letters over the porch of St. Andrews Church and it was this spirit that inspired the citizens of the city to hope for better things in the future.

War-time restrictions were relaxed, clothing coupons, food and petrol rationing were abolished at last, and everyone looked forward to taking up their lives again within a new city.

The Festival of Britain in 1951 gave any impetus that was needed, and 1953 (Coronation year) brought a burst of enthusiasm resulting in a mammoth Pageant of Plymouth which ran for a week at the Royal Citadel, with willing help from the public, the services, the dockyard, amateur companies and local organisations. All combined in one huge effort to revive the communal spirit.

Demands for a theatre were made spasmodically, but official enthusiasm was concentrated on commerce and the vague reference to "a cultural precinct" was pushed aside.

This was the time of the Angry Young Man in the theatre, the time of the outbursts of creative activity from the new generation of playwrights. The works of Beckett, Osborne, Ionesco, Wesker, Genet were becoming fashionable, and were

[222]

included from time to time in the occasional visits to those local halls still remaining.

But the comfortable conservative Devon folk did not take at all kindly to the new realism of the so-called "kitchen-sink" plays, where even amateur productions vied with each other to show "real water" flowing from "real taps". Nor did they very much welcome "Theatre in the Round" (its early Cornish origins forgotten), which was far removed from the tarnished gilt and plush of the Victorian playhouse. The coming of Theatre of the Absurd, of Cruelty and of Fact, of Dadaism, of Brecht and Bond (of which there were quite a number of productions brought down by enthusiasts from universities and cultural companies "to enlighten the natives") were avoided by all except the few devotees.

Plymouth theatregoing suffered, and little wonder when the traditional peacetime apathy is remembered, allied to the now dispersing population, and the advent of mass television. This last was to breed a race of watchers who much preferred to stay at home with an illuminated box, rather than turn out to see an indifferently performed play, involving in some cases travelling five miles each way.

So, except for the summer resorts of Torquay, Newquay and North Devon, the 1950s saw no new theatres and very little of theatrical moment. Plymouth became "a cultural desert"— a term first employed by an ardent amateur actor John Shields Gray, who so described the city at a Dartmoor Commoners dinner in 1962.

Ald. Leslie Paul, then chairman of the Education Committee, declared in a speech in February 1963, speaking of the Plymouth Corporation's apathy towards the theatre:

> During the years since the war the City Council has had no time, no money, and I will freely admit, little inclination to support the Arts in its various ways.

This was the council that in 1937 had pulled down the old Theatre Royal and promised something in its place. Now, over twenty years later, it had not paid one penny towards the arts in any form.

The Palace Theatre was well into its last decade, running

[223]

under the genial managership of William Willis, who had reverted to the popular mixture of variety and revues coupled with the occasional play and musical—with the ever-popular Leslie Howe wielding the orchestral baton over a band which included the loquacious Babs Owen the accompanist (who is still in the summer show business); while backstage, Fred Davenhill ruled as stage manager.

Welsh soprano Anne Edwards, now in international demand for her Verdi roles, has particularly fond memories of the Palace Theatre, Plymouth, for it was here, on a Saturday night in October 1954, that she sang her first ever principal role with the Carl Rosa Opera Company.

She had joined the Company only two months previously as a £10-a-week chorister. At very short notice Anne Edwards was asked to sing the small part of Frasquita in *Carmen*, thus giving her the first step out of the chorus.

Carmen was sung by Marina de Gabarain; Micaela by Estelle Valery; Don José by Thorstein Hannesson and Escamillo by Arthur Copley.

Appropriately enough, Anne Edwards' real triumph came in the real Spain twenty years later, when she sang the only female part in Verdi's *Attila*, conducted by Placido Domingo at the Teatro del Liceo, Barcelona—a performance which placed her in world demand for the most exacting Verdi roles.

But the end was near and the Palace closed down in 1956, to be opened again a year later only once again to be wound up in 1959 with the pantomime *Miss Muffet* as its last production.

Sold for £15,000 in August 1961, it had a brief run of shows (including the D'Oyly Carte Company and the Festival Ballet with John Gilpin, booked by the new Managing Director George Roseman) but it finally succumbed in 1963 and became a bingo hall.

Frustration was in the air with organisations and individuals

FIG. 40 *(facing page)*.—What would be considered innocuous in the permissive 1980s was very daring in 1955, and in the more conservative provincial theatres, then fighting for their very existence against television, such productions were their final fling to attract audiences.

constantly complaining about the lack of proper entertainment, but the 1960s had brought ideas and a faint hope for the future.

The long-established learned society, "The Plymouth Institution" (which before its premises were destroyed in the blitz was housed in the Athenaeum alongside the Theatre Royal), was due to receive a substantial sum in government money as war damage compensation.

One of its most active members, F. Gordon Monk, had been pressing the members for some five years for this to be used not only to rebuild the premises on another site, but also to include a theatre that could be used as a lecture hall for the Institution, as a theatre for public use and also as a studio for the newly-built Westward Television studios next door.

Gordon Monk, a highly intelligent and immensely humane soul, fought against the many objections to his ideas and it

FIG. 41.—The Athenaeum Theatre, Plymouth, which was the first permanent theatre to be built in the city after the devastation of the Second World War.

was mainly through his diligence and perseverance that the building of the Athenaeum Theatre was begun in the first year of the decade.

Seating 350, it reflected the austere building controls of the time. While its stage revolve, mechanical forestage, orchestra pit and backstage facilities are eminently desirable and make it suitable for small productions, its over-all "decor" has been described as "clinical, untheatrical and lacking in atmosphere" by those who revere the red and gold of other times.

Nevertheless, it was all that Plymouth had in the way of a theatre and after its opening in May 1961, it became the home of many amateur groups as well as a venue for an increasing number of visiting professional companies.

The year 1961 also saw the first-ever recognition of the arts by the Plymouth Corporation, who granted £2,500 a year for three years to the newly-formed Plymouth Guild of Music and Drama (later renamed the Plymouth Arts Guild). The Guild was formed to encourage professional theatre and music and later came to be the instrument by which the council grants were dispensed to selected applicants.

It was through the guild's offices that the Richard Graham Company from London became the first professional group to play at the Athenaeum. On 12th September 1961, they staged *The Grass is Greener* to "House Full" notices on the opening night, followed by Nicholas Stuart Gray's *Beauty and the Beast* at Christmas while in the New Year there were a number of exhilarating performances by Spanish dancers, Susana y José.

The Century Theatre Group from Keswick were next, under the direction of Ian Curteis, with that fine actress Joan MacDonald and John Rapley as the lead players. Ian Curteis (now a director for the BBC) visited Plymouth on a number of occasions in the 1960s with his own company, an association climaxed in 1966 by a fine production of John Whiting's play *Penny for a Song*, with Robert Harris, Corin Redgrave (then playing his first roles), Michael Miller and Derek Tansley in the cast. But even with these stars of stature in their midst, Plymothians were reluctant to patronise their one and only theatre, for many now lived much longer distances from the rebuilt city centre.

[227]

That same year came that sensitive and highly professional actor, Richard Wordsworth, together with Stephen Moore, to appear in a marvellous production of *The Caretaker*, just afterwards Peggy Anne Wood, David Markham and Elizabeth Counsell from Windsor played for a week in Shaw's *You Never Can Tell*.

In fact all looked set for a period of conventional theatre-going, until in 1963 a theatrical bombshell burst on the Athenaeum with the arrival of Gerald Frow and Sally Miles (daughter of Lord Bernard Miles and his wife Josephine Wilson, founders of the Mermaid Theatre) with their Margate Stage Company. A volatile group of young actors, they brought originality and vibrant life to peaceful, conservative Plymouth.

Their name originated from the second oldest theatre in the country, the Theatre Royal, Margate, which had suffered many vicissitudes and closures until this lively band of players reopened it in 1960 for a few seasons.

Gerald Frow and Sally Miles were two of a kind—extrovert, highly intelligent, "people of the theatre"—but, for some West Country folk, way before their time.

Plays were performed in different order from the traditional weekly rep, sometimes two different productions in a week. The pr'nted programme resembled a newspaper with "scare" headlines; satire was their *métier*; and established customs and theatrical traditions were set aside, much to the consternation of the theatre die-hards in the city who considered them very much *avant-garde*.

They brought with them a group of players which included Zoe Randall, Powell Jones, Christopher Tranchell, Jack Tweddle, Paul Toml'nson, Mick Hughes, Juan Moreno, Louanne Harvey and Pamela Jackson, whose unabashed extroversion never fitted in too nicely with the wishes of the officers of the Athenaeum theatre, in which they played.

One could not challenge the Margate Stage Company's choice which ran from Molière, a musical on Burke and Hare, another on Al Capone; *Arden of Faversham*; Shaw's *Arms and the Man* (with Frow himself giving a brilliant performance as Capt. Bluntschli); and the first production seen outside London of John Arden's *Sergeant Musgrave's Dance*—a truly

[228]

memorable presentation. It was this last, with the company's refusal to subscribe to the old conventions, that caused a furore among the illuminati of the theatregoers, and the columns of the daily press. Even the city's distinguished librarian, W. Best Harris, fulminated in print against *Musgrave*, describing what was soon to become an accepted school text-book as "basically incoherent, a very poor play and containing little that is significant or new by way of dramatic experiment".

The impact of the Margate Stage Company with its new plays and modern methods had far greater influence on the Plymouth theatregoer, used to the florid nostalgia of the past, than that of John Osborne's *Look Back in Anger* era. They were jerked forward almost fifty years in theatrical history, and did not like it.

The company stayed on for a number of seasons, but their crusading spirit, which was supported to a large extent by the younger and more enthusiastic members of the community, was being frustrated at every turn by some of the senior citizens and councillors. Eventually it came to the pitch when one of them was quoted as saying: "When I hear the words Margate Stage Company, I reach for my gun."

The end came when a most tragi-comical scene was played out in the council chamber in July 1964. The assembled corporation solemnly voted to refuse an extra grant of £500 to keep the company in Plymouth. The argument over this paltry amount (when set against the background of their expenditure of £2 million on a new civic council house) took place amid a debate which, for uninformed speeches from die-hards who had never even bothered to see the company in action, was remarkable.

In more conservative vein, James Roose-Evans paid regular visits for some three years with his Hampstead Theatre Company, and that veteran actor Anthony Roye battled through with such plays as *The Heiress* (with Royce Ryton in the cast) and T. S. Eliot's *The Confidential Clerk* which after its Athenaeum run toured Cornwall.

The patronage of the Athenaeum over those years was erratic. It was good at the commencement after being starved of any kind of theatrical fare for so long, fair when the choice was known and popular, but plummeted to apathetic and poor when anything new and untried was offered.

As if to appease the theatrical appetites of its citizens, the Plymouth Corporation had erected a marquee on the sacred soil of Plymouth Hoe. Furnished with canvas chairs and a stage with a huge tent pole rising up from its front centre it was used during the summer months for holiday shows.

FIG. 42.—The 1950s saw Plymouth's first Civic Theatre—a marquee on the Hoe.

That ex-variety artist and doyen of impresarios Hedley Claxton brought a number of successful productions to "the tent" as it was known locally, when he created a growing demand for this type of show, especially when he brought Gordon Peters, a comedian who was destined to become the favourite of many a local theatregoer.

Bowing at last to public demand, the council eventually replaced the marquee in 1962 with a prefabricated wooden building which they named the Hoe Theatre. Seating 600 it

FIG. 43.—The prefabricated Hoe Theatre which was erected on the same site in 1962.

has been renovated, added to and re-roofed, and remained the only civic theatre in the city.

During the 1970s the Hoe Theatre was used to much greater advantage; for in addition to the annual summer shows (one of which included the then unknown Dave Allen as second comedian) there have been pantomimes—notably those of that good old-timer Jerry Jerome—and latterly the spectacular shows of John Redgrave. The "Theatre For Plymouth Company" played a number of seasons during 1967–9 under the auspices of the Plymouth Arts Guild; and at the present time it is the home of the Plymouth Theatre Company which was formed in 1972 under the Artistic Directorship of Robert Hamlin from Toronto.

Meanwhile, at the Athenaeum, the stormy 1960s finished on a more serene note. Anthony Roye, together with playwright William Douglas Home, brought *The Secretary Bird* for one of its first showings at that theatre—a production that later went on to London to become a renowned success.

Unfortunately not all of Douglas Home's plays fared so well. The Athenaeum Theatre saw the world première of his *The Grouse Moor Image*, attended by the author himself and a fabulous first-night audience which included the Lord Mayor and Lady Mayoress, the Marquis of Bath, Lord and Lady Douglas Gordon from Truro, Viscount Boyd of Merton, Lord and Lady Roborough and many others, giving Plymouth a glimpse of the glitter of a West End first night.

FIG. 44.—Hedley Claxton's company at the Hoe Theatre during the summer show of 1960. Third from left is comedian George Lacy, and at the end on the right, Dave Allen, then aged twenty-three, in his first summer show after appearing as a Butlin's Redcoat entertainer.

But the play was disappointing. It provided pleasant entertainment with a fair proportion of kindly jabs at both political parties; took a knock at the Marquis of Bath and his lions of Longleat; made witty fun at some of the impoverished owners of stately homes; and finished up with the Leader of the

Opposition playing the organ. Yet it lacked action and deserved a much better ending. It may emerge at some later date revised and refurbished into a success—who knows?

The years 1967–8 were indeed vintage times for good theatre in Plymouth. The Bristol Old Vic Company came with *War and Peace* and a remarkably fine production of *Portrait of a Queen* which drew packed houses to the Athenaeum Theatre. Joan Knight and her company did Trojan work in bringing popular plays, while Peter Dews came from Birmingham with a production of *As You Like It* which was described as "wonderfully directed, eminently understandable so that the characters might be living today; gay, laughable, and romantic in turn and devoid of the 'hey nonny no' horrors that sometimes pass for so called 'pastoral' presentations". But once again Plymouth audiences passed it by and the play did not get the support it deserved.

This period was rudely interrupted when the Lord Chamberlain had one final fling banning at the Athenaeum a piece of nonsense called *How Robbers Plan to Steal the Crown Jewels*.

It was part of a satirical revue devised and performed by a band of bright young people headed by Michael Palin, a graduate of Brasenose College, Oxford, who was one of the leading lights in television's record-breaker *Monty Python's Flying Circus*.

The cautious audiences which stayed away that week missed the opportunity of seeing in the flesh that brilliant group of satirists, Terry Jones, Michael Palin and Ian Davidson, whom they so avidly lapped up from the square-eyed box in later years.

It was during this period that a great change of heart took place within the Plymouth Council after "A Survey of the Arts" had been made by the Plymouth Arts Guild.

As had been seen in the past, the city fathers had never given much thought to the arts, let alone finance, and its only noticeable public contribution to the public arts weal over 150 years seems to have been the erection of the Theatre Royal in 1811 (for which it demanded rent with no strings attached) and the building of the Municipal Library and Art Gallery in Tavistock Road.

[233]

But with the inception of the Arts Guild in 1961 it salved it conscience by subsidising—to a very limited extent—certain professional productions until the newly-formed Arts Council of Great Britain began to make itself felt in municipal financial circles, matching grant for grant.

Here it must be freely admitted that the City Council's long-lived parsimony ended. During the next few years, amid a welter of public debates and discussions, it was decided to build a civic theatre of about 700 seats.

Then another bombshell burst. There came a demand for a much larger building to seat 1,500, which would have been economical to commercial users and would have housed the big national shows and stars to which the television-conscious Westcountryman had become accustomed. A "Theatre Action Committee" was formed and sides taken, but unfortunately no compromise came from either camp with the result that the Pattinson Plan (after Ald. Harold Pattinson who was its spearhead) was dropped.

Fortunately the new-found enlightenment towards the arts by councillors in general continued unabated, and year by year grants were increased until Plymouth became one of the largest benefactors of theatrical projects in Devonshire.

Then in 1973 Ald. Ralph Morrell announced plans for a leisure complex to be built with an hotel, shops, offices, concert hall, disco, bars and a theatre as well as other entertainment facilities, all to be erected on that same site surrounding the area of the old Theatre Royal.

As will be seen this proposal was to mark a turning point in West Country Theatre fortunes, bringing in its wake a growing discontent among certain ratepayers which boiled up in 1977–8 into an anti-theatre lobby which fought hard against the project.

It also marked the beginning of a period when Plymothians, after years of neglect and apathy towards the arts could look forward to not one but two major theatres operating in the city at the same time.

At Exeter the stormy 1960s were taking their toll and that fine old Theatre Royal, after battling valiantly under Cliff Gwillim's banner against the new post-war world and an outworn system of dwindling touring companies, was, like so many others in the country, sold, demolished and turned into an office block.

But Exeter was far luckier than most.

A rich man's dream, municipal foresight and a university inspiration, changed within five years a decaying theatre scene into one of the most successful and stimulating projects that has been seen in the West Country for over 100 years.

In 1962, the late G. V. Northcott, a self-made man and an ardent theatre-lover, tried to "save" the Theatre Royal from such a sad fate, but negotiations failed.

Looking back, it was just as well; for shortly afterwards the vice-chancellor of the Exeter University offered an alternative

FIG. 45.—The Northcott Theatre, built in 1967 within the campus of Exeter University, a site which among some Exonians still savours of gown rather than the town for which it was intended. Its exterior was designed to blend with the other university buildings.

[235]

site some three miles from the city on the University campus, a site which did not meet with everyone's approval, as there was at the time much talk of more "gown" than "town".

However, the chancellor won over Northcott to the idea of a theatre giving a service far wider than the traditional fare of rep revivals and popular escapism—a theatre that would serve a regional audience far beyond the bounds of the 78,000 population of the city.

With commendable imagination both the Devon County Council and the Exeter City Council became enthusiastic and each promised an annual grant which has increased yearly to augment Northcott's generous benefaction of £100,000. A further £50,000 from the Gulbenkian Foundation enabled the building of a modern theatre, well designed and appointed, which, when it opened in November 1967, proved an exciting theatrical venture.

The building itself was a departure from the normal pattern of either civic or university theatres, and was based on a steeply-raked fan-shaped auditorium on the amphitheatre style rising from the stage which was on floor level; a design which so far has met every kind of production from box sets to open plan and in the round.

From the public viewpoint it is a pleasant place to visit whatever is shown on its stage, for the uniquely designed foyer with its long, semi-circular bar at first floor level, ex-hibit'on area and box-office facilities offer comfort, refresh-ment and attraction at any time.

Actor Tony Church from the Royal Shakespeare Company at Stratford was appointed Artistic Director and was respon-sible for the theatre's policy.

Tony Church was a man of the theatre indeed, bringing business acumen and a wide theatrical knowledge to work miracles in providing a fair return for the expenditure of public money by the Devon citizens, who had every reason to be well satisfied with its administration.

To the public he gave a varied selection of shows; bowing to the popular with *Charley's Aunt*, to the moderns with Edward Albee and to the traditionalists with Shakespeare.

He maintained a stable resident company with sufficient regular turnover of productions to prevent them becoming stale, and with guest stars and players joining for short seasons, he managed in the first two years to create a great impression in the theatre world at large by touring his company as far as Dorset and Hampshire.

In just over four years the Northcott staged six world premières, which involved such prominent directors as Robin Phillips, Charles Savage and Anton Rodgers; and an impressive list of players included Margaret Tyzack, Derek Fowlds, Davyd Harries, Elspeth March, Diana Rigg, Timothy West and Keith Michell.

On top of this the theatre provided opera, films, ballet and young people's festivals, plus regional tours and an educational service which allowed directors and actors to talk about their work with the public and so create interest in the programme.

Winning audiences was the watchword, and Church rapidly caught on to the fact that television-minded post-war audiences needed the best to beat what the small screen could supply. With the world première of *Abelard and Héloïse* (starring Diana Rigg and Keith Michell) netting an attendance figure of 115,000 in three weeks, Exeter again established itself in the centre of theatre history when the play transferred to London for a highly successful run.

The theatre's reputation was also increased by historical regional dramas like *John Wesley*, and in particular by another première, *The Roses of Eyam*, Don Taylor's immensely dramatic play on the Great Plague, which was later shown on television.

Tony Church left Exeter at the end of 1970 and his place as Artistic Director was taken over by Jane Howell from the Royal Court Theatre, who brought with her a zeal for integration with the people, a taste for modern playwrights and a vivid imagination for theatrical effect. The result was that traditionalists among the audiences had a touch of theatre very different from the three-act, one-set drawing room play so loved by previous generations.

Berthold Brecht's *Galileo* was seen in 1972 and later his *Caucasian Chalk Circle*. Both were fine presentations, staged in the modern style, which upset some who still preferred their "picture-frame" productions.

[237]

There followed a modern *Measure for Measure* (which did not please the Shakespeare "bardolators"); Thomas Heywood's *Fair Maid of the West* (made into a musical by Jack Emery) and then a trio of plays by Edward Bond. Bond's *Pope's Wedding* was seen in 1973 when John Dove directed this unusual combination of lusty life and short-lived marriage with its sinister overtones so reminiscent of Harold Pinter.

Then came his *Narrow Road to the Deep North*, and in November 1973 the world première of his play *Bingo*, a morose look at Shakespeare in his retirement in which Bond dwells on the bigotry, poverty and avarice of Elizabethan times as if these were something new, leaving William to be described by Ben Jonson as being "written out".

The play afterwards transferred to London where it opened with John Gielgud as Shakespeare. It fared reasonably well in the metropolis—better than in the provinces where both audiences and critics alike cared little for the play.

Jane Howell's reign at the Northcott Theatre certainly brought more than a whiff of the new theatre world to the placid West Country folk, who were introduced to realism with property blood, hangings and sudden death in no small measure (especially in such productions as *Judge Jeffreys—A Musical History of the Bluddie West Country Assizes*).

Variety there was indeed from Coward's *Private Lives*, Brendan Behan's *The Hostage*, Joe Orton's *Loot* and a modern interpretation of *The Tempest* with Edward Petherbridge as Prospeo and a bowler-hatted drunken Stephano by Rhys McConnochie. Later followed, in 1973, a rather gimmicky production of part of the Cornish Mystery Cycle.

Director Geoffrey Reeves took over the Northcott in March 1974, this time with a policy of popular plays for the people specially selected to win audiences with known box-office successes and nostalgia. The business of gauging the mood of his audiences began with *The Ghost Train*, Priestley's *An Inspector Calls* and Ben Travers' famous farce *Thark* beautifully directed by Robert Lang with Brian Murphy and Basil Lord in the cast.

These two fine actors were also seen in an excellent production of John Osborne's *The Entertainer* in May 1974, and this

[238]

was followed by *Black Eyed Susan à la* Vincent Crummles, and Chekhov's *The Seagull*, with Hywel Bennett.

The year 1975 saw John McGrath's new play *Trees in the Wind*—not a very successful venture either as a play or as a production; but recompense came with a brilliant presentation of *The Playboy of the Western World* with David Sibley as Christopher Mahon and Mary Yeomans as Widow Quin, performances which earned them great praise from the critics.

In spite of the inflationary 1970s, Geoffrey Reeves's policy of popular plays laced with star names (whenever they were available) paid off, even a summer production of the nostalgic lightweight musical *Salad Days* drawing full houses through the hot summer of 1975.

Here a tribute must be paid to the valuable work for the theatre in the West Country given over the years by the Arts Council of Great Britain and its regional section, the South Western Arts Association (or as it is now known, South West Arts) and the local arts centres. Maligned and castigated as the Arts Council was in the years after its formation for its rather lofty view of the provinces to which it sent small acting groups who exuded an atmosphere of missionaries trying to elevate the natives, it has certainly redeemed its reputation since.

But it must be admitted that those early Art Centres were snobbish places, culturally "toffee-nosed"; they staged much so-called *avant-garde* theatre which was often unrehearsed and unaccomplished, performed by self-indulgent actors. They earned for themselves from local government officers and public alike, a reputation that anything financed by the Arts Council was "way out" and "not for us", a reputation that took some time to dispel when in later years better things came from the Council.

But the development of the Regional Arts Associations and the pressure exerted by Jennie Lee, then Minister for the Arts, on local authorities to participate in the work of the association gave rise to the appointment of a full-time Director, who set about the task of persuading municipal authorities to acknowledge their responsibility for cultural development in the region.

[239]

Northcott Theatre
Exeter

Jan 30 - Feb 16

HAY
FEVER

by NOEL COWARD

Attitudes and outlooks changed radically and so did the programmes of theatrical fare offered to the public.

Local government officers and councillors, who in the past had ignored theatre and culture at any price, were now including special budgets for the arts in their towns and cities, with the result that South West Arts were able to bring to the West Country a number of major events ranging from visits of the National Theatre Company, the Festival and Royal Ballet Companies to the Royal Shakespeare Company and the Comedie L'Ouest from Rennes in France. These events were given excellent support by the public and seemed to have made a decidedly enlightened impression on many Philistines—in particular the Royal Ballet, which played in a mobile theatre in Plymouth for two weeks in 1973 and was completely sold out before it opened.

In addition, the S.W. Arts' responsibility was extended to giving major subsidies to three theatre companies resident in the South West—the Orchard Theatre Company (which serves 1,000 square miles of North Devon), Foots Barn Theatre (which covers the whole of Cornwall) and Medium Fair (which travels South and East Devon) as well as giving annual grants to the Northcott Theatre and to the Plymouth Theatre Company, formed in 1973.

Thus by the mid-1970s, while Plymouth still had its prefabricated Hoe Theatre and Athenaeum, and had established a small resident company which, under the direction of Robert Hamlin, presented five or six productions a year, the artistic pendulum had swung far in the favour of Exeter where the Northcott Theatre was attracting audiences from far and wide.

It is a matter of speculation that if sufficient finance had been available in the two previous decades the same resurgence would have taken place in Devon's largest city with it growing population of a quarter of a million people.

FIG. 46 *(facing page)*.—Geoffrey Reeves' first presentation after his appointment as Director in January 1974 was Noel Coward's *Hay Fever* (welcomed by traditionalists after Jane Howell's three-year term with her penchant for Brecht and Bond and the Royal Court Theatre style of production).

[241]

The direct result of this neglect during those thirty-five years since the onset of the Second World War was that new generations had grown up many of whom had never seen the inside of a theatre or watched a live performance by professional actors save on the television small screen.

It also created a situation where, except for a small minority, theatregoing became a rare occasion among the young, who preferred pop to Pinter, and among adults who were brought up on glitter, gold and emotion. For this was a time when because of inflation, production costs were so prohibitive that the large casts and spectaculars which had attracted popular support in the past were impossible. When taxed with the question of the existence of the professional stage in Plymouth, the reply invariably was: "We have the amateurs."

# CHAPTER XV

# The Great Unpaid

The amateur in the theatre world made his first appearance a long time ago, and was epitomised by Shakespeare in the comical efforts of producer Peter Quince to rehearse Bottom, Snug, Starveling and Flute in *The Most Lamentable Comedy and Most Cruel Death of Pyramus and Thisbe*.

As we have seen, rustic players were in evidence long before this, taking their various parts in the mystery plays of the fourteenth century. In the gaps between, one can merely catch a fleeting glimpse of other amateur endeavour.

Totnes, Devon, 1564. "Paied to the Boys of Totnes which played in the Church before the Mayor of the Towne . . . 5s od." Plymouth, Devon, 1565. "Item. Paide to the Foure Boys of Towne that played at the Mayor's . . . 5s od."

Later on, in 1574, 10s. was paid, again to "the Boys of Totnes which played in the church before the Masters of the Town".

No records exist of any amateur activity in the seventeenth or early eigteenth centuries, which is not, perhaps, surprising considering the effect of the Puritan oppression on the professionals, and it is not until 1786 that an entry in the Plymouth town records recalls a performance of "The Tragedy of Cato by the Young Gentlemen of the Grammar School at the Mayoralty Rooms".

At the beginning of the nineteenth century charades, *tableaux vivants* and minor amateur theatricals began to be popular with the middle classes and certain members of the military with time on their hands. While the learning of lines was irksome there were the rewards of meeting people of the opposite sex as well as appearing to good advantage on a public stage to the admiration of one's friends.

It was, however, difficult for the ordinary working man to enter such lofty circles as the 17-year-old Robert Dyer, of 74 Whimple Street, Plymouth, was to find in 1815.

I became a member of the Stonehouse Amateur Company on the Coal Quay. A member of the company, a corporal in the Marines (you cannot be too select in mixed society) was broken to the ranks, tied up to the halberts and flogged.

I saw him faint under the torture and all for some peculation in the Pay Office to enable him to meet his expenses. A young man of limited means cannot be conscientiously honest in a private theatre. He has to pay his entrance fee, his weekly subscription, for his books, his stage dresses, but here the evil does not end.

After the play it is usual to adjourn to some tavern and there sip ale and flattery until the amateur is intoxicated by the strength of one, and the sweets of the other.

Besides there are strong and irresistible temptations to vice in the female society of a private theatre, and though I know of men who have passed unscathed, I do not know of one amateur lady who has borne an unblemished reputation.

I would advise all young persons to shun even the atmosphere of a private theatre for it will breed in them a love of idle pleasure and unfit them for the duties of respectable men.

Dyer's condemnation of amateur actresses has a distinct Puritan ring, but evidently he must have succumbed to temptation for, as has been related, he himself joined the ranks of the professionals not so long afterwards.

Eight years later, in Exeter this time, the historian William Cotton commented on the growing number of amateur performances in that city, calling attention, some 100 years in advance of his time, to the rather fatuous productions that were being presented to the public, and asking for a more serious approach.

The present wide-spread fashion, if it may be so called, which takes the shape of amateur dramatic societies, may be a revolt against the present neglect of the regular drama. Nor can we regard the fashion as altogether in the same light as the manias which come and go without apparent cause or reason.

In Devon during the first part of Victoria's reign amateur productions became the toy and leisure pastime of the middle classes, and in the many garrison towns an amiable pursuit for both the army and navy. One playbill of 1851 reads:

GRAND AMATEUR PERFORMANCE

By the Officers of the Army and Navy. With New Dresses
by Mr & Mrs Buck.

"DON CAESAR DE BAZAN"

CAST

| | |
|---|---|
| Charles II | Lt Blake R.M. |
| Don José | C. Wheeler Esq. |
| Don Caesar | Capt Disney Roebuck |
| Marquis de Rotunda | Capt Austen R.N. |
| Marchioness | Miss Louise Derette. |

Followed by the farce "THE REVIEW" and

"YOU CAN'T MARRY YOUR GRANDMOTHER"

The servile attitude of theatre owners to people of officer rank was taken to absurd lengths as is shown in "Amateur Night" at the Theatre Royal, Plymouth, of the same year.

J. Lyons with Great Deference informs the Nobility, Gentry and inhabitants of Plymouth, Stonehouse, Devonport and their Vicinities that the Gentlemen Amateurs of the Army and Navy whose performances proved so Fashionably attractive on Former occasions, have kindly proferred their Valuable Services to perform once more in the admired petite comedy of "Charles the Second—or The Merry Monarch", to be followed by "Shocking Events" and "Unfinished Gentlemen".

To be fair, theatre managers did very well out of the amateurs; for they had no wages to pay, and a flattering playbill, however poor the end product may have been, cost no more than the usual weekly advertisement.

A break from the usual run of corny burlettas, rehashed

[245]

melodramas and farces can be noticed in 1868 when T. W. Robertson's drama *Ours* was presented "for the first time in Plymouth by Officers of H.M. 57th Regiment at prices 1 shilling to four shillings for the boxes. Doors open 7.30 p.m. Performance commences at 8 p.m. precisely. Carriages to be ordered for 11 p.m."

The Victorian call for moral and cultural advancement in entertainment was answered in the second half of the nineteenth century by the formation of musical and operatic societies with their select soirées and conversaziones combined with drama groups devoted to study, lectures and play-readings at which mere civilians were welcomed.

One such company performed in 1864 at Stephens Assembly Rooms and again at Gold's Assembly Rooms in Millbrook, Cornwall, where the startling announcement was made that they would perform:

Act two of "Othello" and "The Stranger"
*Which will be delivered from Memory and in Character*
by Mr Saunders, Mr Henri and Mr Clements
to be followed by "Box and Cox"
Front 1/- Back seats 6d

While the professional theatre in mid-Victorian times was considered beyond the pale for respectable genteel folk to visit except on highly recommended occasions, it nevertheless had its effect. There arose that great tradition of family entertainment in the home—songs around the piano from the current popular sentimental music, recitations in sombre and tragic tones as befitted the great tragedians of the day and charades so beloved of Victorian novelists.

This eventually led to the more venturesome forming acquaintances of a like mind outside the family circle, and there began the formation of an ever-increasing number of amateur theatrical societies which would perform for their own amusement, first in private and then at convenient local halls or theatres in front of relatives and friends, thus giving themselves an aura of home-censored respectability. Such a one was the Plymouth Histrionic Club which performed in the Mechanic's Institute in Princess Square.

[246]

In April 1881 they staged a farce *Cool as a Cucumber* followed by a melodrama *Miriam's Crime*, with a cast list that included A. H. Williamson, A. L. Lillicrap, C. F. Fitch, Miss Mitchell and Miss Stewart.

Like all Thespians through the ages, the Victorian amateurs' ambitions knew no bounds and like their present-day counterparts they often chose plays and characters wholly unsuited to their talents and powers, with the inevitable result that what was intended to be taken seriously often ended in fiasco.

Whitfeld relates the havoc which the broad Devon dialect played in an amateur performance of *The Duke's Motto* in 1880 when one of the actors playing a soldier, having pursued another character Legardère off stage, returned to arrest the chief officer with this declaration: "Leegurdare is ded. Bind'n with koards and pitch'n overboard. Wunst to the bottom he'll nivver cum op agaen!"

An amateur production of *Hamlet* at the same period must have surely got off to a rousing start when, in the battlement scene, Francisco, on guard over the castle of Elsinore, challenged Horatio with the classic Devon greeting: "Who cums yur?"

The traditionally accident-prone *Macbeth* ran into trouble in one amateur production seen by Whitfeld when one of the gentlemen playing "an evil spirit half way between Heaven and Earth" suddenly crashed on to the stage below amid uproarious laughter and an agonised cry of "Oh me toe! Me toe!"

Even in late Victorian times amateur dramatic societies were mainly in the hands of service people and there was an abundance of ranks among the names of the officers of the various groups. Major Rendle was responsible for a number of productions at the Theatre Royal and at the Volunteer Depot in Catherine Street, aided by such others as Capt. Jack Stevens, Capt. Alf Dyer, Capt. Holmes and Capt. David Brown, plus two civilian names, Lovell Dunstan and Fred Dunstan who were to become more distinguished in civic life during the years to come.

But at first it was music more than speech which sparked the compulsion to perform in public, fostered by the rapidly rising craze for the sentimental song, the burletta and the

## THEATRE ROYAL, PLYMOUTH.

N° 73 ]  Lessee and Manager,—Mr. J. R. NEWCOMBE, 5, Mount Pleasant Terrace, Plymouth.  [ N° 80

A GRAND

# AMATEUR PERFORMANCE,

## By OFFICERS of the

# DEVON MILITIA,

UNDER THE DISTINGUISHED PATRONAGE OF

LIEUT.-GENERAL

# Sir HARRY SMITH

BART., G.C.B., AND

# LADY SMITH.

## On THURSDAY, JUNE 29th,

The Performances will commence with TOBIN's elegant Comedy, in Five Acts, of The

# HONEYMOON.

| | |
|---|---|
| The Duke Aranza | Mr. COLERIDGE, S.D.M. |
| Count Montalban | Mr. DEVON, D.M.A. |
| Rolando | Capt. MARSHALL, D.M.A. |
| Balthazar | Capt. B. RUSSELL, D.M.A. |
| Lampedo | Capt. TURNER, 29th Regt. |
| Lopez | Capt. BULLER, S.D.M. |
| Jacques | Mr. HODGKINSON, S.D.M. |
| Campillo | Capt. STEVENSON, S.D.M. |
| Pedro | Mr. BARWELL, D.M.A. |
| Olmera | Mr. NEW, D.M.A. |
| Juliana *Her First Appearance these Four Years* | Mrs. HUDSON KIRBY, |
| Zamora | Mrs. G. SMYTHSON. |
| Volante | Mrs. WARDE. |
| Hostess | Mrs. HARDING. |

SONG—" The Soldier tired "—from ' Artaxerxes ' .................................Dr. ARNE.

MISS CLARA ST. CASSE.

Pas Transylvanien ...............................Master and Miss BARNUM.

IN THE COURSE OF THE EVENING, THE BAND WILL PERFORM

| | | | |
|---|---|---|---|
| OVERTURE  " Le Domino Noir" | AUBER. | QUADRILLE—" Constantinople " | D'ALBERT. |
| POLKA "Rigi" | DAVIS. | " War Galope " | D'ALBERT. |

To conclude with an original Farce, entitled The

# MOUSTACHE MOVEMENT.

| | |
|---|---|
| Mr. Simon Swosser, in the Law | Mr. NEW, D.M.A. |
| Captain Altamont Kidd, in the Army | Mr. COLERIDGE, S.D.M. |
| Lieutenant Cornelius O'Pake, formerly in the same, Swosser's Nephew | Mr. HODGKINSON, S.D.M. |
| Anthony Soskins, a Lawyer's Clerk | Capt. BULLER, S.D.M. |
| John, a Waiter, as may be anticipated | Mr. BARWELL, D.M.A. |
| Butcher, with a Moustache | Mr. STEVENSON, S.D.M. |
| Baker, with ditto | Mr. DEVON, D.M.A. |
| Two Individuals, in the Police | { Capt. MARSHALL, D.M.A. <br> { Capt. RUSSELL, D.M.A. |
| Louisa Fitz-Johnson, a Milliner | Mrs. G. SMYTHSON. |
| Eliza Swosser, Swosser's Daughter | Mrs. WARDE. |
| Sally, a Housemaid, as will be naturally expected | Miss WYATT. |

Tickets to be had of Mr. R. LIDSTONE, Box Office, George Street, where Places for the Boxes may be secured.

PRICES AS USUAL.]  THE CURTAIN WILL RISE AT EIGHT PRECISELY.  [KEYS, PRINTER, PLYMOUTH.

Gilbert and Sullivan operas which were later to take the whole country by storm.

Most of the long-established amateur operatic societies which still exist started life with music, either as choirs or operatic societies, giving static concert versions of opera and oratorios. As might be expected, Cornwall, with its historic theatrical background and Celtic touch for song, has, in Liskeard, one of the oldest companies in the South West. Formed in 1870, originally called the Liskeard Choral Society, it performed many such concert versions in the town and surrounding villages until it graduated into the Savoy operas that are still performed today by the Liskeard and District Amateur Operatic Society.

Even the venerable Plymouth Shakespeare Society began with a musical evening in December 1887, when a score of citizens met together in Treville Street to arrange a programme of music and excerpts from *Julius Caesar*; from this meeting there emerged the Plymouth Shakespeare Literary Society which went on to present further "excerpts" each year.

In 1902 they staged *Othello* at the Masonic Hall, Princess Square, and the next year *The Merchant of Venice*, with W. Greenland chosen for the part of Shylock because he was the possessor of a fine flowing beard.

Later on the word "Literary" was dropped and the company under the guidance of such personalities as W. J. Taylor, Donald Pengelly, Hilda Dennis, Thomas G. Read, Leslie Briggs and Ian Trigger (now a professional actor of repute in America) continued presenting at least one of Shakespeare's plays annually for some seventy years right up to 1977 when owing to diminished membership they resigned themselves to play-readings, lectures etc., a policy which is still continued.

Just as the Savoy Operas and musical comedy had fired the imaginations of the Victorian amateur singers, so also were

FIG. 47 *(facing page)*.—Comedy and farce became the mainstay of the amateur theatre as long ago as in this one-night performance in 1856. The Miss Clara St. Casse, who sang the appropriate *The Soldier Tired* in the interval between the two pieces, was a professional actress of the time who had appeared in the previous week's production at the theatre.

amateur actors, at the turn of the century and later, inspired by the hero worship given to Irving, Tree, Lewis Waller, Wilson Barrett and Martin Harvey. The ladies also were infected by the glamour of Ellen Terry, the vivacity of Ellaline Terriss and the tragedy queens Sarah Bernhardt and Eleonora Duse.

At the beginning of the twentieth century there were dozens of similar societies scattered all over the South West. Exeter had its enthusiastic personality C. B. Kay, who was a great organiser of amateur productions including *tableaux vivantes* in which many county people took part. He was also an official of the Exeter Musical Comedy Company which presented a performance every year.

The still flourishing City of Plymouth Amateur Operatic Society was formed in 1899 with a performance of *H.M.S. Pinafore* presented at the Royal Naval Barracks in Devonport. They then aspired to the Theatre Royal with other Savoy operas until 1910 when they branched out into Gaiety theatre musicals, staging one every year either at the Royal, Alhambra, Globe Theatre or the Palace right up to the present decade when they play at the Athenaeum or the Hoe Theatre.

Reginald Ball was the first Musical Director of the company and in 1900, as behoves a group calling itself after the City of Plymouth, many prominent citizens became members and have had long connections with the society either as players, on committee or backstage.

A group of Exonians, who were snared by the delights of musical comedy and Gilbert and Sullivan, formed the Exeter Amateur Operatic Society. This was established in 1904, giving its first performance in February 1905 at the Royal Public Rooms with *The Pirates of Penzance*, which was later toured by the company to Tavistock, Tiverton and Exminster. They are still in existence and with the gaps caused by two world wars excepted, have presented an annual show ever since.

Truro in Cornwall founded its company in 1912 opening with *Trial by Jury*. After running through all the Savoy Operas in turn, including *Utopia Ltd.*, eventually added musical comedy to their repertoire which they still present annually.

The first quarter of the twentieth century saw more and

more groups being formed for the promotion and appreciation of a theme or one author's or composer's works, and like the Shavian and Shakespeare societies, the Bach and Handel Festivals, there soon appeared the Plymouth Gilbert and Sullivan Fellowship, dedicated to the Savoy Operas and performing no others.

The Fellowship first saw the light of a stage in 1923 when the company played at the Repertory Theatre in *The Mikado*. Later they also appeared at the Theatre Royal, the Alhambra, the Globe, and the Palace. At present, they play at the Athenaeum Theatre, leaving a trail of such names as Ida Lander, Harry Greene, Norman and Horace Bickle, Harry Andrew, George Ayres, Edward Aldridge, Cifford and Margaret Tolcher, Ivor Bryan, Jennie Ellis, Frank Urell and Stella Whiteway. In recent years their many first-class productions were invariably directed by such talented Savoyards as Leo Sheffield and Richard Dunne.

Mention must also be made of the renowned Mrs Arthur Picken, of Whimple Street, Plymouth, who formed her own company of actors and presented in fashionable style a number of successful productions at the delightful Globe Theatre.

Then there was Kenneth Spooner's Dramatic Society which performed at the Repertory Theatre staging such plays as *A Rose Without a Thorn* (a gorgeously dressed production) with Frank Hughes as Henry VIII, Peggy Bardon, Angus Smith and Jocelyn Woollcombe in the cast, and *The Middle Watch* in 1933 at the Alhambra Devonport.

As was to happen in the ensuing years, a dissatisfied member of an amateur company would break away from the parent group and form another. Such a one was Suzanne Wagner, wife of Dr R. H. Wagner. After a difference of opinion with the Plymouth Amateurs she formed her own society—Mrs Wagner's Company—which enjoyed a successful run for some years at the Theatre Royal until it folded just before the 1939 war.

This pattern of splinter groups was to be found on many occasions in the future and was the main cause of the proliferation of the large number of dramatic societies which came into being in the 1930s and later.

One of the most stable and successful of the Plymouth

companies were the Tamaritans, founded in 1931 with actress Lillah McCarthy (Lady Keeble) as its first president. This was one of the few with enough energy and enthusiasm to aspire to having its own theatre. In fact they have had two, the first being bombed during the war and the second (the Little Theatre in Lambhay Street) still being used regularly.

From an opening membership of some twenty or so, the number of acting members rose to 120 in just over two years. "The Tams", as they became known, staged fifty full-length plays in the first decade of their existence. The list has increased steadily since the war.

For many years the indefatigable Eileen Thomas and James Knape looked after the company's affairs as well as appearing in their productions, while other stalwart members included C. C. Cooper (their first chairman), Irene Hall, Stella Essery, Cyril Penrose (who was one of those responsible for converting the Little Theatre), Dennis Jeffery, Joan Warn and Pat Giddy.

The British Drama League, under Geoffrey Whitworth, was coming into prominence in the 1920s, and the amateur movement grew fast. It was also beginning to have side-effects on the state of the professional theatre, which became either a curse or a blessing, depending upon which side of the fence one sat.

The amateur who preferred to "do his own thing" was disdained by the professional actor (who conveniently forgot his own beginnings) and was praised on the other hand by those who had never before had the opportunity of appearing in any kind of live entertainment and who now realised the novelty.

Figures are not available for the number of pre-war societies, but in the early 1950s it was estimated that there were some 30,000 amateur players in Great Britain, and while there might have been some radical changes in organisation in the past twenty-five years, the present estimate of some half a million people being actively engaged in amateur theatre is by no means an exaggeration.

This figure was confined to those engaged in established dramatic and operatic societies who performed regularly on theatre stages, while if one includes the vast numbers in smaller groups—the aspiring "popsters", the dancers and the hopeful concert artists—the total is greatly exceeded.

At the time this book was written there were some twenty dramatic and operatic societies operating all the year round in Plymouth, some of them presenting three shows a year. The Bristol area with its half a million population, had over thirty, a quarter of which were operatic and musical. Cornwall, with its scattered area, could muster nearly fifty societies of various kinds, while Exeter in the 1970s could easily name half a dozen, and these figures do not take into account the large number of groups affiliated to churches, schools, institutes, guilds etc. who only perform at intervals throughout the year.

This preponderance of amateur entertainment is also common in other parts of the country outside London, particularly in places in the North, the Midlands and in Ireland where large sums are often spent on professional directors who are engaged to stage bigger and better productions each year.

The result is that while some of them may be bigger, they are not always better.

The influence of the amateur movement in Devon and Cornwall on the work of the professional theatre cannot be over-emphasised, for, while it may well be described as "The Nursery of the Paid Theatre", the infants in the nursery of today have grown to become disdainful and oblivious to the work of their "adult" commercial brethren.

Where one would suppose that a close affinity would exist between amateur and professional—as in the sporting world— in the South West there is a marked lack of interest in appreciation of the commercial theatre, repertory movements, national projects, ballet and opera.

One paradox leads to another; for while the amateur actor dedicated to "the drama" to a point of fanaticism will give every moment of his spare time from office, shop or workbench to his hobby, he is often far too busy to support visiting professional companies and so, perhaps, learn a bit more from them, or something of their technical skills.

Another paradox is that audiences will willingly patronise amateur productions of plays and musicals in large enough numbers to often warrant "House Full" notices to be dis-

[253]

played on many occasions, yet visits by professionals, with high standard presentations, invariably play to handfuls. The exceptions are those rare appearances of the Royal Ballet or the Royal Shakespeare Company at which an appearance among the audiences has a certain snob value.

In case the foregoing should be considered a cynical generalisation, the Plymouth amateur scene is a fair example over a period of 150 years.

In the early 1820s Robert Dyer (then a professional actor) changed his tune and was soon fulminating against half-empty houses and blaming amateur competition. Thirty years later James Doel and George Wightwick were both to comment on fashionable theatricals taking business away from the established theatres while in 1900 Whitfeld blamed the amateurs for not caring.

If, in the 1930s, the support given to amateur productions had been devoted to the professional players, the repertory theatre could have been saved from extinction and it might also have helped to save the Theatre Royal from the house-breakers.

In the 1950s a generous offer by the Palace Theatre management to give every facility and encouragement (even rehearsal space on the stage) in return for organised amateur support was ignored, at a time when the box-office trade drawn by amateur societies was in excess of that earned by visiting professional companies.

The professional on the subject of amateur players will inevitably be suspected of prejudice, but the remarks of André Van Gyseghem at an Arts Council conference in 1948 are worth noting.

A number of amateur theatres exist solely as a means of exhibitionism for their members. They like to get up and be seen on platforms by their friends and enjoy these mutual admiration societies. Such amateur societies are of no use to either man or beast; they should be closed down.

In my adjudications I have told them that quite half of the groups who belong to the Drama League ought not to be in existence because they are not serious. If they are not serious theatre productions I don't care two hoots for them. If the art of the theatre becomes a secondary consideration to some other

[254]

object, then I am not interested, for this is not the ground in which the seeds of the healthy theatre should be sown. We see in the amateur theatre bumptiousness and jealousy. We have heard those people who say that their society has done the particular play presented by a professional company and that they have "Done it rather better".

We have all met the man who has played for a long time in his local society and who seldom goes to see a professional production and this is not a very unusual attitude. Isolation from the general life of the theatre is a very bad thing, and if you cut yourself off from contacts you become sterile and your work is of little value.

While it is painfully true that an over-large amount of amateur theatre activity has done great damage to the provincial theatre as a whole, the profession itself must take a measure of responsibility. Jealousy, bumptiousness, conceit and exhibitionism are just as much a part of some professional actors' make-up as they are of the amateur player, and to these may be added a certain contempt and forgetfulness among some of them of the way they first trod the ladder to becoming a paid performer.

A large proportion of the theatrical profession, legitimate or otherwise, began their careers on the amateur stage and in recent years many of our leading players freely admit to learning the elements of their trade on its boards and make no bones about it.

Edith Evans once appeared as an amateur at Streatham Town Hall; Irene Vanburgh played in an amateur production in Exeter; Alfie Bass began acting in London Boy's Clubs; John Slater appeared with the Taverners playing in pubs, and the list ranges far and wide from Michael Redgrave, Alec Clunes and Mrs Patrick Campbell to Fred Karno, Flora Robson, Eric Portman, Peggy Ashcroft and Christopher Fry. All have acknowledged their amateur debt and what is more, have gone out of their way to encourage and stimulate others.

The south-western part of the country during the past twenty-five years serves as a classic example of the amateur movement overtaking the professional theatre. This, in no small part, is due to the paucity of suitable theatre buildings and, in consequence, to a lack of regular visiting players to a region which is still considered "off the beaten track". This phrase, in these days of television, has come to mean too far for the actor to go from the London telephone whence his next (more lucrative) appearance on the "box" may come.

But there is a positive side to this distressing situation, for over the years the amateur movement has progressed from mere theatricals. Today there are many instances of companies providing much imaginative thought in their productions and choice, and while these may not always be brilliantly sophisticated in presentation they are works which, because of economic and other factors, could not possibly be staged by the commercial theatre.

It is this factor above all others that gives the responsible amateur the right to exist and to be heard; for what professional company these days is going to tour Devon and Cornwall (or any other county for that matter) with *Oedipus Rex*, Shakespeare's histories, Sheridan's *The Critic* or even *Rose Marie* and the big musicals of yesteryear which demand large casts and costly sets?

It was the Carmenians Amateur Operatic Society (a splinter group from the Plymstock Operatic Society) which staged the first-ever production of *The Mayflower*, the spectacular musical written by Tommy Connor and Ireland Cutter, a show specially written for Mayflower Year, 1970. They were also the first, in 1971, to present the same writers' *Gentleman of Stratford*, the musical about William Shakespeare based on John Brophy's novel.

A number of première productions have been staged by the small, but energetic, Lyric Players who first brought Irish playwright John B. Keane's work to England. Notable among these were *Many Young Men of Twenty*, *Sive* and *The Iron Harp*, plays which brought more than a touch of genuine Irish humour and pathos to this country and which gave a penetrating look at the lives of ordinary folk in present-day Ireland.

This company was also instrumental in producing for the first time in this country *Tamarinda* and *Execution of a Patriot* by Dutch author Hans Keuls, plays which revealed the serious and dramatic approach that the Netherlands expects from its own theatre.

The contributions made by the Royal Navy to the field of

FIG. 48.—The television personality Angela Rippon (right) as a Cockney gum-chewing pop-singer in an amateur production of the comedy *It's a Record* at the Hoe Theatre, Plymouth in 1964. (Photograph by Jack Collins, The Western Morning News Co. Ltd.)

drama in their annual festivals should not be forgotten. For although a certain number may be classed as "lower deck" entertainment there have been outstanding examples of fine theatre.

There were the original plays of Lieut. Cmdr. Charles Evans who wrote and staged *A Sound of Bugles* and *The Last Day of June*, a dramatisation of the Nore Mutiny of 1797, at Manadon College.

There was the production at H.M.S. *Raleigh* and *Fisgard* of *Caligula* and John Finn's production of *The Visit* by Durrenmatt, the Pinter plays at Manadon College and a never-to-be-forgotten modern naval dress *A Midsummer Night's Dream* by Cmdr. Peter Osborn which for sheer brilliance by amateur performers and imaginative direction has never been equalled.

One would hardly expect to find pantomimic brilliance in

[257]

the tiny town of St. Blazey in Cornwall or, after Wilkie Collins's drastic visit in the nineteenth century, a star amateur attraction in Redruth.

Yet these two places vie with each other every year in pantomime productions in which settings, costumes and performances are more than equal to most of the professional touring pantos which nowadays despise such traditional adornments as transformation scenes and only offer a few token thieves out of the forty!

Who would have thought that the Devonport dockyard could ever have recruited a competent company to stage such a highly commendable production of Shaw's *Major Barbara* which (apart from the film) had never been seen "alive" in the West Country? Or who would believe that the combined Plymouth amateurs could resurrect Sir George Etherege's *The Man of Mode* in a brilliant production which ran in the Tithe Barn at Buckland Abbey for a week under the direction of Henry Whitfeld?

All these and many more have come about through the dedication of imaginative and enthusiastic amateur players and directors of which the following are but a token number: Angela Collins, surely a pro in her own right who has acted and produced so many West Country musicals; the talented Elizabeth Heighway and John Dicks (from the late lamented Mandrake Company, who after graduating through the Northcott theatre is now well on his way to the London stage); Peggy Hitchins, Geoffrey Bersey and Dorothy Harwood from the Plymouth Amateur Operatic Society, and those two outstanding players from Truro, Peter Stribley and Jennifer Roebuck.

Exeter amateurs gave us James Whiteside and Harold Gayton, and also from the Devon Players their Director, Ernest G. Pitts. Plymouth produced Margaret Bailey of the Rapier Company, while Mary Larson of the Lyric Players has probably unearthed more original plays than all the rest of the amateur groups in the South West.

From time immemorial it has always been the elusive mystique of the theatre that has lured the amateur, fired his imagination and stimulated his desire to emulate the professional.

[258]

Whether he aspires to be a dashing leading man or a glittering pop star, such ambitions are inherent in human nature.

With the mass media daily parading examples of rags to riches in the entertainment world before him, these aspirations are increasing, particularly in schools and colleges where drama is now an accepted subject and "theatre in education" has become more widespread.

Fig. 49.—The amateur theatre can even claim a Foreign Minister has risen from its ranks. Doctor David Owen, M.P., then aged twelve (third from left, front row), as Tommy, one of the babes in the pantomime *Babes in the Wood* staged by the Plympton Wranglers in 1951. (Photograph by Dermot Fitzgerald.)

The impasse of not being able to obtain Equity membership until one has professional experience, without which it is impossible, does nothing to encourage budding talent, and the present imbalance of top-class theatrical fare in the provinces has left the gates wide open for the amateur companies to take over what was once a professional field, and unless this is drastically altered in the future the multiplicity of such companies will continue.

So far as audiences are concerned, the middle-class taste for popular plays and musicals by amateurs will remain unabated until the professional theatre moguls can lift such taste with productions and players that can be seen to be of a far better quality than some of those provided on run-of-the-mill tours in recent years. The past decade has shown that the theatre public is becoming increasingly aware of what high standards are being offered in other places and will not be fobbed off with second best at the prices demanded.

CHAPTER XVI

# Full Circle

In the early 1970s it looked as if the even tenor of run-of-the-mill drama and entertainment would continue to be the fare well into the 1980s, but forces had been at work during the last two years of the decade which were to culminate into something just short of a miracle for Plymouth and a shot in the arm for many other communities in the South West.

To appreciate this change of heart it is necessary to see what had happened just previously to create such a revival of interest and enthusiasm among a population inured over the years largely to second best and resigned to the status quo as the price to be paid for living so far from London.

If anything can pinpoint this change of heart it was the decision in 1974 of the Royal Opera House Covent Garden to embark on a national experiment to bring the Royal Ballet to the regions in a specially designed mobile theatre which would seat 2,500 at a time.

That Plymouth out of all the towns in Britain was chosen to see the Royal Ballet in all its perfection was the direct result of the encouragement and foresight of the Arts Council of Great Britain coupled with Plymouth City Council, the energy of Ian Watson, Director of South West Arts, and the financial support of the Midland Bank.

To the surprise of many pessimists who viewed ballet with a jaundiced eye, the whole of the season was completely sold out before the opening night. It became an instant success, with some 30,000 people paying far more for tickets than theatres in Plymouth in the past had ever dared to charge—and coming away entranced.

Such was the enthusiasm created by this first visit that negotiations were immediately begun for another, and it was this, in 1976, when the Royal Opera House staged a three-week season again with the full London company, on the vast stage of the mobile theatre with full orchestra and all the elaborate scenic effects from Covent Garden, that the full impact of theatre magic with all its enthralling beauty and high drama was felt. In a glittering programme which included *Les Sylphides*, *Swan Lake* and *Elite Syncopations* (with Plymouth-born Wayne Sleep as a Principal Dancer) it was the production of Kenneth Macmillan's *Romeo and Juliet* together with Prokofiev's superb music that really captivated and fired the public's imagination.

Anthony Dowell's performance as Romeo and Natalia Makarova as Juliet together with the perfection of the whole company drew superlatives from the Plymouth press. It was described as: "The most marvellous, the most fabulous and the most dramatic performance ever seen in the theatrical life of Plymouth. But mere words such as these fail to match the beauty and the tremendous impression of great theatre which will surely live for ever in the minds of those lucky enough to have been present."

It was this performance more than any that seemed to inspire thousands of West Country folk and make them aware of what had been missing over the years; and it was from the hot summer of 1976 that the renaissance in more serious and ambitious theatre fare was noticed.

This was exemplified in the growing number of notable productions which poured into the Plymouth and Exeter theatres during the following two years, many of them playing to packed houses. The improvement in the demand for first-class entertainment was also noticed nationally, so much so that it inspired other well-established companies which had so far not deigned to tour so remote a region as Devon, to reconsider their itineraries.

The year 1977 saw the Nuffield Theatre Company at the Northcott in Exeter with Shakespeare's *A Midsummer Night's Dream*, *Twelfth Night* and *Othello*, with Barry Stanton as the Moor.

The famous Actors Company came on a tour of Devon and Cornwall in *The Importance of being Earnest* starring Edward

Petherbridge and Tenniel Evans; and the television idol of the times, actor Ralph Bates, Warleggan from *Poldark* (based on Winston Graham's books of Cornish romance), forsook his villainous television image to appear as Fancourt Babberley in the Plymouth Theatre Company's production of *Charley's Aunt* thus giving the company one of its first tastes of success at the box-office. But this was just a beginning; for 1978 brought a new name to the Northcott Theatre, Exeter—Richard Digby Day, a brilliant Director who raised the standard of choice and production even higher than it had been before. His reign was firmly established with a superb production of Tom Stoppard's play *Travesties* which in spite of all its wordy content and intellectual witticisms was a masterpiece of acting and production earning a press comment as being "the most brilliant production seen in the West Country for many years".

There followed Phyllis Calvert and Geoffrey Toone in a lovely production of *Old World* and Shaw's all talking, all sit-down play *In Good King Charles' Golden Days*, which proved in this revival that the original critics were right and it was not such a good play after all. There was a production of *Elektra*; a caustic version of *Cabaret* and a Shakespeare season with Frank Barrie and Margaret Wolfit (daughter of Sir Donald Wolfit) in *Macbeth* and *As You Like It*, followed by John Ford's *'Tis Pity She's a Whore* in November 1978.

The Royal Shakespeare Company came to Plymouth in October 1978 with two magnificent productions of *Twelfth Night* and Chekhov's *Three Sisters* starring Ian McKellen, Edward Petherbridge, Bridget Turner, Suzanne Bertish and Emily Richards, a cast which drew packed houses at every performance; and enthusiasm for the live theatre spread even more when the company moved on to Redruth in Cornwall.

The Sadler's Wells Royal Ballet came with the mobile theatre in 1978 with *Coppelia*, *La Fille Mal Gardée* and *Swan Lake* to dance again to packed houses. It was during this season that the Royal Opera House conducted another public experiment to try out the effect of touring Grand Opera in the Big Top. Four artists from the English National Opera Company, Henry Howell, Eric Shilling, Lyn Barber and Joy Roberts, together with the full Opera House orchestra, gave

[263]

Fɪɢ. 50.—Director Richard Digby Day brought a vivid and polished new look to his revivals of popular successes, and his caustic version of the musical *Cabaret* in 1978 proved a great attraction and an eye-opener to theatregoers who expected the current "cosy" style of production.

an operatic concert which, by its success with the audience as well as technically in voice and acoustics, proved the mobile theatre eminently suitable for such a project.

The Kent Opera Company saw the advantages of the hitherto untapped audience potential, and after two very successful productions of Mozart operas at the Festival Theatre, Paignton, settled down to regular visits which were eagerly awaited.

After a far too long absence professional Shakespeare came to Cornwall for a second time with Ian McCulloch, Phillipa Gail and the New English Shakespeare Company giving performances of *Macbeth* at the Cosy Nook Theatre, Newquay— the first time that the classics by a professional group of players had appeared on its summer show stage.

William Gaskill, the eminent National Theatre Director and one of the pioneers of the Royal Court Theatre, rejuvenated The Joint Stock Company (a touring group which had achieved some renown but had disbanded) in Plymouth to give a memorable performance of *The Ragged Trousered Philanthropists* prior to its going on tour and eventually to London. It was based on the classic trade union book by Robert Tressell about the working conditions of the depressed British working man in Victorian times, and Gaskill, a great stickler for detail, had his cast working full time at manual labour in a derelict warehouse in Union Street so that they could assimilate the atmosphere of low paid drudgery.

Comedian Max Wall of the funny walks, the extrovert Jazz entertainer George Melly, Clive Dunn from the perennial television series *Dad's Army* and Dickie Henderson brought star status names even to the Hoe Theatre.

The Plymouth Theatre Company began to increase its casts and staged Wilde's *An Ideal Husband* followed by *Under Milk Wood* with Bernard Bresslaw, Shakespeare's *The Merchant of Venice* and a fine production of *Equus* with Philip Bond and Robert Morgan. At last even *Hair* came to the Princess Theatre, Torquay, but this had dated badly since its first controversial beginnings so that even Torbay citizens scarcely raised an eyebrow.

These varied happenings in and around the South West peninsula, while perhaps sounding commonplace events to more sophisticated ears in the metropolis, were manna to a part of Britain which had been woefully neglected, for some thirty years, and the abundance of fare offered to the public at large spread a mood of optimism for the future.

To a great extent this revitalisation of the West Country theatrical scene was due to the valiant efforts of South West Arts, who struggled hard to persuade companies of national standing to visit the region. This in turn encouraged a number of industrial organisations to support various enterprises with subsidies or to guarantee against loss. Not the least of these was the Plymouth-based Westward Television company which regularly financially assisted the Northcott Theatre and the Plymouth Theatre Company, thus integrating themselves in the work of the community within the spirit of their charter.

This revival of the age-old custom of patronage of the arts, albeit transferred from the sixteenth-century lord to the twentieth-century board of management, proved a vital factor in raising considerably the artistic standards of the whole area.

The name of John Redgrave had been associated with Plymouth since 1974 when he presented a series of annual summer shows at the Hoe Theatre. A former company manager for the *Black and White Minstrel Show*, he had become an impresario presenting a growing number of productions in resorts around Britain.

After a very successful 1978 summer season at the Hoe Theatre with Dickie Henderson, Redgrave announced that he had purchased the long derelict Palace Theatre in Union Street and it was opened at Christmas—thus personifying once again the opportunist private enterprise of the optimistic theatre-owners of the past.

This brought a huge wave of nostalgia followed by intense enthusiasm from the public which was expressed in the box-office returns when the New Palace Theatre re-opened on 24th December completely refurbished, repainted and with new carpets and seats (the original 80-year-old carpet in the stalls was still there in reasonable condition) for a nine-week season of *Cinderella*, the longest run in the theatre's history.

The pantomime broke new ground in provincial productions by having no less than six stars in the cast, headed by

[266]

Frankie Howerd as Buttons, Julian Orchard and Terry Gardener as the Ugly Sisters, John Boulter, a renowned tenor, as Prince Charming, with television stars Peter Jones and Nicholas Smith playing the "nasty parts". It was a lavish spectacular which drew audiences from all over the South West, confounding the critics who said it would not pay.

This success was followed by promises of visits from companies providing ballet, plays and musicals, and from such artists as comedians Ken Dodd and Larry Grayson who up to now had been precluded from playing in the city as there was no theatre large enough to hold a viable audience.

As if this was not sufficient to satisfy the artistic appetites of theatregoers, in January 1979 the Plymouth Council in full session, after nearly five years of deliberation and indecision voted by 36 votes to 25 to sign the tender of Richard Costain Ltd. for the building of a Civic Theatre at Derry's Cross, to be completed in 1981 at a cost of £5.8 million (expected to rise by inflation to £6.7 million on completion).

There was a storm of objections from the Ratepayers Association and other individuals who demonstrated at every

FIG. 51.—The architect's model of the proposed Civic Theatre for Plymouth due to be completed in 1981.

turn (on the grounds that this inflationary figure was extravagant and an unnecessary expenditure), and who pointed out vociferously that the Palace Theatre alone was already fulfilling the requirements of a Plymouth Civic Theatre.

However the Council won the day with its plans for a "Flexible Theatre" which again aroused much controversy from those who wanted a much larger functional theatre, a concert hall or an all-purpose building.

The theatre was designed by one of the most distinguished theatre architects of the day, Peter Moro, in conjunction with Martin Carr of the firm of theatre consultants Carr and Angier of London.

Situated opposite Derry's Clock in front of Foulston's original site of the old Theatre Royal, it was planned as an octagonal building constructed to seat 1,300 in its main auditorium. This figure could be reduced by hydraulically closing the circle to seat 700, and still further to 500 if required. In addition there was to be a "Studio Theatre" seating around 200, designed for the use of the Plymouth Theatre Company and experimental productions.

Work began on the site on the 1st April 1979 and it came as no surprise that the name chosen for the new building was "The Theatre Royal".

So it came about that during the final months of the 1970s a new and optimistic atmosphere came over the Devon theatrical scene. Delayed by almost forty years since the devastation caused by the Second World War, the West Country could at least look forward to a promise of more inspiring and invigorating theatrical fare in the 1980s.

# CHAPTER XVII

# Enter the Stars

One cannot say that the seed of drama planted in Cornwall 700 years ago has flourished over a period of long and gradual cultivation into an eventual flowering of the arts, culminating in a glorious new age in the world of live theatre in the West.

Instead it has wilted under bigotry, been enlivened by great events and plunged into stagnation by apathy, blossoming only at infrequent intervals.

Neither can the last decades of those seven centuries be dismissed as the last dying gasp of an outworn mode of entertainment, for if eventually the live theatre in this country, as we know it now, expires (indeed some have buried it already) then other forms of entertainment and cultural activity will also suffer.

For despite its shortcomings and old-fashioned ways the provincial theatre has been, and always will be, the cradle of drama, opera, variety, films and ballet in whatever mechanical or electronic devices these arts may be encapsulated in the future, and the talents employed will still spring directly from the ordinary people of the big cities and provincial towns and villages as they have done in the past.

It has become the fashion since the 1950s to talk about a revolution in our theatre which has been brought about by a new generation of playwrights whose work has been dispensed by fringe, regional or *avant-garde* groups to a steadily diminishing public audience.

The great mass of the public have little time for such presentations which generally have nothing new to offer except for a little less inhibited dialogue and which are designed for the self-indulgent, the morbid, masochistic and the "way-out". They are often performed on bare stages, in rooms and on street corners where illusion is banished and a certain embarrassment takes its place.

Such a "revolution" over a few short years must be set against the background of the long-established conservative approach bred in provincial audiences, for the West Country has seen many similar unheavals far greater than the present one and has gazed at them with a jaundiced eye.

As has been seen, the history of the West Country theatre is a saga of the boundless hopes and supreme optimism of the professional entertainer, be he actor, playwright or manager, forever coming forward time and time again in the confident belief that given a reasonable venue in which to perform, the audience will flock to see him.

It is also a saga of frustration, of persecution, a struggle against bigotry, indifference, neglect and ignorance by authority and against low taste of audiences condemned by virtue of their geographic isolation to be content with raucous comedy, crude drama and the often second-rate, while other parts of the country received more enlightened fare.

Amid the present-day flood of permissiveness in the theatre, films and television, there is the apparent nation-wide paradox —a desire for nostalgia and a revival of past glories. One also sees and reads daily about the cult of personalities as if that were a new thing imported with the electronic age.

Surely behind this façade there lies the craving for hero worship, the star, the personality who can rise above his fellow men, be he Edmund Kean or Donny Osmond.

We have with us today the age of the Director and the Designer, who seem only to think in terms of high intellectual exercise, obscure plays and gimmicky settings. We also have the "instant playwright" who thinks up depressing family situations where belts and braces with the wife in curlers are shown as shining examples of "social awareness" in plays which are liberally laced with four-letter words "to be in character".

It has become the habit to bypass the well-constructed play which has a beginning, a middle and an ending and to sneer at emotion, enjoyment and laughter in the theatre and write them off as "middle-class".

"Entertainment" has become a dirty word; but "enthralment" is far more appropriate here, as it is the main ingredient that the long-suffering British public lacks in these basic pragmatic times, and it is left to the few discerning playwrights like Robert Bolt, Alan Ayckbourn, John Mortimer and the late John Whiting to provide some means of enlightened escape to the world of real theatre.

But there is one that even transcends the playwright.

Over the years we have passed through the ages of the actor/manager, the actor, the playwright and the scenic designer and we have seen the Theatres of Naturalism, of Comedy, Melodrama, Cruelty, Surrealism, the Absurd and of Fact.

The public at large will have none of them except one— the actor.

When all the rest have finished their work, he alone remains, and when the play is done, it is his performance that lingers.

Alone among the world of culture, the ephemeral art of the theatre leaves "not a rack behind" except within the memory, and call it nostalgia, hero worship or what you will, great acting performances can shine thereafter, in men's minds throughout a lifetime.

The play may have been the thing to the first Elizabethans, but times have changed since then, and now the player has become the king.

Ask anyone for reminiscences of theatregoing and they will quote individuals. They have remembrances of Henry Irving, Martin Harvey, Matheson Lang, Donald Wolfit, Robert Morley, Laurence Olivier, Edith Evans, Richard Burton, John Gielgud, Peggy Ashcroft, Margaret Rutherford, George Robey or Morecambe and Wise, but the play, the words, the lighting, the scenery, the costumes etc., all are forgotten, leaving only an impression of some moment of magical communication and intense enjoyment or emotion in which the actor or performer alone transcends everything else, and so makes his impact for posterity.

The likes and dislikes of audiences have been debated by everyone in the theatre business from impresarios to the stage-door keeper over a hundred years in an impossible effort to find the "open sesame" to success at the box-office.

[271]

Every device has been tried to unravel the secret of what audiences really want when it comes to entertainment, whether it is spectacle, humour, music, comedy or tragedy, and only one element seems to remain constant in this paradoxical profession: this is the role of the actor.

The English have always liked their actors to be actors, people who can arouse emotions not. so much by the words put into their mouths by the author, but by sheer force of personal magnetism, exquisite technique and the power to hold an audience in the palm of their hands.

It is true that much of the actor's charisma today is destroyed by the player himself, for gone are the days when an actor was "a being on a higher plane", instantly recognisable and aloof from ordinary mortals.

The public enjoyed this difference for it bolstered their illusion of players being somehow apart from ordinary folk.

Today, with actors being turned out of drama school in a mould to fit in with those nondescript workaday characters that seem to people most present-day plays, it is perhaps no wonder that they find it hard to recapture the majesty and mystery of another world—which do not go well with jeans and jersey.

Perhaps the days of realism have indeed gone too far when in a recent professional production of *Hamlet* the actors, who were only conversant with the modern conversational television style, had to receive elementary lessons in speaking Shakespeare's blank verse with its attendant gestures, in order to fit in with a costumed production. Even lines were clipped and words changed so that they could "make it understandable to the audience" thus following Thomas Bowdler's expurgations of 150 years ago.

This is no plea for the return of the old-fashioned ham of Victorian times, the stilted idiom of the 1920s or for theatres to be festooned with baroque trappings of gilt and plush and the flat scenic effects of a bygone age.

But a study of West Country audiences suggests that we might have gone too far in the opposite direction. The theatre has been influenced too much by the "naturalism" of the television documentary which has to show every speck of dirt and bloodstain to be "real" and demands speech in

[272]

restricted tones unless the sanctity of the microphone be shattered.

We now have open stages where every lantern and spotlight in the place is in full view of the audience; where backstage effects and scenery hands are openly displayed; where settings and costumes are not related to the play at all (one remembers *The Duchess of Malfi* performed in sweat shirts and jeans around a jumble of steel scaffolding) and the proscenium arch is criticised as being an anachronism, with the result that we have lost illusion and the magic and mystery of acting.

This hankering after tradition is perhaps understandable in Devon and Cornwall where there is a larger proportion of retired folk than in most other areas—not by any means senile, but vigorous, intelligent, and more than willing to be vitally interested in the stage and what it has to offer.

On the other hand there is an equally large number of members of the younger generation who have been brought up from school years under the auspices of a qualified drama teacher or such, who has instilled into their minds the art of improvisation, of mime, movement and "the total involvement" said to be so necessary to modern methods of theatre. Yet there is little evidence that appreciation of modern drama extends beyond the school-leaving age.

Generally speaking, there is no antagonism against the unorthodox methods or the production of *avant-garde* plays, for they, like the pop world, have their Top Twenty among the hundreds of lesser projects.

But the West Country has had a surfeit of them until they have become synonymous with the slapdash, the unscripted, the unrehearsed and the sleazy, in which none but the very few seem interested.

But looking objectively at, say, Fugard's *Sizwe Bansi is Dead*, at Edward Bond's *Pope's Wedding*, at plays by John McGrath, Samuel Beckett, even Genet's *The Maids* (which ought to have drawn on the score of sheer notoriety) and others—all of which have stated in emphatic terms examples of glaring social injustice, the plight of the underprivileged and by word and symbolism have outlawed the old conventions through direct approach to the audience—it cannot be truthfully said that any of these productions have caused much of a revolution at the box-office or more than a mere ripple among theatrical conversationalists.

A survey undertaken in Plymouth in 1972 revealed that whereas repertory and plays were in the minority (by plays one takes this to mean the four males, three females, one-set productions upon which the present generation has been mostly reared) there was almost a unanimous demand for spectaculars and musicals, from which it seemed that only an almost unbroken series of *The Sound of Music* and the *Black and White Minstrel Show* would satisfy.

The survey also showed a demand for "a large theatre", but gave no hint that it would be supported for fifty-two weeks in the year. Neither did it give any indication of an alternative type of entertainment that would be acceptable to the West Country public at large.

This refusal to take theatre seriously was evidenced by some Plymouth councillors who seemed to regard drama as frivolous and not falling into the category of higher things such as education, libraries, art galleries, swimming pools, shops, drains and roads or civic dignity.

Plymouth's half-hearted attempts over the years since the Second World War to build a theatre made the city into something of a laughing stock in the theatre world, and its reputation is only just now about to be redeemed with its proposed Civic Theatre to be completed in 1981.

Whether the newly-opened Palace Theatre will prosper in the coming years under private ownership and without Arts Council support can only be conjectured, but its success with the public at its rehabilitation certainly shows that the spirit of theatregoing is by no means dead as many would have it.

The Plymouth Athenaeum Theatre, after its early prickly start, has settled down to a comfortable compromise of a learned institution living in harmony with theatrical people, and provides a first-class venue for amateur productions, laced with occasional visits from professional touring companies.

The Northcott Theatre at Exeter, since it opened in 1967, has seen different policies under directors Tony Church, Jane Howell, Geoffrey Reeves and Richard Digby Day, who have presented the classics, the moderns, the musicals and the popular comedies and who between them have created a very fine example of genuine Regional Theatre possessing a high standard of production and performance.

Whatever theatrical revolution there has been must surely have occurred in the more rural areas of Devon and Cornwall which up to the 1950s saw precious little of anything. This was radically altered when in 1972 Foot's Barn Theatre Company began its work from a base in Liskeard travelling the whole length and breadth of the county taking original plays (some of them, admittedly, beyond the ken of their onlookers) into pubs, tents, clubs and the open air, bringing with them their own individual extrovert style to a slightly bewildered audience.

Then there is Medium Fair which serves South and East Devon, also with much-travelled shows of drama and variety in the modern style, while the Orchard Theatre in North Devon under Andrew Noble brought regional theatre through the farmhouse door with an eighteenth-century *The Archers* Style localised documentary as well as touring a full production of *Henry V*—the first time it had been seen in Devon for some forty years.

The newest theatre in Devon is the Plough at Torrington, which opened in April 1975 with a festival of twenty-two events, the first of which featured that great actress Edith Evans.

Although changes and vicissitudes have attended many of Devon and Cornwall's theatres over the years, there have been triumphs, too; and there are many instances of the glamour of the provincial theatre sparking off inspiration and impetus to a large number of people who saw their first live theatrical performance in a West Country theatre or local hall.

An Arts Council exhibition of the Georgian Playhouse was held in London in October 1975, and among the exhibits was an extract from *The Theatric Tourist* of 1820 which quoted James Winston's dismal entry: "Devonshire has never yet been famous for producing theatrical geniuses." The following list may go some way to redress the balance and do justice to some renowned West Country names.

There was Thomas D'Urfey, the Exeter dramatist and songwriter of Restoration times, who suffered prosecution for

[275]

profanity in 1698 for daring to defy convention and publish witty plays. William Farren made his debut in Plymouth and later appeared at the Exeter Theatre. He was head of a great theatrical family of which the most famous was Nellie Farren, his granddaughter, who as one of the first-ever Gaiety Girls became the darling of the musical comedy public and was to have the historic honour of being the first to appear in *Thespis*, the first-born Gilbert and Sullivan opera.

Then there was the great Samuel Phelps. Devonport-born, yet unwanted by his own people, he left the city for London where he was engaged by Macready, earned a reputation as a tragedian and was the first to make Sadler's Wells the home of Shakespeare, training in the process a number of actors who in later years boasted that they "had played the Wells under Phelps".

Where would the musical comedy world have been today had not Barnstaple given us John Gay with his *Beggar's Opera*? This ousted the old Italian style and introduced a new fashion in entertainment the pattern of which is still very much with us today.

Remember, too, the comedian Jimmy Doel of Devonport, one of the first "stand up" comics in his later years; and William Dowton, son of an Exeter innkeeper who became an actor of the Garrick School, who Leigh Hunt described as "one of the finest comic geniuses of the day"; also the gifted Sheridan Knowles of Plymouth who became a playwright and gave Macready his play *Virginius* which became a vehicle for some of his greatest triumphs.

It was the Exeter Theatre that was the first to give the fabled Edmund Kean a real opportunity to reveal his dazzling talents to the world, and it was from the West Country that he entered the London theatre.

Then there was the Cornish-born Charles Incledon, the great tenor of his time.

Plymouth was the town which gave birth to those two actresses Maria Foote and Cora Pearl, the first of their kind to earn notoriety and cause scandal in high life. There was Henry Arthur Jones, the playwright (author of those money-spinning plays of Victorian times. *The Silver King* and *The Liars*) who lived in Exeter and had his first two plays staged in the city's theatre thus giving him the first taste of success and the spur to greater efforts.

The great tragedian Osmond Tearle was born in Adelaide Street, Stonehouse, and after earning a high reputation in this country became one of the leading actors at Wallack's in New York. He left his son Godfrey Tearle to carry on his great tradition and to become a British star of the theatre and of films.

Who, out of the many thousands who have visited the London Palladium, the London Coliseum or the dozens of Empire Theatres all over the country, would connect these buildings with the delightful Devon market town of Newton Abbot?

Yet they were all designed by a Devonian, Frank Matcham, born in the town in 1854 who was to become one of the most prolific theatre architects of his period, responsible for the Chiswick Empire, the well-known Empire Theatre at Finsbury Park, Hull's Palace of Varieties, the "Met" in Edgware Road, the Lyric Theatre at Hammersmith—scene of so many of Nigel Playfair's triumphs. "Matchless Matcham", as he came to be called, designed so many theatres in the late Victorian boom that the precise number cannot now be calculated, but the list also includes the Tivoli, the London hippodrome, the Richmond Theatre and the old Paragon in 1893.

Where would the famous Charlie Chaplin have been if it were not for the eccentricities of Fred Karno, who was born in Exeter and was responsible for starting so many careers on the variety stage? These include Stan Laurel, Max Miller, Billy Bennett, Will Hay, Naughton and Gold and Sydney Howard. Remember also Henry Irving, who, as young John Henry Brodribb, although born across the border in Somerset, spent most of his early years deep down in Cornwall absorbing that rare Celtic romantic atmosphere—if ever a genius came out of the West it was Irving.

Tiverton in Devon was to give us that delightful actor, Ronald Squire, who was born in that town; Violet and Irene Vanbrugh, born in Exeter, were to become great ladies of the theatre; and then there was Walter Fitzgerald from Keyham, Devonport, who played with Mrs Patrick Campbell, Martin

Harvey, Seymour Hicks and who also made a name for himself in America as a film actor.

One wonders what Noël Coward would have done without the services of Gladys Calthrop, the artist and designer, born at Ashton in Devon and who became his confidante and close friend for so many years; or the light comedy stage without the presence of Frith Banbury from Plymouth; or the Music Hall and radio without those two "Cads", the Western Brothers—both Devonians, Kenneth from Exeter and George from Crediton.

(Photograph by courtesy of The Western Morning News Co. Ltd.)
FIG. 52.—Eden Philpotts (1862–1948), the playwright who brought Devonshire humour to the theatre with his West Country comedies *The Farmer's Wife, Yellow Sands, Devonshire Cream* and many others which he wrote in conjunction with his daughter Adelaide.

The legitimate stage was greatly enhanced by Dartmouth-born Rachel Kempson, married to Michael Redgrave; and by Michael Shepley, another Plymothian; and what would the Whitehall Theatre have done without R. F. Delderfield the author from Exmouth, whose *Worm's Eye View* kept audiences roaring with laughter for years?

[278]

Talking of playwrights and laughter, there was Eden Philpotts who wrote those very funny Devonshire comedies *The Farmer's Wife* and, with his daughter Adelaide, *Yellow Sands*.

Who will go down in theatre records with greater impact than Agatha Christie, author of *The Mousetrap* the longest-running play in British stage history? Born Agatha Miller at Torquay in 1890, she was to become the author of some fifteen plays and seventy books, which were acted and read all over the world.

Then there was Jack Train from Torpoint with a million or

FIG. 53.—Plymouth-born Wayne Sleep who became one of the Principal Dancers of the Royal Ballet and a talented and versatile artist in many branches of the entertainment world.

[279]

more fans listening to his Colonel Chinstrap, and who was one of the first radio impressionists; there was Jack Tripp, the talented dancer and comedian who hailed from Plymouth; Edward Murch the Dousland playwright, responsible for over thirty short plays that have found a ready market all over America and Canada as well as in this country; and that delightful Plymouth-born actor, Donald Sinden.

What about that Principal Dancer of the Royal Ballet, Wayne Sleep, a Plymothian who began his career under Pat Rouse of the Valletort School of Dancing, thence to a ballet school, and was to become one of the top dancers in the greatest ballet company in the world; or that equally talented and much neglected John Gilpin from Dawlish who passed top in the 1940 Plymouth Festival and went on to become one of the leading dancers with the London Festival Ballet and guest artist for the Royal Ballet in Covent Garden?

While to many the word "provinces" may appear dull, and the mention of Cornwall and Devon may in theatrical terms evoke visions of a remote peninsula far removed from sophisticated civilisation, the Royal Court and the Round House, the fact remains that the halls and theatres of the South West have also provided many a stepping stone to national success.

Broadway's "Oscar" for the Best Actor of 1967 was given to Paul Rogers for his performance in Harold Pinter's *The Homecoming*. Grandson of "Big Bill" Rogers (Superintendent of Plymouth Police and Captain of Plymouth Fire Brigade in the days when the engine was drawn by horses), Paul was born in Plympton.

Educated at Plympton Grammar School and Newton Abbot Secondary School, he trained as an actor under Michael Chekhov at Dartington Hall, and after his return from the Navy in 1946 he joined the Old Vic and went on to become one of the most sought-after members of the Royal Shakespeare Company in London at the Aldwych and in Stratford-upon-Avon.

Another boy from Plympton was Ian Trigger, now a respected actor in the West End Theatre and America. He appeared regularly with the Plymouth Shakespeare Society while still a pupil at Devonport High School for Boys, before taking

FIG. 54.—One of Plymouth's most respected sons is the celebrated
Shakespearean actor Paul Rogers, seen here with his wife Rosalind
Boxall who he met in the cast of the Old Vic production of
*Love's Labour's Lost* at the New Theatre in 1949.

up the stage as his career. Then there was Peter Cook from
Torquay of *Beyond the Fringe* fame, who together with Dudley
Moore has established himself as one of our foremost original
humorists.

Danny La Rue, the greatest drag artist of them all, spent
his early days at Kennford, near Exeter, and later on served
behind the counter at Bobby's of Torquay; Bruce Forsyth,
then almost an unknown artist, was "discovered" by Billy
Marsh one wet Sunday afternoon while he was playing at the
Babbacombe Theatre in Devon.

[281]

One remembers Eleonor Bron with her Cambridge Mummers playing the small role of Ursula in *Much Ado about Nothing* at the Athenaeum Theatre; Dave Allen the television comedian as an almost unknown second comic to George Lacy in the summer show in a tent on Plymouth Hoe; and Royce Ryton the very successful author of *Crown Matrimonial* playing a small part with the South West Theatre Group.

From just over the Devon border in Taunton comes Jenny Agutter, now a very much sought-after film actress, who began her acting career as a child and progressed to teenage roles. She has now begun an adventurous and promising contract in the Walt Disney Studios.

That renowned baritone Frederick Harvey was born and bred in Plymouth and as a boy sang with St. Andrew's Church choir. His reputation soared after his many radio concerts, and his name became synonymous with those heroic songs of England and the West Country, songs like "Drake's Drum", "The Fishermen of England" and "Glorious Devon", recordings of which have been reissued on a number of occasions some ten years after his death, and are still popular.

From Saltash in Cornwall comes one of Britain's leading pianists Moura Lympany who has travelled all over the world giving solo recitals as well as appearing with all the great orchestras on the concert platform.

From Grenofen near Tavistock comes that famous television personality, the first ever BBC woman national news announcer, Angela Rippon, known to millions of viewers both in this country and over a large part of the rest of the world.

As a young girl she had danced on the Palace Theatre stage, and it was in her early years while working in a Plymouth newspaper office that she regularly appeared as a competent amateur actress with the Western College Players, revealing then a commanding personality on the stage, thus laying the foundations for her very professional appearances before a world-wide audience.

There are many others who first tried out their professional careers in the South West—Michael Palin of *Monty Python's Flying Circus* fame appearing before he was "known" in a satirical revue at the Athenaeum Theatre; Christopher Cazenove, also at the Athenaeum Theatre, when a student with the

Bristol Old Vic Theatre School being noticed well above the rest, even then; also the appearance of Angela Pleasance, daughter of Donald Pleasance (who himself appeared at the old Plymouth Rep in 1939) in one of her first major roles in Plymouth in 1967.

There are vivid memories of Charles Lewsen, now a dramatic critic of *The Times* giving his delightful one-man show in a tour of Devon, and of Arthur Lowe in *Lock Up Your Daughters* at the Princess Theatre, Torquay, long before *Dad's Army* was ever thought of.

Looking back on these names and the countless others who have served the West Country and the provincial theatre over so many years, one is sustained by the thought that, although this part of England may seem to some eyes rather remote from London and the North from which much of our theatrical inheritance is born, dramatic inspiration, and indeed genius, has emerged from Devon and Cornwall, and from the town of "The Theatre of Splendid Misery" itself.

This phrase, born of a period when humanity was a severely class-ridden society, aptly portrayed the conditions existing in the early nineteenth century, conditions which have since emerged into a "Theatre of Missed Opportunity". The West Country is now poised to enter the last two decades of the twentieth century with a much broader appreciation of artistic entertainment, which will embrace the larger part of the population.

Enterprise and enthusiasm is now being noticed among civic administrators as well as among actors: qualities which have always been the essential ingredients which go to make up the player's own philosophy—a "Theatre of Optimism".

# Bibliography

*Plymouth and Devonport in Times of War and Peace* by Henry Francis Whitfeld (published privately by E. Chapple 1900)

*Cavalcade by Candlelight* by Eric R. Delderfield (The Raleigh Press, Exmouth 1950)

*Fifty Years of Vaudeville* by G. Earnest Short (Eyre & Spottiswoode 1946)

*The Minack Open Air Theatre* by Averil Demuth (David & Charles 1968)

*Fanny Kelly of Drury Lane* by Basil Francis (Rockliff Publishing Corporation 1950)

*Portrait of Plymouth* by J. C. Trewin (Robert Hale 1973)

*Last Theatres* by Max Beerbohm (Rupert Hart-Davis 1970)

*Macready's Reminscences* ed. by Sir Frederick Pollock (Harper, New York 1875)

*A Plan for Plymouth* (Underhill (Plymouth) Ltd. 1943)

*The Seventh Star* (Exeter University 1961)

*The Actor and his Audience* by W. A. Darlington (Phoenix House 1949)

*It Came to our Door* by H. P. Twyford (Underhill (Plymouth) Ltd. 1945)

*Theatre Royal Drury Lane* by W. J. Macqueen Pope (W. H. Allen 1949)

*Specimens of English Dramatic Criticism* ed. by A. C. Ward (Oxford University Press 1945)

# Index

# INDEX